FREEDOM IV
Armed and Extremely Dangerous

*"Man's impenitence precedes
his own destruction,
just as righteous judgment precedes
eternal life!"*

– Ed Marr

FREEDOM IV
Armed and Extremely Dangerous

The Investigation of True Repentance
continues in the New Testament...

by Ed Marr

Christian Literature & Artwork
A BOLD TRUTH Publication

Dedication

I've always wanted to honor those men that Almighty God has brought into my life. Of particular mention, are four men of God, who I love and cherish as God's precious jewels which He has bestowed upon me. They are: my first Pastor in the faith, Doctor Dwaine Lee, my spiritual father, Doctor Phil Oslin, Rev. John Davis (a mighty Preacher of Repentance), and Revivalist "Big" John Hall, [who in my estimation is one of God's generals, and I thank God for the opportunity to have been his armor bearer].

To these men of God, I hereby dedicate this investigation. My dearest brothers in Christ, I love you all, even in your absence!

FREEDOM IV - Armed and Extremely Dangerous
Copyright © 2019 by Ed Marr
ISBN 13: 978-1-949993-06-6

FIRST EDITION

Printed in the United States of America

BOLD TRUTH PUBLISHING
(Christian Literature & Artwork)
606 West 41st, Ste. 4
Sand Springs, Oklahoma 74063
www.BoldTruthPublishing.com ▪ *beirep@yahoo.com*

Available from Amazon.com and other retail outlets. Orders by U.S. trade bookstores and wholesalers.

Quantity sales special discounts are available on quantity purchases by corporations, associations, and others. For details, contact the publisher at the address above.

Cover Art & Design by Aaron Jones

All rights reserved under International Copyright Law. All contents and/or cover art and design may not be reproduced in whole or in part in any form without the express written consent of the Author.

Printed in the USA.
07 19   10 9 8 7 6 5 4 3 2 1

Unless otherwise indicated, Bible quotations are taken from the King James Version of the Bible. Copyright © 1988 by B. B. Kirkbride Bible Company, Inc.,

Some quotations are taken from the Thompson-Chain Reference Bible, 5th Improved Edition. Published by the Kirkbride Bible Company, Inc.

Copyright 1995 by The Zondervan Corporation and the Lockman Foundation. Scripture marked AMP are taken from THE AMPLIFIED BIBLE, Old Testament Copyright 1965, 1987, by the Zondervan Corporation. The Amplified New Testament Copyright, 1958, 1987 by The Lockman Foundation. Used by permission.

"Scripture quotations taken from the Amplified® Bible *Classic Edition* (AMPC), Copyright © 1954, 1958, 1962, 1964, 1965, 1987 by The Lockman Foundation. Used by permission. www.Lockman.org"

The Strong's Exhaustive Concordance of the Bible. Copyright © 1990 by Thomas Nelson Publishers.

The Works of Josephus, Copyright © 1987 by Hendrickson Publishers, Inc.

Volume One Repentance: The Doctrine of God and the Knowledge of Salvation (in the Old Testament) Copyright © 2004 by Xulon Publisher.

Table of Contents

Author's Preface .... *i*
   The Bible Codes... *ii*
Introduction: From a Baptism to a Lifestyle 1
   The Handmaid to Theology... 2
   A Heritage of Faith and Repentance................................. 4
   The Higher Call.. 5
   The Wisdom of God... 7
   God's Plan, His Hidden Plan and His Revealed Plan........... 9

BOOK 4: FREEDOM IV
Chapter 1: Repentance in the Book of Matthew 21
   The Encumbered Soul.. 21
   Repent Means to Renew and Change............................... 24
   The New Testament Church Must Acknowledge
   Her Heritage of Disobedience…...................................... 26
   Repentance, the Fourth Baptism..................................... 28
   The Agricultural and Horticultural Process
   of Repentance.. 32
   The Multipurpose Tool of Repentance............................. 34
   Water unto Repentance Precedes the Fruits
   of Repentance.. 38
   The Leaven That Coagulates.. 39
   The Baptism with the Water unto Repentance................ 42
   Trees of Religion.. 43
   Trees of Righteousness.. 45
   A Condition of Stasis... 46
   The Four Faculties of the Mind.. 47
   Impenitence as Evidence Used Against Us...................... 50
   The Wisdom of Repentance... 51
   Why Sackcloth and Ashes?.. 52

Sackcloth is a Symbol of the Blood......53
Worthy or Unworthy......55
The Customary Practice of Servant Hood......55
Consciousness of Guilt/Carnality Denotes Culpability......57
The Blasphemy of the Holy Ghost......58
Wells Without Water......60
Transfigure Means Repent and Repent Means to Renew......61
We are All Given Ample Opportunities to Come
to Repentance......61
That Word which John Preached......62
Our Enemy Cannot Betray Us......63

Chapter 2: Repentance in the Book of Mark......65
  The Prophet 65
  The Last Old Testament Prophet......68
  John's Duty......68
  The Horns of the Altar and the Horn of Salvation......69
  The Power of Repentance, R R R......70
  The Force of Righteous Words......72
  Who Recognized John the Baptist as a Prophet?......73
  A Prophet's Reward and A Righteous Man's Reward......74
  John's Fidelity and Our Righteous Charge......75
  Repentance Heals the Withered Hand of Carnality......78
  The Timeline of Prophecy......79
  Your Spiritual Time Line......81
  The Decapitation of the Church......83
  Pulpit Puppeteers......85
  Grace is the Expression of God's Love......87
  The Remission of Carnality......89
  The Copulative Characteristics of a Baptism......89
  Salted Meat in God's House......92
  An Explanation of Frankincense
  (as the Secret of Jeremiah, the Prophet)......94
  Amputations and Bodily Disfigurements......96
  Carnal Snails......97
  Carnal Maggots......97

Salt, Colloquially Speaking..98
The Dung Hill of Self-Righteousness...............................98
Substitution Salt..99
Harvested Salt..100
The Anointing and the Salt..101
The Curing Process of Repentance................................102
Self-Righteousness as a Sacred Cow 102
Salt as Repentance...103

Chapter 3: Repentance in the Book of Luke....................105
The Birth of a Prophet...105
The Wisdom of the Just...106
He Tutored Me in Rabbit Trails.....................................107
The Preaching of Repentance..108
The Force of the Doctrine of Repentance......................110
That Word which John Preached...................................111
The Error of Tradition...113
Vomit is Spewed Pre-chewed Food................................114
Health is a Fruit of Righteousness *(Repentance)*...............116
We Must All Acknowledge the Justice of God..............118
A Lifestyle of Repentance Caters to Jesus.....................119
But Wisdom is Justified of All Her Children.................120
A Walking Gospel..121
Obvious Success is Never a Reason to Gloat.................122
There is a Generation That..124
That which Belongs to and is Intended for the
Devil Alone..125
The Things that Make for Peace....................................127
Obsessive Compulsive Disorder or is it Unsuppressed
Carnal Dysfunction..129
A Kingdom of Priests and the Politics of Religion............130
The Filibuster of Carnality...131
The Sign of Judgment..132
Two News Worthy Events..134
The Tower of Repentance...135
Preexisting, Symptomatic Conditions of Carnality...........138

We Have Lost Control!..138
Where Have All the Leaders Gone, Long Time Passing?......139
Contaminated Blood is Useless..141
Mingled Blood..141
The Call of Repentance, Refused...143
Cast Sheep..144
A Fireman's Carry and His Footprints in the Sand..............145
The Ninety-Nine Sheep..145
A Boxer Named Sabu..147
Boundaries Are Essential..148
Coming of Age or Come to Your Senses................................149
We Have Only Ourselves to Blame...150
A Lifestyle of Repentance as Portrayed by the
Rich Man and Lazarus..153
    Point Number One: A Desire for Crumbs. 153
    Point Number Two: My father, Abraham......................155
    Point Number Three: Lay up Uncertain Riches.............156
    Point Number Four: Salvation Through
    the Living Word..157
Repentance Restores Health..158
Repentance is Not an Audacious Public
Display of Self-Righteousness...159
Lost Opportunities..160
The Theory of Relativity..162
Ability, Opportunity, Jeopardy..162
The Pointed Stakes of Carnal Jeopardy.................................165
A Heart's Desire for Incarceration..167
The Penitent Thief...169
That Which Must Be Taught and That Which Should
Be Preached..172
Four Kingdoms and then Some..174
Immigration is Translation..175
Repentance as a Command...176
The Call of Repentance..177
Profane Views Against Nature and Nature's God................178
The Elephant in the House..179

False Peace is not Genuine Peace..180
Same Sex Marriage and Nepotism..180
We Have Ruined Our Country! 181
Repentance, as the Doctrine of God Should be
Preached to All Nations 182

Chapter 4: Repentance in the Book of John 185
It's Just a Matter of Interpretation 185
The Spirit of the Law 186
The Technique of a Thorough Witness..189
Pacifying Responses...191
Paradox Versus Paradigm..192
The Capacity and the Utility of the Mind....................................194
Give Me This Water!..195
Is There a Doctrine in the House?..196
The Will of God and the Doctrine of God..................................197
Scriptural Truth is Absolute Truth...198
The Four Quadrants of Love..200
Revelation Versus Philosophical Pursuits.....................................201
Penance, Penitence and Repentance...202
Repentance and Judas Iscariot..204
Blinded Eyes, Calloused Hearts and Dementia...........................207
Other Synonymous Expressions of True Repentance.................211

List of Axioms **Truths of** Repentance...213

BOOK 5: FREEDOM V
Chapter 5: Repentance in the Book of Acts
To Maintain or to Multiply
Through the Agency of the Holy Ghost
Barabbus is Preferred Over the Word of God
The Times of Refreshing
A Negligent Landlord
Refreshing is a Clean House
Signs, Wonders and Miracles
What Do We Really Know About These Two People?

The Shock and Awe of a Miracle of Judgment
The Gift of Repentance
The Bone Box
The Depravity and the Wickedness of Simon, Who Said
The Thoughts and the Intents of Another's Heart
The Gall of Bitterness and the Bond of Peace
What Has Made You Bitter?
The Posterity of Bitterness According to "NORAD"
A Defense Code Against Carnality
The Color Code of Bitterness
Bitterness Denotes Your Soft Spot
Real and Imagined Bitterness
The Root of Bitterness
The Bond of Iniquity
God is a Respecter of the Gift
The Published Baptism of Repentance
The Gift of, Is a Life Towards
Repentance as the Message of Salvation
Taking Aim at the Shell of Carnality
The Wildfires of Carnality
Carnal Beetles
Fighting Fire with Fire
The Preparatory Command and the Command of Execution
A Sharp Rebuke
A Two for One Baptism
Faith and Repentance Go Hand in Hand
Works Meet for Repentance as Exculpatory Evidence

Chapter 6: Repentance in the Book of Romans
A Lifestyle of Repentance is a Consecrated Life
The First Principles of Righteousness
Carnality Is Not a Constitutional Element of Design
The Four Quadrants of Righteousness
Quadrant One: Saving Faith Begets Obedient Faith
Quadrant Two: Obedient Faith that Begets God's Righteousness

Quadrant Three: Righteousness Begets Sanctification (Holiness)
Sanctifcation Must Become the Object of a Reasonable Pursuit
The Language of an Unlawful Command
The Language of a Promise
Quadrant Four: Justification is that which Satisfies the Divine Law
Obedience By Proxy
The Essential Conditions of Gospel Justification
The Ground of Gospel Justification
To Satisfy the Mission He was Sent to Fulfill
Historical and Religious Despots
What the Atonement is Not
What Then is the Atonement?
That Which is Equivalent
A New Quality of Spirit Being
A Multiple System Shut Down
The Doctrine of Imputed Righteousness
Conscience, Colloquially Speaking
A Microscopic Detection of the Spirit of the Mind
The Spice of Life
Trial and Error
An Error in Judgment
Specific Classes of Truths
Conscience: The Credential of God
The Law of Conscience and the Measure of Faith
The Rescission of a Reprobate Mind
The Unconscious Condition of Impenitent Men
The Purpose For and the Reason of Conscience
Cauterize and Catharsis
The Law of Sin: A Self-Evident Truth which Requires Proof
We Have No Excuse!
Conscience: A Fail-Safe Mechanism
The Hand Clasp of Repentance
The Real Function of the Law as a Condition of Estoppel

The Forbearance of God
Those Who Know the Law
Legal Claims
Discontinued Intercourse
To Satisfy the Urge to Acquire
The Principle of Sin and the Subject of Carnality
Carnality as a Rule of Action to the Law of Sin
The Law of the Mind
How Shall Impenitent Men be Judged and with What?
The Principle of the Dead-Fall
A Horrible Pit
Turning State's Evidence
Endure and Be Saved

Chapter 7: Repentance in the Book of 1st Corinthians
A City Wide Over View
A Rebuttal Against Established Carnality
Under the Control of the Ordinary Impulses of Carnality
Be Saved By Fire
Let a Man Thoroughly Examine Himself
Operations, Administrations and Gifting(s)
Under New Management
A Demonstration of Man's True (Holy Ghost) Conviction
Corruption, Incorruption, Decomposition, and Mummification
Cremation is Legalized Superstition
Paradise Lost
Earth Defaults and Man's Unsuppressed Carnality

Chapter 8: Repentance in the Book of 2nd Corinthians
Unethical Pulpits
Ethics Must Involve Sound Principles and Specific Truths
A Good House Keeper
A Repentance that Leads to and Contributes to Salvation
Our Laughter Condones the Abominations Around and About Us
Benefits of Repentance

Presumptuous Sins In and Outside the Church
A Lifestyle of Repentance and the Ministry of Reconciliation
Repentance as the Probationary System of Discipline
That We Might Become the Righteousness of God

Chapter 9: Repentance in the Book of Galatians
Carnality as Another Gospel
Carnality as a Spy
The Right-Hand of Fellowship
The Left Side and the Left Hand of Fellowship
Here I Am Verses I Am Here
Carnality: the Device of Satan
There Just Ain't No Getting Around It
Carnality is Satan's Royalty
Carnality That Bewitches
The Satisfaction of a Bond
Jesus Christ, Our Stand In
Carnality: The Weak and Beggarly Elements of the Flesh
The Progression of Carnality
A Dental Procedure
Our Living God Demands a Living Sacrifice
Cast Out Carnality
A Call to Freedom
A Rat's Nest
You Dirty Rat!
The Leaven of Carnality
To Be Rich or To Be Enriched, That is the Question
That Residue of Sin
The Fruits of the Spirit
Reconciliation and Restoration
Repentance as a Proven Work of Righteousness
The Rule of the Gospel
The Rule of Law and the Rule of the Gospel
Officers of the Court
Repentance Presupposes Carnality
Presuppositional Apologetics

Capturing Our Thoughts

Chapter 10: Repentance in the Book of Ephesians
    Carnality Contrasted to True Holiness
    We Grow Faster Spiritually than We Do Physically
    The Body of this Death and the Graveyard of the Dying
    The Wiles of the Devil and the Attributes Thereof
    The Armor of God
    The Truth of the Matter
    The Breastplate of Righteousness
    The Preparation of the Gospel of Peace
    The Booby-Traps of Carnality
    The Shield of Faith
    The Helmet of Salvation
    The Sword of the Spirit
    Carnality as a Concealed Weapon of Suicide
    Prayer to the Lord of Hosts

Chapter 11: Repentance in the Book of Philippians
    Cultivated Salvation
    Carnality as Dung and Putting on the Dog
    Beware of the Concision

Chapter 12: Repentance in the Book of Colossians
    Repentance as a Surgical Operation
    Close Deliberations and the Secret of God

Chapter 13: Repentance in the Book of 1st Thessalonians
    To Turn is to Occupy
    Sanctification is a Result of Righteousness

Chapter 14: Repentance in the Book of 2nd Thessalonians
    To Be Counted Worthy of the Kingdom of God
    God Shall Repay and the Impenitent Shall Pay
    Neglected Properties of God
    The Falling Away

  The Mystery of Iniquity that is Already at Work
  What Do the Gnostics Believe About
  The Stockholm Syndrome

Chapter 15: Repentance in the Book of 1st Timothy
  Great is the Mystery of Godliness
  The Bridge, the Currency and the Route

Chapter 16: Repentance In The Book of 2nd Timothy
  The Opposite of Courage is Conformity
  To Recover Ourselves
  Many Enlist, but Very Few Make the Grade
  Repentance as Instructions in Righteousness
  A Doctrine, a Dogma and a Diatribe
  Scripture that is Profitable for Reproof
  Conviction of Sin
  Correction of Error
  Discipline in Obedience

Chapter 17: Repentance in the Book of Titus
  The Passion of a Lifestyle
  Righteousness as a Song
  Shed Does Not Mean "Hut, Hut, Hut"

Chapter 18: Repentance in the Book of Philemon
  Prisoner of War

Chapter 19: Repentance in the Book of Hebrews
  Absolute and Straightforward
  The Defragmentation of the Spirit of the Mind
  God is Not the Author of Confusion
  Six Basic Doctrines
  Stunted Growth and Development
  The Choke Point
  We Must Make More Room
  This Worm and the Proverbial Butterfly
  The Word of His Power and the Power of His Word

The Slope Principle
To Renew Them Again Unto Repentance
The Power of an Endless Life
Having Respect Unto the Recompense of the Reward
Men of Whom This World was/is not Worthy
A Lifestyle of Repentance is not a Blood Sacrifice
No Repentance, No Birthright
No Place of or for Repentance
No Repentance and No Place of Repentance
The Baptism of Repentance is Sound Doctrine
Coming to do Your Will
In the Volume of the Book
That Which is Beneath His Feet is Trampled Under Foot
Those Who Consecrate Themselves Are Made Holy
Imprinted Laws on a Renewed Mind
Law Breakers and Other Violators
Absolute Remission
He Who Rules Over the House of God
Cleansing Water
He Is Faithful to His Word
The Strength of a Man's Name
Those Who Deliberately and Willfully Sin
Profaning, Insulting, and Outraging the Holy Ghost
Vengeance Is Mine
The Voice of Words
The Contour of the Heart
Repentance as the Spiritual Science of Carnal Dynamics
Maggie's Drawers
Go Out Side the Box

Chapter 20: Repentance In the Book of James
The Thing I Need to Save My Soul
Save Our Souls
The Satellite
Substance Must Precede Evidence
A Burial at Sea

    Reasoning that is Contrary to the Truth
    The Wisdom of this World
    Repentance as a Memorial
    Anything Else is in Bad Taste
    Repentance as a Antihistamine
    There is No Genuine Escape for a Fugitive

Chapter 21: Repentance in the Book of 1st Peter
    Due Diligence
    Due Diligence Means to Walk Circumspectly
    Disbelief Begets Disobedience
    Believing Without Knowing
    Repentance as a Spiritual Sacrifice
    Becoming Peculiar is to be a Nonconformist
    The Power of His Resurrection
    The Love of Life and the Pursuit of Peace
    A Mere Desire is not a Pursuit After Righteousness
    Arm Yourself with the Same Mind as Christ
    Judgment to Begin in the House of God
    The Commercial and Corporate Enforcement of Judgment
    Eternal Life, Defined
    The Spiritual Pathologist
    There's No such Thing as a Partial Rapture

Chapter 22: Repentance in the Book of 2nd Peter
    The Knowledge of Salvation
    Repentance is the One Thing that Must Remain the Main Thing

Chapter 23: Repentance In the Book of 1st John
    The World Verses The Word
    The Sin Not Unto Death
    What is Sin?
    The Three Conditions of the Sin Unto Death
    Peremptory or Preemptive

Chapter 24: Repentance In the Book of Jude
    The Incursion of Carnality
    Caught in Plain Sight
    Man's Abandonment Caused by Carnality
    The Bastard Seed of Carnality
    The Hidden Reefs of Carnality
    The Cross Triangulation Process of Repentance
    Clouds Without Water
    Trees Without Fruit
    They are Rogue Waves of the Sea
    A Wandering Star is a Black Hole
    To Execute Judgment Upon All to Convince All
    Distinctions and Divisions
    It's Just a Matter of Opinion
    Inter-Faithism

Chapter 25: Repentance In the Book of Revelation
    They that Dwell in Caves and Who Inhabit Islands Shall Behold Great Works
    A Very Special Delivery
    No Two Objects Can Occupy the Same Place at the Same Time
    "Or else" is Another Example of Case Law
    Man's Carnality is His Own Self-Fulfilling Prophecy
    Have We Been Mistaken?
    Heaven's Least Wanted
    Bedlam and the Doctrine of Balaam
    The Alluring Power of a Woman
    The Bar of Judgment and the Doctrine of the Nicolatians
    The Frankenstein Monster of Man's Unsuppressed Carnlity
    The Whys and the What Nots
    Repentance as the Hidden Manna
    The White Stone and a Touch Stone
    From the Bar, to the Bench to the Bema Seat

The Gospel Message is only Secondary to His Return
Do You Feel a Draft?
A Space-Time Continuum to Come to Repentance
Repentance Means to Provoke Ourselves to Righteousness
Sackcloth and Ashes
The True Church is not a Red-Light District
The Rendering to be the True Remnant
On Thee and Upon Thee
Our Sackcloth Here Shall Be Exchanged to White Raiment There
Shame for Sin is the Law of the House
The Faith and the Patience of the Saints and the Word of His Patience
The Watchmen of the Heart
They Cast Dust on Their Heads
The Editing Process
God's Trash Bag and His Bottle
A Spiritual Transfer
The Glad Rags of Repentance
Dress Right, Dress!
Our Glad Rags Here Shall be Exchanged for Our Holy Garments There
The Enemy is In-A-Me
God's Judgment at Man's Request
Philosophical Faith in a Carnal Church
The Three Signs of Jonah
The Only Thing that God Can't/Won't Do
A Jury Trial by Our Peers
The Judicial Power of Judgment
An Earthly Trial and a Heavenly Sentence
Another Prolonged Trial
Jesus Christ Will not Judge, but He Shall Preside
The Saints to Judge
God's Judgment is a Spiritual Principle of Consequence
The Little Book of Repentance

Unsuppressed Carnality Proliferates Anarchy
   The Great White Throne Judgment
   That Which is More Costly than Human Life

Chapter 26: Born Again and the Scriptural Meaning of Salvation
   Overview
   A Critical Analysis of That Which is Written
   Man's Perspective: Who
   Scriptural Perspective: Who
   Man's Perspective: Where
   Scriptural Perspective: Where
   Man's Perspective: When
   Scriptural Perspective: When
   Man's Perspective: Why
   Scriptural Perspective: Why
   Man's Perspective: What
   Scriptural Perspective: What
   Man's Perspective: How To
   Scriptural Perspective: How To
   A Pendulum Swing
   A View Towards Water Baptism
   Water Baptism as a Religious or Institutional Panacea
   Carnal Christianity
   If You Cannot See, then You Cannot Enter
   The Essential Condition of Must
   Salvation is the Outcome of Being Saved
   The Difference Between Discerning and Perceiving
   The Nomenclature of Salvation
   The Scriptural Assignment of Praise
   How Do I Get inside?
   A Made to Order Salvation
   Customized Salvation
   "Ye Must Be Born Again"
   A Toast and a Drink
   Like a Scrubbed Up Pig, Some People Will Eat and

Drink Anything
The Blood and the Water
The Blood of Vengeance and of Mercy
The Blood Covering and the Sackcloth Unto Repentance
The Assimilation Process
Drinking the Blood, Metaphysically
Apprehension is the Effect of Assimilation
Pleading the Blood, Judiciously
The Power of the Blood (to Forgive Sins)
Faith in the Blood
Repentance as a Nazarite Vow
Once Saved, But are We Truly Converted
The Cart Before the Horse
God Hates the Sin, But He Loves the Sinner
Soul-Mate and a Helpmate
The Playmate of the Soul
The Genesis of a General

Truths of Repentance, Catalogued

Author's Preface

Since completing my Freedom Book Series of this vital doctrine of God, I have received wonderful comments from those to whom I have provided bits and pieces of that work. However, some have voiced their concerns over the strong statements contained. My only response to these concerns, is that the strong statements made are scripturally based. Scripture, is replete with very strong rebuke and chastisements. Every prophet had something hard to say to the impenitent people of his day for their long standing disobedience. Even the New Testament writers, made severe demands with their harsh words of divine import. When you consider the deplorable condition of stasis in which the Church is in, you can readily determine for yourself that something—is definitely wrong! It is my opinion, that due to insipid and passive preaching, our spiritual leaders have permitted the Church as a whole to wane in her morals, for she has been permitted to become strengthened in her carnality. Obviously then, it is apparent that the present methodology of innocuous sermonizing has not stemmed the flow of immorality within the Church, nor has the Church made any kind of substantive impact on this unrighteous world! Therefore, another tact must be considered to augment God's righteousness, and *the Doctrine of Repentance* is the tool which shall accomplish the spread of God's righteousness within the Church and eventually into this wicked world! Where my FREEDOM Books represent repentance as a compulsive law, these three New Testament works, shall present repentance as a command; in fulfillment to the spirit of this same law! This suggests that the Laws of God are superseded by a spiritual principle, which is just as binding as the written Word, itself. This is because God's commands,

His laws and His promises are equally the same, for without our compliance to these commands, His promises shall never be enjoyed, and man's salvation shall be jeopardized.

The Bible Codes

Moreover, just as the Bible Codes reveal that the volume of the Book speaks of carnal man's history in his impenitence, likewise Scripture reveals that penitent men may prevent such self-destruction, because of the righteous judgment which they *could or might* apply to the carnality within their souls! In other words, just because the Bible Codes reveal certain historic events, as well as giving notable mention of individuals, does not mean to say that certain destruction must occur or that all that has occurred was preordained of God. What it does say however, is that all of humanity has a choice, and the fact that these things are revealed in Scripture implies that consistently, *the wrong choices of impenitent men have been made throughout history!* This then clarifies a misunderstood concept of prophecy, and provides unequivocal testimony of the pure purpose for prophecy. In other words, *man's impenitence precedes his own destruction, just as righteous judgment precedes eternal life!*

So as you progress through this work, please remember that our righteous God commands all men everywhere, to come to repentance, for His benefit, as well as for our own! And should you have any resentment towards the strong statements of truth found herein, please admit that your resentment is an attribute of that spoiled, little child within, namely your iniquitious thoughts (Lie Based Thinking) and that your carnality will kick up a fuss; because, that is all it knows how to do and can't help but do so.

Introduction

From a Baptism to a Lifestyle

I have had difficulty continuing this investigative work of and about repentance into the New Testament. Understanding the heritage of repentance from a western civilized perspective is difficult to comprehend simply for the lack of a cultural perspective. But this must not be our excuse for our ignorance! It is essential that the Body of Christ grow in grace in her knowledge of God, so that she may appreciate repentance as the means to becoming Armed and Dangerous and then apply these spiritual truths as a cultivated lifestyle of repentance. And like my Freedom Books, which contains **258 Truths of Repentance,** this work also contains hundreds of Truths which are self-evident to the subject matter at hand.

There must occur a paradigm shift from that which is predictable to that which is paradoxical! From the old to the new; from an old, stale tradition to a new, vibrant transition. Almighty God expects His people to transfer their allegiance from a limited, and predictable heritage of church as usual to spiritual transitions, as a right of passage from carnality to righteousness and then holiness and justification! Therefore, a mood, tenor and urgency of a compulsive lifestyle of repentance tends to become a baptism unto the waters of repentance in the New Testament, which is a precedent and is the basis for that very same lifestyle!

As pertaining to the ordinance of baptism, there are essentially three methods or processes of application of this ordinance. For the purposes of this investigation, they are *immersion, submersion* and *emergence. Immersion* is immaterial in that a sinner is baptized into Jesus Christ upon his conversion (coming to faith). *Submersion* is that event in a convert's life when he or she is baptized into and beneath water by a minister. This baptizing represents an outward expression of that which has spiritually taken place inwardly upon his or her conversion. And *emergence*, pertains to the baptism of the Holy Ghost with the evidence of speaking in tongues of which Scripture teaches that Jesus Christ does Himself.

The Handmaid (Political Correctness) to Theology

The Hebrew nation was in Egyptian bondage for four hundred years. During these four hundred years of silence, God's Word was precious among men, in that Almighty God never intervened in the affairs of impenitent man. Similarly, there was an approximate four hundred year span of time between the Old Testament, which concluded with the *Book of Malachi,* and the commencement of the canonized New Testament with the *Book of Matthew.* (Actually, the Old Testament era did not conclude until the crucifixion of Jesus Christ.) Through the passage of time, Almighty God did intervene through Moses and again, with the advent of the New Testament, (the Church Age) Almighty God once again made Himself known to fallen humanity through the birth of His Son, Jesus Christ, who is the Word made flesh full of grace and truth! And let me just add that who Jesus Christ was to his disciples and the people of His day, the Holy Spirit is to and for humanity today!

John 14:16, 26
"And I will pray the Father, and He shall give you another Comforter that He may abide with you forever." "But the Comforter, who is the Holy Ghost, whom the Father will send in my name, He shall teach you all things and bring all things to your remembrance, whatsoever I have said unto you."

Introduction

Throughout these four centuries between the historic Testaments, philosophers such as Herodotus, Aristotle, Plato and others developed a systematic ground of political and secular thought of human wisdom known as *philosophy*, that *(Handmaid to Theology)*. To properly understand this view, please know that a handmaid is one who is an assistant to her master. She is subordinate to her owner. She is the minor to the major. *However, through the centuries, this philosophic handmaid has usurped her position of servitude and has over thrown the master's weakened position through her insubordinations!* Today we could call this *Political Correctness!* This was accomplished because impenitent men eliminated repentance from the pulpit as well as from their living! Such was the case between Abraham's wife, Sarah and her Egyptian handmaid, Hagar as read in *Genesis 21:1 –14*.

The contributions of this societal influence, questions the origin of man, of God, of the mind and such *Life Altering and Eternal questions* that man has pondered throughout his existence. I call these inquiries, man's eternal questions, because all of us at one time or another in our lives have asked these questions for ourselves; is this not true? Such philosophical influences have infiltrated governments, institutions of higher learning and the world's civilizations, having the time to entrench themselves deeply into the respective cultures. Consequently, it seems that the written New Testament exists to address these presiding philosophical mind sets and to provide answers to these eternal questions, then and now. In short, the *Hand Maid of Philosophy (Political Correctness)* has been allowed to take the prominent position and view for centuries!

Sometime ago, I was casually reading a paperback book entitled, *The Great Philosophers* and their teachings. Immediately, I recognized a parallel between the philosophical bent and the scriptural truth. Through this unintended discovery on my part, the Holy Ghost revealed to me the reason why such New Testament truths were so documented! To wit, the scriptural content of the New Testament is not a nebulas, esoteric statement, spoken by men and women of God as fillers on a page or in a book! They were all spoken and then recorded to address the societal influence of humanistic, philosophical ideologies and pagan practices of all sorts! *Whereas, these philosophers seemingly inculcated humanistic speculations of natural truth, Scripture counters with the declaration of divine truth!* For example, Samson spoke a riddle to the Philistine nobles at his wedding, *(Judges 14)* which was the answer given masqueraded in a question which he provided! But the philosophy minded nobles did not have the answer, but only questions. Jesus Christ, who is thee Answer, came to provide the solution to these eternal questions then and even now for humanity today!

A Heritage of Faith and Repentance

The Hebrew nation had its own heritage which was conscripted in their Talmud, from which they were to understand the heart of God and His intervention with them. They were to comprehend the elements of the Mosaic law, which mandated compliance to God's law or else. In the New Testament however, Almighty God presents the spirit of these same laws of His Righteousness (even morality), which He still requires humanity to live by today! However, as the apostle Paul instructs in *Romans 3*, the Law of (obedient) Faith is the ordinance by which men are to obey the spirit of these Laws of God, as these laws represent the full counsel of God's eternal Word to all generations. Through this knowledge, the saints of God are to obtain the knowledge of the Laws of Faith and of Repentance, and with this knowledge we are to obtain understanding and from this understanding, we should obtain divine wisdom that *Wisdom of the Just.* The philosophers of antiquity and those philosophies of the individual must never replace the truth of God's Word, nor must the true Church tolerate philosophical addendums, additions or supplementals to God's Word as that insubordinate handmaid to scriptural theology, because God's Word stands alone. Should man do so, then the church becomes insubordinate as well and becomes another handmaid to this same theology. *(cf. Rev. 22:18 –19)*

Throughout the history of the Old Testament, the heritage of repentance was evident to the Hebrew people, as a condition of the covenant relationship between the Lord their God and themselves. However, in the New Testament, the Holy Ghost urges the saint into a *Baptism unto Repentance,* for the remission of past sins, which is in compliance to the spirit of the Old Testament law.

Consider that the Holy Spirit was then and is now actively involved in the affairs of men, just as He was actively involved in the creation of the earth. *(cf. Gen. 1:2)* Scripture teaches that the Holy Spirit is the self-same Spirit, for there is no other. *(cf. 1 Cor. 12:4)* Do you see a difference in the motive of operation? The difference of the *motif operandi* is this: In the Old Testament, the Holy Spirit went before and walked beside mankind, but now in the New Testament, the Holy Ghost lives and works inside each man (saint) as well as for the benefit of all of creation through Whom all things do consist. *(Col. 1:17 –18)* It's the self-same spirit, but working in different ways or capacities. It's the same as when you or I are at home and when we are at work. We are the same individual, but we function in different capacities wearing different hats. Simple right?

The Higher Call

The predominate message from the pulpits today is that we must have more of God. I disagree, because this mind set implies that perhaps Almighty God is intentionally withholding Himself from His Church. God cannot be any more than what He is, for He is Almighty! I do concur that God is ready to communicate with His Church, but her conversation with Him has not been proper! *What any nebulous conversation may be to lip service, holy communication with God is a pure heart expression!* *(cf. Eph. 4:29-30; Col. 3:8)* It's not that we need more of God, we need to make more room for God! However, the means by which we are demanding more of God's presence is what concerns me. Simply quoting Scriptures without resolve to live according to the standards of a *higher call* will avail us nothing, because man's unsuppressed carnality still abounds within. *(cf. Isa. 22:14, 59:2)* You see, the *higher call* is intended to be discovered by those who are the *highest of creations!*

A Lifestyle of repentance as that **Wisdom of the Just** enables each saint to give and communicate more of himself to Almighty God. Through the spiritual disciplines of *due diligence* and *suppression*, the saint is regurgitated from the filth of his Iniquity and his carnal mindedness and at the same time, he enlarges his capacity for more of God. I believe that the Apostle Paul spoke of this higher call which the saints of God are to apprehend. *(cf. Phil. 3:11 –14)* Consider this, not once did Paul mention any of the three other baptisms as being a pinnacle of spiritual maturity! *His desire in life was his passion to know Christ and the power of His resurrection, having fellowship with His sufferings being made conformable to His death.* Paul never emphasized the baptism of immersion, the baptism by submersion, neither the baptism of the Holy Ghost (emergence), although he experienced all three! He did however, speak of a *higher call*, which I believe to be the fourth baptism of repentance which the New Testament church has intentionally avoided or ignored! Paul spoke of the baptism of repentance as the word of this salvation, and Scripture bares this out! *(cf. Acts 13:24 – 27; Lk. 1:77, 3:3)*

Specifically, in *Acts 28: 23 –31* Paul spoke of the Kingdom of God as to its nature, its glory, its purpose and design that it is heavenly and spiritual, sealed in the minds of men, and shines not in external pomp of will-worship, but in purity of heart and life. Paul instructed the Jews and the church at Rome of their misunderstanding of the Kingdom of God in that it is not by their observation *(cf. Lk. 17:20)* of ceremonial liturgies. As to the teachings of Jesus, Paul taught the whole history of Jesus as pertaining to His incarnation, God's doctrine, His life, His miracles, His death, His resurrection, His ascension—all that related to the mystery of godliness! (Matthew Henry Commentary, *Acts 28:23 –31*) Whereas, the twelve apostles were taught of God during the three years of Jesus Christ's earthly ministry, the apostle Paul was taught of God three years in the wilderness, for as he says, *"For I neither received it of man, neither was I taught it, but by the revelation of Jesus Christ." (cf. Gal. 1:11 – 12)* Like Paul, I too have not received this *wisdom of repentance* from any man, neither was I taught it by any man, but I did receive it by direct revelation. I therefore, attest to you that this *Doctrine of God* presented herein is not after the fashion of any man!

The Wisdom of God

Job 38:36
"Who hath put wisdom in the inward parts? Or who hath given understanding to the heart?"

Matthew 13:11
"He answered and said unto them, Because it is given unto you to know the mysteries of the kingdom of heaven, but unto them it is not given."

1 Corinthians 2:7 –12
*"But we speak **the wisdom of God** in a mystery, even the hidden wisdom, which God ordained before the world **unto our glory:** Which none of the princes of this world knew: for had they known it, they would not have crucified the Lord of glory. But as*

*it is written, eye hath not seen, nor ear heard, neither hath entered into the heart of man, the things which God hath prepared for them that love Him. But God hath revealed them unto us by His Spirit: for the Spirit searches all things, yea, the deep things of God. For what man knoweth the things of a man, save the spirit of man which is in him? Even so, the things of God knoweth know man but the Spirit of God. Now we have received not the spirit of the world, but the Spirit which is of God: that we **might know** the things that are freely given to us of God."* (emphasis mine)

Ecclesiastes 7:23 – 24 AMP
"All this have I tried and proved by wisdom. I said, I will be wise independently of God–but it was far from me. That which is, is afar off, and that which is deep is very deep–who can find it out [true wisdom independent of God]?"

Repentance, as the wisdom of God, resides in the deep things of God and cannot be ascertained without Him (Holy Spirit)! Nor can Repentance, as the doctrine of God, be comprehended with shallow renderings and trite recitations, because what repentance is to the *wisdom of God* becomes for the saint the **Wisdom of the Just**! Had corrupt men known of this wisdom, they would not have crucified the Lord of glory! Like a precious metal that must be excavated, the wisdom of repentance is presented to us in a hidden mystery, and this investigation exists to uncover this mystery. God intended it to be so, so as to protect this wisdom from corrupt men who are not deserving of its treasures or of its benefits! Therefore repentance, as the doctrine of God, remains *the wisdom of God and of the Just* even in a mystery, which God predetermined before the world began *for our glory,* for as Scripture states in *Proverbs 25:2, "It is the glory of God to conceal a thing, but the honor of kings is to search out a matter." (cf. Dan. 12:4; Amos 8:12)* This then means that carnal men must come to repentance with the understanding that they must conduct a reasonable pursuit towards a lifestyle of repentance. Otherwise, they will forever remain ignorant of their iniquity, of their carnality and of God's Righteousness and fall short of the glory of God! *(cf. Rom. 3:10 –11, 17)*

Proverbs 24:3
"Through wisdom is an house builded; and by understanding it is established."

God's Plan, His Hidden Plan, and His Revealed Plan

- **God's Plan:** Satan is frustrated because He cannot understand the gift of repentance or salvation. More specifically, Satan does not want carnal men to understand God's Righteousness either; so he keeps impenitent men in the dark by means of their iniquity! An impenitent man remains ignorant of his iniquity and of repentance which leads towards salvation, nor can carnally minded man comprehend the wisdom behind these attributes of God's amazing grace. As the adversary of all men, Satan fights against humanity to prevent us from coming into this revelation of our iniquity and of repentance ourselves!

Because Satan does not understand God's Righteousness, he will stop, block or otherwise impede the message of repentance. The fact the Gospel message is presented the world over, indicates that Satan has failed in his attempts to thwart the salvation message and God's plan of redemption! Satan cannot conceive or conceptualize eternal life, because he has already been sentenced by Almighty God unto eternal death! It is not within him, therefore, it is hidden from him. This shows God's wisdom. He hid it and kept it to himself. The wisdom of God which includes His knowledge, His plan, His organization and His vision were all kept from the devil, therefore Satan does not have a snowball's chance in Hell to understand or comprehend repentance or salvation! Hallelujah!

- **God's Hidden Plan:** Don't let the *left hand* know what the *right hand* is doing! *(cf. Mt. 6:3)* Notice I said, Don't let the left hand know what the right hand is doing. I didn't say, *"Don't let the **right hand** know what the **left hand** is doing."* As an explanation, consider that the *left* represents those who are sinister, evil, unrighteous, even self-righteous; while the *right* represents those who are of the truth, who are righteous and who are good. I said, that which the right hand knows or does, is not to be revealed to the left hand, which represents those who are carnal! They have no lot or portion to the things of God. This exclusivity then remains a mystery to the left hand.

If the right hand never reveals to the left hand, then it is the wisdom of the right hand, because the left hand is always left in the dark! This then intimates the wisdom of God! In other words, a lifestyle of repentance is righteous, just and good; while man's carnality remains sinister, self-righteous and corrupt. This is wisdom, for it is the masquerade of the plan of salvation, and repentance is that wisdom of God towards that end or final outcome and for the suppression of one's carnality! As a case in point, consider President Donald J. Trump (the right hand). God placed this man into office as the President of the United States of America at the right time and for such a time as this. Where one and all of the oppositional left fully anticipated his defeat by Hillary R. Clinton in the 2016 election, the fact that he is now our lawfully elected 45th President baffles and enrages the left. President Trump has been groomed by God Almighty with the wisdom of God so much so that he is capable of playing 3 even 4 dimensional chess against the strategems of the *demoncrats* and their nefarious ways. In short, God has placed Donald J. Trump into the Presidential Office so that he will drain the swamp and allow God's righteousness to prevail in and throughout America and the entire world! Hallelujah!!!!!

Introduction

According to Satan's devices, his knowledge of Heaven, and of the things pertaining to Heaven and all that he thought he knew in all the knowledge of who he thought God was and is, has only accomplished one thing for the devil-devastation and frustration! Why? Because the devil cannot comprehend what repentance is all about, even after all this time, and as such it still remains the wisdom of God, even as a mystery of godliness!

■ **God's Revealed Plan:** God's plan of salvation is not hid from those who are truly born again, because these saints of God have entered into His Spirit. For instance, suppose there existed a high rise building which possessed no doors and no windows. It was completely encased top to bottom and three dimensionally. Now suppose that people lived inside this building, which is impenetrable from without. The question is, How can you get inside? The only explanation is that you must be born into it from within! And so it is with salvation. We are born into God's Spirit from within His Spirit, and a lifestyle of repentance evinces this spiritual reality.

Scripture says that the things of God knoweth no man. *(vs. 12)* This means that the natural man cannot receive the things of God, and this includes repentance as the wisdom of God! Do you suppose that the devil has become knowledgeable about the things pertaining to salvation? I am telling you that he has not, because he cannot comprehend salvation; neither can he understand repentance as an attribute of true conversion! Satan cannot understand it, but we saints have the mind of Christ, which is the mind of the Spirit. Hallelujah!

Since every man born is an eternal spirit being, Satan cannot kill God's highest creation. Although man may torment himself, Satan is still shooting blanks in the dark, because he can't understand repentance or comprehend salvation. And so it remains with carnal men, who choose to sit in their self-imposed impenitence of darkness. *(cf. Jn. 1:5)* Traditionally, the mind set has been to cast the blame on somebody else and Satan is often given this culpability. Personally, I don't even give him this much recognition. If Satan could kill me, then he would have done it long ago to prevent the propagation of the Gospel message. But you might say, *"Well, he's done a pretty good job of it thus far!"* My reply is this, *"No, you did a pretty good job of it, yourself."* If Satan had the power, I wouldn't be writing this investigation on and about repentance. I would be digging some ditch somewhere or in a cave hiding from him. People! Satan does not understand the joy and the peace of God! Neither does he receive it or know from where it comes. He can't understand repentance, salvation or anything about its effects or its attributes! *(See Rom. 5:14-21)*

Scripture teaches us that Jesus Christ witnessed the fall of Satan, who was as lightning from Heaven as he was booted out of Heaven and fell to the earth. *(cf. Lk. 10:18)* I do believe that Satan is still sporting a very large footprint on his backside! Consider this. Although a lame man may hobble in his temporal physical condition, Satan has a continuous limp for all eternity! Since Satan failed in his attack against God directly and having been booted from Heaven as something that is cast before the dogs, his only other option, as plan B, was to attack God's creation, specifically mankind. Satan thought that created man was the next best thing to attacking Almighty God, Himself! So that man would transgress against the Laws of God, Satan foiled the communication and relationship between God and man, thereby causing man to be tarnished in and through his carnality and lose His image, his dominion, his portion, his office, his domain, his identification and the kingdom he was placed in. Satan, knowing that he could not destroy God, would attempt to destroy that which God had created! He has succeeded only in the guise of iniquity/carnality, which all men have and deny even to this very day!

Satan surmised that the next best way to destroy God would

be to wreak havoc on all of creation, especially man, the highest of all that God created. Satan's intent was to get man to transgress against His Creator, in a covert and clandestine operation to undermine the rule of God and of His house! Because Adam sinned, death reigned from Adam to Moses. *(cf. Rom. 5:12 – 21)* All descendants of Adam therefore acquired the mark of death (iniquity) and the penalty for it. Because of Adam's transgression, all people at all times have inherited this carnal nature, as a rule of action of their carnality! Once iniquity entered the world, then it would run its own course as evinced in man's carnal history as the rule of action to sin. The devil then would only have to sit back and watch sin proliferate. It kind of reminds me of a salesman who sits back and enjoys the profits earned through *residual sales* of an initial product which he initially sold to the public, such as fuel for the automobile or the cosmetic for a woman's face. **Truth#1: To wit, what residual income is to a product continually sold, resident iniquity (Lie Based Thinking) is to Satan's reproduced deception in the history of the soul of humanity!**

- **Mystery Described:** A mystery is just knowing bits and pieces. It's just enough revealed to keep the truth hidden. For many, the Bible is a mysterious book. But it does not have to be! It only remains so because people refuse to allow themselves the opportunities to examine the pages of Holy Writ, having the discipline or taking the time necessary to grow into spiritual maturity. As I understand it, there are at least four dimensions of inspiration from the Word of God. They are as follows: 1. What is only heard. 2. A cursory reading of the Word. 3. A structured academic program of the Word. 4. The inspiration of revelation that only comes through a diligent search of the Word. These four dimensions are in keeping with the tenets of critical thinking, which in its most simplistic expression means, thinking how one thinks.

In an ordinary, carnal sense, *mystery* implies knowledge withheld; but the scriptural significance is the truth revealed! Terms like, *made known, manifested, revealed, preached, understand, enlightened, etc.* are keynote expressions to alert the reader of *divine secrets* found throughout the scriptural text. Among the ancient Greeks, the mysteries were religious rites and ceremonies practiced by those initiated or indoctrinated into such secret societies. Those involved in these mysteries where entrusted with certain knowledge. These *enlightened ones* were called the *Perfected of Society*. However, *1 Cor. 2:5-16 (Amplified)* describes the *Perfected Ones* as the full grown, spiritually mature disciples, whose faith did not rest in the wisdom of men (philosophy), but in the wisdom and the power of God!

- **Mystery Defined:** Vine's Expository Dictionary, page 97 states: *"It is a secret. That being outside the range of unassisted natural apprehension. And that which is made known by divine revelation and is made known in a manner and time appointed by God and to those ONLY illuminated by His Spirit."*

God's wisdom pertaining to repentance and His plan of salvation was established through one man (Jesus Christ) as His plan to be fulfilled. God ordained this plan as a mystery/wisdom within Himself. Therefore, God's plan was kept within His Spirit and it has never been revealed to Satan. Because Satan is not of God's Spirit, he cannot understand God's Spirit or that which is kept in God's Spirit. For instance, animals cannot understand man or his ways and nature, because they are of a different nature. Man understands the passions of man. Animals understand one another within their own species, because they are of a different nature, unique to their species. Animals know and understand without saying a word. Although any man may recognize certain mannerisms of an animal, as a tendency only, he will never completely and fully understand animals, because of their different nature. For instance, you may be a good horseman, but horses cannot understand you fully. They can only understand that portion of you which you have revealed to them in the context of the situation such as any correction, teaching, rescue or rehearsal, but only within the framework of their mind. This is so, because man was created in the image of God to dominate.

God (the right hand) remains a mystery to Satan (the left hand), but Satan is never a mystery to God! Satan can't understand God, because he is of a different spirit! He is a different creature and is therefore a lower species of a spiritual creation. There is no way that Satan can understand God! But God can bring Satan under subjection, subdue him and can overpower him. God understands Satan, but Satan cannot understand God.

We speak the wisdom of God in a mystery—even the hidden wisdom which God ordained before the foundation of the world unto our glory! This is God's wisdom of repentance and therefore the wisdom of the just. In effect, He said, *"I'm going to hide this thing. Nothing outside My Spirit is going to know my plan, because I've hidden it within Myself!"* Herein lies a powerful truth for you and I. Hide that which Almighty God has revealed to you! Keep it within your heart, for it is protected and preserved there within your heart.

Jesus spoke in parables. He exposed, but He didn't reveal. He spoke in parables, but His disciples could not understand them. Hence, Jesus Christ remained a paradox to those who were paradigms (traditional, predictable, carnal). He was a paradox to others, because Jesus spoke spiritual truths which were contrary to common beliefs or were controversial to established religion or instituted order. Jesus showed them, but they could not see! Even Phillip said, *"Show us the Father!"* In reply, Jesus said, *"When you have seen me, you have seen the Father!" (cf. Jn. 14:8-9)*

If the princes of this world had only known, they would not have crucified the Lord of glory. That which is hidden from the hearts of unrighteous men remains concealed (hidden) in the Spirit of God. This speaks of repentance as the wisdom of God as well as the carnality of men, which all impenitent men deny. Had the princes of this world known that it was Jesus, they would never have crucified the Lord of glory and the plan of God would never have occurred. *(cf. 1 Cor. 2:8)* However Almighty God, knowing the end from the beginning, conscripted Jesus Christ to die for the sins of all humanity just the same, for carnal men remain blind to their carnality and by choice remain impenitent before a just and holy God!

It's kept even today within His Spirit, for what man knoweth the things of a man save the spirit of man which is in him? What do we really understand about another man? Don't we all know and understand what it is to be broken hearted? Most animals cannot express to man, unless it is a severe pain. Otherwise, their discomfort often goes unnoticed by man. The only way that any man may come to know the mystery of God is to come into His Spirit, because God's wisdom is contained within His Spirit. So then, in many respects the enigma that exists between any created species on Earth exists because each is of a different spirit, nature or flesh. *(cf. 1 Cor. 15:39 – 41)* To be a mystery, bits and pieces must be leaked out and expressed in parables. Since Satan does not know the wisdom of God, he remains ignorant of the doctrine and wisdom of repentance as part of God's overall plan of salvation! *This then intimates that the very thing that the devil will attempt to use to destroy man in and through iniquitous thoughts, God shall also use for victory through faith and a lifestyle of repentance!*

Throughout antiquity, Satan attempted to stop the very mention of the Messianic Prophecies, by killing the Prophets and hindering their utterances even to the point of the very crucifixion of Christ, the Messiah! He did so to prevent the preaching of righteousness against sin begot by iniquity. The problem was that impenitent men, who bought into Satan's lies rejected repentance, for they simply did not want to be told what to do! There-

Introduction

fore, in their denial and ignorance of their own carnality, they did in fact murder the Apostles and the Prophets to satisfy their carnal propensities perpetrated by their moral depravities. Because they were natural and altogether carnal, these impenitent, even self-righteous men could not receive the spiritual things of God, for they are spiritually discerned and acquired. They failed to realize that the Prophets and the Apostles they murdered were the very embodiment of God's spiritual gift to an unrighteous world. It is for this reason why the New Testament Church, for the most part, has become desolate to this very day! *Because the office of the apostle and the prophet have been relegated to antiquity, in that they are no longer considered essential for the post modern era and its erroneous theologies.* Jesus Christ implies that the carnal church shall not see Him henceforth until the brutish church embraces repentance and the preachers of righteousness who present this message! *(Mt. 23:32 – 39)*

Satan knows but he cannot comprehend that Almighty God would accept His Son (Jesus Christ) Who would be obedient and overcome. Not one time did Jesus Christ ever transgress against God, for had He done so, just one time, this one man could not become sin who knew no sin! Therefore, Satan is a nervous wreck! He is so frustrated. Many people are in his shoes, because they have chosen for themselves to receive Satan's condemnation. The condemnation which Almighty God has intended for Satan alone, has been deflected upon man so that impenitent men would receive the condemnation meant just for the devil only! Consequently, Hell is their destination and eternal torment is their condemnation along with Satan! It was never intended for man! But carnal men receive Satan's condemnation, because they choose to reject repentance as the wisdom and doctrine of God! Initially, Almighty God made Hell just large enough for Satan, his demonic horde, and the fallen angels. But, the Bible clearly states that Hell has enlarged herself, due to carnal propensities of impenitent men which are never satisfied! *(See Isa. 5:14; 1 Jn 2:15 –17)*

Romans 5:16 –17
"And not as it was by one that sinned, so is the gift: for the judgment was by one to condemnation, but the free gift is of many offenses unto justification. For if by one man's offense death reigned by one; much more they which receive abundance of grace and of the free gift of righteousness [repentance] shall reign in life by one, Jesus Christ." (brackets mine)

In essence, God said I'll choose one man and redeem them all back! Because Satan remains ignorant of God's wisdom he says, I'll just torment each one, one at a time. The time of his frustration has caused Satan to become a nervous wreck. He's gone berserk, as the times of the Gentiles are coming to a close, his demise comes ever closer! Humanity must also come to know that our time of repentance is also coming to an end, in that, each man's lifetime on Earth is for each individual his time to come to repentance! *(cf. Zeph. 2:1 – 3)* Like the prisoner on death row, Satan is watching the calendar of his doom get ever closer! In fact, the torment that he might inflict on man is only a small flicker of the Hell bound torment he feels within himself!

John 1:5
"And the light [of the Word] shineth in darkness: and the darkness comprehended it not."

There are only two spirits in the world. Darkness cannot overcome light; this is because, darkness can't comprehend, take in, or grasp mentally, or embrace light. If you want something to truly be hidden from sight, place it in the light! Just as a blind man would stumble over, upon or into something which he cannot see in his darkness, likewise the devil is blind in the light of the glorious gospel, because he cannot grasp the wisdom of God, which is first light! No wonder God said, *"Let there be light!"* Because impenitent men love darkness more than light, they that love darkness will receive the reward of darkness—condemnation! Those who love the light will receive the reward of light, repentance which leads to salvation through faith in the shed blood of Jesus Christ to which a lifestyle of repentance infers! *(Acts 20:21)*

In closing, humanity bares the image of the first born (Adam) but upon conversion and coming to repentance, we are born again and bare the image of the one man born of God (Jesus Christ). As saints of God, we can bare the image of the spiritual and not of the carnal. It is my heart's desire for you, that when you discover for yourself, repentance as the wisdom of God, hide it! Hide it deep. Sell everything you have and by the whole field. It is there for you to find. *(cf. Prov. 25:2)* God's plan was by one man. Almighty God hid His plan in the light (Jesus Christ). His revealed wisdom is to all those who love the Light. *(cf. 1 Cor. 1:30)*

Proverbs 23:23
"Buy truth and sell it not; also wisdom, instruction, and understanding."

Notes:

FREEDOM IV

Chapter 1
Repentance in the Book of Matthew

The Unencumbered Soul

The Lord commissioned me to investigate repentance as the doctrine of God on January 11, 1999. Since I had no previous understanding of repentance outside of the shallow rendering which most people had; therefore, I found myself at a great loss. I had no game plan, I possessed no concept of layout, I had no idea as to how, and in which direction I would have to follow to even initiate this project! As I mused over this huge dilemma, I basically told God, He would have to assist me, if He expected me to fulfill this assignment. Consequently, my method of investigation evolved into a three pronged filtration system. To ensure myself that everything I would write would be strictly Gospel, I first researched every Scripture which included the word *repentance* and its derivatives. I did this via the *Strong's Concordance*. Second, as I read through my *Thompson-Chain Bible*, I noticed that in the margin of each page were printed literally hundreds, if not thousands, of keynote words which expressed the primary thought or intent of each verse. *Repentance, penitence, impenitence, righteousness* and *carnality* are just a few of these words, which did appear many times page after page, chapter after chapter and book after book. So, I highlighted those words pertinent to this investigation, from *Genesis to Revelation*. Third, I read through my *Amplified Bible* looking for any verse in which *repentance* was written. An example of this, is found in *Zephaniah 2:1-3* in which the Authorized King James does not specify repentance within these passages as does the Amplified Bible.

I came to realize that I had little or no earnest understanding or knowledge of iniquity, carnality nor any specific knowledge about repentance or righteousness, singularly or as a doctrine of Scripture! In effect, the Word of God was precious [rare, scarce, inadequate] to me pertaining to these doctrines of God. And here I am a Bible School graduate, and a seasoned veteran of God, and I had no comprehensive knowledge of iniquity, carnality, repentance or righteousness, beyond the average rendering which the carnal church currently possesses! So, I did embark on this quest. I thought, since I am this ignorant about iniquity and carnality and since I have a misunderstanding of repentance and righteousness, I wondered just how many other people were ignorant like me, misunderstanding these doctrines themselves. So, I took a census. I asked spiritual leadership, the churchgoer, and the man on the street to either define or describe for me *iniquity, carnality, repentance* and *righteousness*. To my amazement, their responses were no better or different than my own! Consequently, this census revealed to me that the denominational church's tenet of carnality was simply to be carnal minded, an undefined and nondescript expression, and that repentance meant to turn from sin and a return back to God, while righteousness meant standing uprightly before God or to be in right standing with Him: And the word *iniquity*? Nobody could define that for me! I did not know nor was I ever taught *that carnal mindedness which consists of iniquitous thoughts, extends to the four quadrants of the mind!* However, having completed this investigation, I have learned that *iniquity* and *carnality* are afflictions and conditions and that their overall effect upon the soul is carnal mindedness and death. I have learned that anyone who is carnally minded is afflicted in the four faculties of the spirit of the mind by his iniquitous thoughts (aka: Lie based Thinking). Specifically, in his will, his consciousness, his reasoning and his intelligence. But more about this later.

When I asked these people whether they had successfully overcome their carnality, I learned that no one had successfully accomplished this in their own life, although many did state that they were not carnally minded! After awhile, a pattern began to appear; specifically, not a single person, with whom I spoke (cross denominationally) possessed any working knowledge of and about repentance, righteousness, iniquity or carnality! Since this depravity was evident, the question Almighty God asked me was, *"Why did John the Baptist tell the people of his day to repent?"* Knowing that I did not have an answer, the Holy Ghost said, *"Because John knew that the people were aware of their heritage, as well as their nation's long standing rebellion against the Mosaic Law."* Immediately, I learned a powerful truth of and about iniquity, carnality, repentance and righteousness! **Truth #2: The New Testament Church does not know her heritage pertaining to either, neither does she genuinely recognize her own long standing disobedience in her own carnality against the Word of God!** Therefore, **Truth#3: Repentance as the Wisdom of the Just is the doctrine of God, which the saints of God should comprehensively know if they are to overcome carnal tendencies within their lives, for without this knowledge, righteousness remains unknown and the resultant holiness shall not be obtained!** *(Rom. 3:10 –18, 6:16 –19, 22; 1 Jn. 5:16 –17)*

In my first three Freedom books I investigated the heritage of Israel's long standing rebellion to the Mosaic Law. Here in this investigation, I shall investigate the church's long standing disobedience to the spirit of these same Laws of God. To wit, what rebellion was to Israeli history, disobedience is to humanity, the New Testament Church and ultimately to our country! I say this because the word, *rebellion* is strictly of Old Testament origin, for it does not appear in the New Testament text. However, in its place the word *disobedience* does. (Strong's Exhaustive Concordance)

In this investigation, the Body of Christ can learn of *Repen-*

tance as the Doctrine of Salvation to correct this scarcity and her insubordination! Scripture tells us that knowledge is power. Therefore, it is reasonable to say that without a working knowledge of iniquity, carnality, of repentance and of righteousness, the saint remains powerless to renew his mind of the iniquitous thoughts therein. *(Lk. 1:77; 1 Tim. 4:8, 13 –16; Jam. 1:21)*

Although his spirit may be reborn, as if it never existed before, the saint's soul is another matter! **Truth #4: Repentance pertains to man's soul wherein his carnality resides, and righteousness is the expression of his true penitence. Without a working knowledge of his iniquity and carnality, man's disobediencce will never be suppressed and neither shall a soul be reconciled back to God!** *(cf. 2 Cor. 5:17 – 21)*

In fact, the New Testament opens with John the Baptist preaching repentance to an impenitent people and Scripture closes with the two witnesses preaching repentance to another future generation of impenitent people, and as you will learn, *repentance remains the prevailing theme throughout the New Testament text, just as it is in the Old Testament text!* Even Jesus Christ, stated that repentance should be preached throughout the nations, beginning at Jerusalem! *(cf. Lk. 24:47; Rev. 2:5, 16, 21 – 22; 3:19, 11:3)* He said this to undergird that word of righteousness which John the Baptist had preached. The fact that Jesus Christ did not preach another Gospel, nor teach another doctrine different from John, denotes that John possessed a revelation about repentance as the doctrine of Almighty God. It is my hope that as you continue to read this investigation, you too will acquire this same revelation for yourself.

Repent Means to Renew and Change

Matthew 3:1-2
"In those days came John the Baptist, preaching [repentance as the knowledge of salvation] in the wilderness of Judea and saying,

Repent ye for the kingdom of heaven is at hand." (brackets mine) (*cf. Lk. 1:77, 3:3*)

Truth #5: What metaphysical is to the supernatural, repentance is to the meta, as that which facilitates metamorphous! Now, John the Baptist, was a cousin to Jesus, the Christ. He said to the people of his day, *"Repent ye!"* Here, the word *repent* in the Greek is translated *meta*, which is a prime root of the word *repentance*. It means, *"to think differently, reconsider."* Of interest is the phrase, *"Consider your ways"* which appears four times in the *Book of Haggai*. As used in the text verse however, *repent* also means, "metamorphous as a *transformation*, a transfigure and therefore a *change, renew*." (Strong's Exhaustive Concordance Greek ref. #3340, 3339, page 47) Renew means, "to restore, renovate, repetition, intensity." (Strong's Greek ref. #303, 340, 341, pages 10 and 11) This infers that whenever you read the words *change or renew*, they each imply repentance or more specifically, coming to repentance, and God's Word intends that impenitent men must come to repentance no matter which translation you read! For instance:

Romans 12:2 AMP
"Do not be conformed to this world (this age), [fashioned after and adapted to its external, superficial customs], but be **transformed (changed)** *by the [entire] renewal of your mind [by its new ideals and its new attitude], so that you may prove [for yourselves] what is the good and acceptable and perfect will of God, even the thing which is good and even the thing which is good and acceptable and perfect [in His sight for you]."*

Matthew 3:11a AMP
"I indeed baptize you in (with) water because of your repentance [that is, because of your **changing** *your minds for the better, heartily amending your ways, with abhorrence of your past sins]...."*

Therefore, *change, repent, renew* and *transformed* are uniquely related in that they imply something to be transfigured, and that something is every aspect and faculty of the mind! Think of an existing house that would be restored or renovated. The reconstruction of it often requires the restoration of all that is internal, that is to say, all which is within the perimeter walls and beneath the roof and above the flooring. Although it may have a street address, the occupation of it would only be determined by those who reside in it, for without someone's occupancy, the house would remain an empty structure. Since Scripture tells us that the saints of God are the house of God *(cf. Heb. 3:6)*, then it is also reasonable to deduce that through a lifestyle of repentance, the saints of God possess the same attribute as *transfigure*, because of the occupancy of the Holy Ghost! Consequently, the saint is not an empty structure, for he is a holy residence! **Truth #6: Renew then, is to restore as repent is to change or turn! When a saint acquires repentance as that Wisdom of God, his soul is regenerated, because he has purposed in his heart to renew his mind so as to save his soul by and through a lifestyle of repentance!** *(cf. Mt. 17:1 – 8; Jn. 1:14; Rom. 6:16 –19, 12:1 – 3; Eph. 4:21 – 24)*

The New Testament Church Must Acknowledge Her Heritage of Disobedience

According to the Amplified Bible commentary, the Talmud to the Jew, was a compilation of their legal decisions, but it was also a repository of knowledge about religion, philosophy, history, astronomy, ethics, medicine and folklore. Since this is the case, then the Jews derived intellectual stimulation from their Talmudic studies, and because of this, they knew the heritage of their long standing disobedience to the Laws of God. This was abundantly shown in my 3 Freedom Books. Knowing this beforehand, and in order for John to demand the people to come to repentance, he too must have known that the people knew of their God dishonoring heritage. Personally, the only thing I ever knew of carnality or repentance was from my Roman Catholic upbringing pertaining to absolution, the confessional box, three Hail Mary's and the Rosary! In retrospect, this abuse of sacrament seems to mimic the practices of the Pharisees, Sadducees and temple priests who did levy taxes and sold, for their financial gain, animals and birds for the temple sacrifices. It was for this reason, that Jesus Christ became indignant with the merchants who merchandised the basic tenets of the Mosaic law within the house of God; for their own selfish gain. *(cf. Mt. 21:12)*

Gullible people [today], simply live out their lives day to day as assembly-line workers. For us Gentiles, the workforce has become our sanctuary of modern times, whereas, the Jews had their temple as the hub and center of their culture. **Truth #7: Through a lifestyle of repentance, the saints of God shall learn God's will for their lives, because repentance must be based on the specific knowledge of carnality and not upon some slick trick of merchandising or religiosity!** *(cf. 1 Jn. 1:6 – 8; 2:4; 2 Cor. 7:10 AMP)* Through a lifestyle of repentance, the potential exists for each saint to reach thousands of people, impacting their lives for Almighty God. People will be attracted to a properly presented word of and about repentance, for as they say, *"If you want to draw a crowd, just tell them to repent!"* John certainly did just that. But what has been the typical method of presenting repentance? Out of ignorance, preachers have presented repentance with heavy-handed tactics! Just as there are two sides to every coin; likewise, there is another way of presenting repentance that leads to edification, exhortation and comfort. Rather than beat somebody over the head with repentance, as with a hammer or an ugly stick, teach the HOW TO of repentance through the use of metaphors, analagies and life associations, of which this complete investigation contains.

Repentance, the Fourth Baptism

According to the Vine's Expository Dictionary, pages 96, 97 *Baptize, Baptist* and *Baptism* are described as the process of *immersion, submersion* and *emergence*. The doctrine of baptism is seen with the following reference:

Baptize defined: (BAPTISMA) with (a) John, the Baptist (b) of Christian baptism (c) of the overwhelming afflictions and judgments to which the Lord voluntarily submitted to on the cross (d) of the sufferings His followers would experience, *not of a vicarious character*, but in fellowship with the sufferings with their Master. *Baptism* defined: (BAPTISMOS) the ordinance is used of the ceremonial washing of water of articles. *Baptist* defined: (BAPTIZO) a Baptist, is used only of John the Baptist, and only in the Synoptists, 14 times.

Since *baptism,* is a predominant doctrine of Scripture, it would be reasonable to review this tenet of biblical text. Now, I am aware there presently exist within the halls of universal Christendom, divergent premises on and about baptisms, which seem to pertain more to the traditional implications among the various denominations. For a short period of time, I attended a Baptist church in San Diego, where I was told by the pastor, that to become a member of his church, I had to be water baptized! Conversely, other church teachings insist that a person must be baptized in the name of Yahweh only! While there are still others that sprinkle or are baptized in Jesus' Name only. Be that as it may, I choose not to contest any of these; rather, I simply want to point out the mention of four baptisms from my own understanding, however flawed it might be in the light of established tradition. For some, this review would be elementary, but for others, this segue will be most interesting.

According to the traditional church perspective, there are primarily three baptisms. To my understanding these baptisms are: *in the Name of the Lord Jesus* [into Christ] *(cf. Acts 19:5;*

Rom. 6:3 – 4; Gal. 3:27 – 29) into one Body (cf. 1 Cor. 12:12), and *that of the Holy Ghost (cf. Acts 11:16)*, all of which are or may be ceremoniously celebrated in water baptism. However, there are a few influential denominations which claim that there are just two baptisms, meaning that the Baptism in the Holy Ghost is not considered! In any event, the Scriptures reveal that there are actually four distinct baptisms! One is ceremonial, and the others are not. First, and as I understand it, upon coming to faith the new convert would be baptized *into* the Body of Christ, and as a command of Scripture and his compliance to it, the convert would then be ceremonially baptized in water by a minister. This ceremonial observance, is the outward expression of the rebirth [born again experience] of a new convert's spirit man from the old, dead spirit to a new reborn spirit. *(cf. 2 Cor. 5:17)*

The second baptism, is the baptism *into* Jesus Christ which is symbolic of the death, burial and resurrection of Jesus Christ, as well as, the convert's acknowledgment, identification and regeneration of the soul, through his confession of saving faith. It seems, that this baptism is a concurrent event with baptism in water. However, and in spite of this, the churches are filled with a bunch of wet sinners and soggy saints! *(cf. Col. 2:12 –13)*

The third baptism has been most controversial among the rank and file of the major denominations. I'm speaking of the *baptism of the Holy Spirit* with the evidence of speaking in other tongues. This particular doctrine has caused church factions and conflagrations between, among and within the halls of Christendom, for decades! I, for one, have been baptized with the Holy Spirit and I do speak in tongues; however, this unique capability is not my primary focus. Rather, the fruits of the Spirit are my primary aim, for they denote the character of godliness that should be evident in my life. The speaking in tongues, is secondary, and by writing this, I'm sure that to some I have just committed a sacrilege! *(cf. Mt. 3:11; Acts 1:8; 2:1 – 4; 1 Cor. 14:1, 38 – 40)*

Concluding, let me just say, that I have not been the same since! Truly, for me, this encounter with Almighty God was a genuine baptism of divine proportions! Since I've had this encounter, I know firsthand the baptism of the Holy Spirit is a genuine event, which every saint should experience for themselves if they choose. *I learned by this experience that knowing the reality of a thing is far better than believing in that thing, because anybody can contest or challenge a belief.* Although, there is so much of Scripture which I do believe, it is wonderful in deed when the Holy Spirit will allow me to truly know a spiritual thing, and it is my intent that you dear saint would come to experience a lifestyle of repentance, so that you too may know this spiritual thing of God as I have.

I mentioned that there are four baptisms. By now, you are probably guessing that repentance to be that fourth baptism. How perceptive you are! Permit me to elucidate. First, it is abundantly clear to me that presently, the traditional church does not have any concept of the baptism unto the waters of repentance, which this investigation pertains. What it does have, is a convoluted evangelistic, ceremonial observance, which in their minds qualifies the convert's lifelong confession of faith and his profession of faith. (See Freedom 2, chapter 26 for insights pertaining to the difference between a *confession* and a *profession*.)

Interestingly, the folds and ridges on the *surface of the brain* are called "convolutions". (Webster's) Concerning the *surface rendering* of repentance, which cultural Christianity promotes today, the societal *convoluted* mindset of its errant theology on or about this baptism, leaves the people with a twisted and entwined denominational doctrine and dogma! No wonder church people are coiled and ready to spring a rebuttal against any whose attestation would contradict or otherwise challenge the talisman of their particular dogmatic bent or fetish! For most church folk, their denominational affiliation, is just that—a talisman, for their allegiance to it over the Word of God, is as a charm, fetish or amulet! They fail to realize that *repentance, is the doctrine of God and the knowledge of salvation,* and it is for this reason that repentance must be taught! The baptism of repentance is sound scriptural doctrine, which every believer must experience, for this gift of God has been granted to all nations.

Acts 11:18
"Then God has also granted to the Gentiles repentance that leads to eternal life [that is real life after earthly death]."

Without any further castigation of the traditional church system and its particular doctrinal penchants, let me proceed with the many metaphors and allegories which are *true to Scriptures, true to Reason* and *true to Life* which this investigation contains. Since repentance, is a spiritual thing of God, then physical associations and parallels are necessary, so as to fulfill the law of language and interpretation. Namely, that before any two people can fully understand and comprehend what the other may say or mean, a common denominator must be established to facilitate such acknowledgment. Having said this, I believe that our intelligent, all knowing Creator has been trying to communicate to intelligent and albeit impenitent humanity as one intelligent being to another, but due to man's iniquitous thinking/carnality, our minds, ears, eyes and hearts have all been impaired to receive this truth from Him. It is for this reason why confusion and conflicts remain. And as I said, whenever a denominationally minded person is challenged in his doctrine or dogma, conflicts, confusion and chaos shall arise. Therefore, please allow the following metaphors and allegories to assist you in your comprehension of this gift of God, which He calls *repentance* and what I believe to be the *Doctrine of God and the Knowledge of Salvation.*

The Agriculture and Horticulture Process of Repentance

The *fruits* mentioned in the first passage below refers to the fruits of the Spirit, which are found in the *Book of Galatians* chapter 5. In both instances, the word *fruit* implies, means or refers to the saint's character/conversation of Godliness, which should be exhibited in our righteous conduct and our holy behavior!

Matthew 3:7 – 10
"But when he [John] saw many of the Pharisees and Sadducees come to his baptism, he said unto them, O generation of vipers, who hath warned you to flee from the wrath to come? Bring forth therefore **fruits meet for repentance**; *And think not within yourselves that we have Abraham to our father ...And now also the* **axe is laid unto the root of the trees,** *therefore every tree which bringeth not forth good fruit is hewn down and cast into the fire." (cf. Lk. 3:8, emphasis mine)*

Galatians 5:22 AMP
"But the fruit of the [Holy] Spirit [the work which His presence within accomplishes] is love, joy (gladness), peace, patience (an even temper, forbearance), kindness, goodness (benevolence), faithfulness, gentleness (meekness, humility), self-control (self-restraint, continence). Against such things there is no law [that can bring a charge]." (cf. Jn. 15:1 – 2; Rom. 11:16 – 25)

Horticulture, is the science of growing flowers, *fruits,* vegetables, shrubs, etc. in gardens or orchards. (Webster's) When I consider the scriptural import of seed, time and harvest, I think of *horticulture*. Another word that comes to mind is *agriculture*, which is the art or science of farming, and it is the work of *cultivating the soil, producing crops,* and raising livestock. (Webster's) As a side note, Scripture points out that there are *seasons and purposes* for everything under the sun. *(Ecclesiastes 3)* With this concept or truth in mind, *the time release (TTR),* is found universally in and throughout creation, even micro-sphereically. Elsewhere, Scripture teaches *seedtime and harvest (STH),* as a spiritual principle for fruition of all things in life. This spiritual principle is applicable micro-sphereically in *plants* that grow from the *seed* that is *planted* which in time becomes a tree after its own kind, to a thought that in time becomes a reality.

Regardless, STH is evident as a process of growth, and that intentionally! By design then, things occur as a consequence of action, of word or of thought. So then, TTR is equivalent to STH and this occurs in nature, even pathogenically. There are even certain medicines that are TR remedies pathologically. My defective heart valve for example as a pathogenic condition of my anatomy, is a TR malady that I have had for decades and without knowing it! And even though this has been determined medically and scientifically, there does exist a TR for its healing, its cure, a miracle waiting for me! It already has my name on it. This remedy is waiting for me (in time) to simply show up, arrive or catch up! This remedy was *ahead of time,* because previously *it wasn't time.* I was *behind the time,* but now that *time* has arrived and is NOW, my healing, my cure, my miracle provision of health is NOW, expressed and to be embraced by me at the appropriate time. In other words, *TTR cure is equivalent to TTR malady and both speak of STH universally, as well as individually!*

Here in these verses, I find a conjunction of both sciences. John the Baptist meant that the penitent saint must become knowledgeable in his ability to grow *fruits* meet for repentance, which pertain to a demonstrated *character* of godliness, and at the same time be skillful in his ability to *cultivate* the soil of his soul, so as to *dig up the weeds of iniquity/carnality,* which reside therein. Both apply towards one's character, for we are all known by others through it, whether our character be a righteous one or not. *(cf. Psa. 1:3; Rev. 22:2)* Presently, there is a television minister who persistently refers to *Matthew 3:7 – 10*. In his televised ruse, he urges his viewing audience to contribute large sums of money for his particular cause. In effect, he implies that if given, then God would be compelled to give more fruits of righteousness! What this minister, who reminds me of a used car salesman, insinuates is that giving money to him was equal to a righteous cause or character! John the Baptist never demanded any such thing! No wonder the Body of Christ is so confused when there are Slick Willeys out there, who have a freehand to merchandise the Gospel! And no wonder people dispute each other, for nobody wants to be told that he or she is wrong or has been taken! **Truth #8: Although he might be made the righteousness of God in Christ, spiritually, the saint's righteousness is not a quick acquisition, because a man's soul character takes a lifetime to develop; neither does righteousness ever pertain to fiscal achievement!** *(cf. 1 Cor. 15:34; 2 Cor. 5:18 – 21)*

The Multipurpose Tool of Repentance

Ecclesiastes 10:10
"If the ax is dull and the man does not whet the edge, he must put forth more strength; but wisdom helps him succeed."

Matthew 3:7 – 10
"But when he saw many of the Pharisees and Sadducees come to his baptism, he said unto them, O generation of vipers, who hath warned you to flee from the wrath to come? Bring forth therefore **fruits meet for repentance***; And think not within yourselves that we have Abraham to our father …And now also* **the axe is laid unto the root of the trees***, therefore every tree which bringeth not forth good fruit (of character) is hewn down and cast into the fire."*

Inherently, garden and farming tools are used to accomplish

particular tasks. Spiritually however, Scripture reveals that repentance is the shovel the saint must use to get this job done! *(cf. Deut. 23:12-14* – See also Freedom 1, chapter 6 for additional insights.) Here in *Matthew 3,* John introduced the axe that was laid unto the root of the trees. He used the axe as an interesting analogy, for John spoke of it as a tool which possesses spiritual significance. Therefore, *it seems that repentance is actually a multipurpose tool, combining a shovel to dig and an axe to cut!*

Through the years, I've heard denominationally minded pulpit ministers say, that this axe speaks of Jesus Christ. Well, consider another comparison, which in my opinion, is more appropriate. Like the *shovel called repentance*, which I spoke of in Freedom 1, there is an *axe called repentance* as well! Both are spiritual tools by which the saint becomes a fellow worker with Christ. *(cf. Col. 4:11)* The difference is in there use. By design, a shovel is used to dig, scoop, grade or otherwise cultivate or excavate dirt [agriculture]. An axe, by its design, is used exclusively for cutting, chopping, severing, lacerating trees or timber [horticulture]. The application of the axe as cutting may also be regarded as pruning! **Truth #9: Therefore, what the shovel of repentance is to the dirt of our carnality, the axe is to the pruning of the fruit of our character!** Both tools are essential to develop a lifestyle of repentance. This infers, that they work hand in hand, just as faith and repentance go hand in hand. But the problem has been that our hands have become withered as an arthritic hand that impedes dexterity; or like the horse whose tendons have been strung to impede its run! In Jesus' Name, Stretch forth thy hand that it be made whole! **Truth #10: Whereas, a withered hand prevents spiritual quickening, the arthritic condition of carnality impedes righteousness. This is due to the fact that the cultivation of a soul unto repentance and its pruning of the growth and fruits of repentance have been long since neglected!** Since trees have their roots in the dirt, the meaning of John directed the people of his day to consider the roots of the trees [themselves] and the dirt within their soul. Ergo, that which the shovel could not accomplish, the axe could! So let me ask you, which potting soil is your character rooted in?

Look at any tree, specifically its sprawling branches. These branches reflect the unseen extensive root system beneath the ground. Therefore, that which is seen above ground mirrors that which is unseen and beneath ground! *(cf. Mt. 12:35)* Now, should the roots be severed from the tree, the tree would topple over and die, because the root system, as that which also anchors the tree to the earth, has been compromised. When John said that the axe is laid to the root of the trees, his meaning was intended to inform the people, and especially the religious sect, that all of man's traditions [carnality] which have been his foundation and anchor to all that is earthly/worldly shall be severed and these trees/deeds of carnality shall topple over and die! Therefore the axe, as a implement of husbandry, helps to preserve the fruitfulness of the tree [saint] ahead of time!

Moreover, although a tree may lean to one side or the other, basically, a tree stands vertically, does it not? Now, consider any man. He stands and walks upright. **Truth #11: A lifestyle of repentance shall become, for the saint who truly seeks after God's righteousness, a shovel to expose the root of iniquity (Lie Based Thinking) and an axe that cuts the traditions of carnality from beneath the saint, so that he may stand uprightly before a holy and just God as a pruned tree of righteousness!** Without the root system intact, the tree could be toppled by a stiff, hot, dry wind. This wind shall become to the penitent saint a wind of judgment, which he permits and allows God to direct, against his own iniquity, effectively blowing this carnal element from his soul, so that he won't be toppled over by God's stronger wind of judgment unto eternal damnation! *(cf. Jer. 4:11 – 13; 2 Cor. 7:8 – 11; Eph. 3:17)* For you see my friend, the choice to change—is always ours.

But alas, most people refuse to change because they are fearful or ignorant. They fail to realize that to change *willingly* now will prevent the abrupt change brought on by adversity later.

As another example, have you ever landscaped your yard or another's property in which all hands had to remove existing trees or shrubbery? If you had to do this by hand, that is to say, without heavy equipment, then you know that the hand tools which you used were probably a [pinch] pry bar, a shovel, an axe or hatchet, pruning saw or shears, even a chainsaw. Not to mention the rope or chain used to pull the tree stump or bush out of the ground. Get the picture? In retrospect, each tool was used interchangeably, were they not? What one tool could not accomplish, the other might or could. Either way, that was backbreaking, hard work!

As for myself, I once landscaped my property in San Diego, California, where I had planted and pruned 93 rosebushes. But before I could plant, I first had to cultivate the soil and uproot existing shrubs and trees. To successfully accomplish this task I, without knowing it, applied the principles found in the science of horticulture and agriculture. Occasionally, I used an axe to prune away the larger unwanted branches, which were too large in diameter for the pruning shears, and I used the shovel to dig. But either way, the same application of cutting/pruning was employed. So in this sense, it would be reasonable to consider the use of the axe, as spoken by John, to also reflect the pruning of the tree as well, for even Jesus referred to the pruning of branches in His discourse to the disciples in *John chapter 15:1 – 3 (AMP). "I am the True Vine, and My Father is the Vine dresser. Any branch in Me that does not bear fruit [that stops bearing] He cuts away (trims off, takes away); and He cleanses and repeatedly prunes every branch that continues to bear fruit, to make it bear more and richer and more excellent fruit. You are cleansed and pruned already, because of the word which I have given you [the teachings I have discussed with you]." (cf. Mt. 3:7 – 10)* Do you see it? Jesus said that the saint that receives His Word of righteousness, is cleansed and pruned already, and that the doctrine of repentance, is that hand tool which gets the job done!

Water Unto Repentance Precedes the Fruit of Repentance

Matthew 3:11
*"I indeed baptize you with **water unto repentance:** but he that cometh after me is mightier than I, whose shoes I am not worthy to bear: he shall baptize you with the Holy Ghost and with fire:"*

John 3:5
*"Jesus answered, Verily, verily, I say unto thee, Except a man be **born of water** and of the Spirit, he cannot enter into the kingdom of God."* (emphasis mine)

For myself, this reference of water unto repentance has been a mystery for me for many years. All I know of water is that which is commonly known by everybody else; it's wet! Often times, Scripture is taken out of context, and what is left is a pretext. Inaccurate surmising and pretensions regarding scriptural meaning have often left me with a sense of disappointment. To find rest, my mind demands accurate truth and specific knowledge which must be proved or demonstrated. Such was the case with Nicodemus in *John 3:5*. I have heard and have been taught that this particular verse *(John 3:5)* speaks of the birthing of an infant, and only after the mother's water breaks; but there is one thing though that should be mentioned. **Truth #12: The water unto repentance as agitated water, is living water, whereas stagnant water, is polluted and dead. This is because the water unto repentance brings life to an otherwise carnally tainted, dead soul!** But, John the Baptist eluded to a spiritual truth that has yet to be fully grasped by the Church! This is because the wisdom of God resides in the deep things of God! He intended it to be so, so as to protect it from carnally corrupt men, who are not deserving of it's blessings nor of its treasures! **Truth #13: Therefore, to be deserving of the provisions of a lifestyle of repentance will require one to become knowledgeable with the agricultural excavation process of his soul and the horticultural growth process of the fruits of his salvation!** Since people are in denial of their carnality and remain ignorant of their iniquity they don't understand righteousness consequently, repentance remains a mystery to them also! This fact substantiates what Paul, the apostle, said to the Romans in his discourse to that church in Rome. He said,

Romans 3:10 – 11
"There is none righteous, no not one. There is none that understand, there is none that seek after God."

It is common knowledge that natural sunlight and water are essential elements for the growth of crops as well as the sustenance of trees and all earthly life. However, inordinate volumes of water will either kill a plant or utterly destroy everything in its path, especially if the water becomes a torrent. **Truth #14: The water unto repentance insinuates the gradual, gentle moistening of the saint's soul, so as to irrigate the sludge of his carnality so that his carnality may be exposed, acknowledged and identified for what it truly is, SIN! Unlike the deluge of Noah's day, which covered the entire Earth for forty days and nights as divine judgment against man's wickedness, the water unto repentance is the lesser judgment which the saint must levy against the iniquity/carnality within his own soul!**

The Leaven that Coagulates

Here's one of the spiritual insights the Holy Spirit gave me back in 2018. It concerns the *water unto repentance*. Religion and tradition coagulates the consciousness of men, for without the cleansing of the water of repentance, all temple furnishings remain soiled with the stench of coagulated blood! Whereas, the coagulation of blood creates blood clots that potentially damage the brain, so too does religion thicken the iniquity that corrupts the consciousness of man! *Leviticus 17:11* states that life is in the blood. Spiritually and medically, this is a proven fact (anatomically)! But the unique thing here is, that whatever kind of life you may have or live (toxic or not) or whatever the condition of your blood is, this condition is indicative of the lifestyle that you live! It's for this purpose that the water was used to cleanse the Old Testament Temple furnishings, because the water (of repentance) removed the sacrificial blood splatter (left behind by previous sacrifices) from the Temple furnishings, thereby cleansing the temple before another sacrifice was accepted or offered. What the water was to the O.T. Temple cleansing, the Holy Spirit (as the Living Water) is now the cleansing agent to the Temple furnishings of and within man! *1 Corinthians 3:16 – 17* and *1 Corinthians 6:19 – 20*. Why? Because our iniquity is as the stench of ROADKILL! What iniquity is to my Lie Based Thinking, the stench of it is as the decomposition of my flesh before Almighty God! Again, what my iniquity is to the script I have written or write [of]which I base my life upon or from (self deception), the Holy Spirit (as the Living Water) invites me to drink and bathe in the truth of my identity, in order to cleanse my internal spiritual furnishings of the stench of my own iniquity; aka roadkill! So what are the furnishings of the Temple for men today? They are our: consciousness, subconsciousness, mind, heart and soul. *(Heb. 9 – 10; 1 Cor. 3:9 – 17; Eph. 2:22)*

Fruit bearing trees cannot have fruit unless they first have nourishment, which is found in the ambient conditions of the earth and this includes, sunlight and water. Where the heat of the sun facilitates chemical photosynthesis enabling the plants to convert energy and produce oxygen, the washing of the water expedites their nutrition! **Truth #15: Similarly, coming to the Son in faith, oxygenates the soul, facilitating its salvation, while the water unto repentance accelerates the growth of the fruits of repentance unto Godliness. This water unto repentance works in harmony with the saint, to lead him towards and into a lifestyle of repentance, because repentance expedites the soul's cultivation and nutrition in righteousness, for without the Spirit and the water, the soil (soul) would not be moistened or cultivated!** Herein, I discovered a simple truth of association. Specifically, what faith is to the Spirit, repentance is to the soul! In this, they become soulmates to each other!

Being baptized with the water unto repentance precedes a lifestyle of repentance. This baptism exposes the Lie Based Thinking (iniquitous thoughts) in life and *a lifestyle of repentance suppresses the carnality that is still resident within the soul, living. (cf. Isa. 22:14)* **Truth #16: Just like you or I would drink a glass of water to conduct the nourishment of the foods to our physical bodies; likewise, when the saint drinks/assimilates the water unto repentance, he quickens the washing and cleansing of his soul from the carnality entrenched within it!** *(cf. Titus 3:5)*

Had the Pharisees accepted the words which John and Jesus had spoken, they too would have eventually presented fruits meet for repentance, for they would have accepted God's Word as their washing! However, their self-righteousness precluded their entry into Heaven, which Jesus Christ addressed in *Matthew 5:20*, because they chose not to be *born of water*, which Jesus also spoke of in *John 3:5*. Similarly, I believe the denominational church institutions have also fallen into error concerning their systemic priorities. *Their erroneous dogmas accentuate the head count only, but not the heart beat of its congregations!* A conversion experience alone never qualifies a person's profession of faith with God, for so many return to their previous state of wickedness and carnality! This is because of the scarcity of the knowledge of carnality, (repentance), as the mainstay of insipid preaching! *(cf. Psa. 1:1 – 6; Jer. 10:19 – 21; Eph. 5:25 – 26; Titus 3:5)*

In effect, the Pharisees, who were rulers over the people, compelled the people in and through their burdensome religion, and at the same time, they coerced those whom they oppressed. They were not as *Nicodemus*, whose name literally means, "ruler among the people." John the Baptist, on the other hand, compelled the people to come to repentance, as demonstrated righteousness in their living whereas, the Pharisees repulsed the people in their own self-righteousness!

Isaiah 5:13
"Therefore, my people are gone into captivity, because they have no knowledge; and their honorable men are famished, and their multitudes dried up with thirst." (cf. Mt. 5:6)

The Baptism with the Water unto Repentance
Matthew 3:11 AMP
"I indeed baptize you in (with) water because of repentance [that is, because of your changing your minds for the better, heartily amending your ways, with abhorrence of your past sins]. But He who is coming after me is mightier than I, Whose sandals I am not worthy or fit to take off or carry; He will baptize you with the Holy Spirit and with fire."

It has been my experience that when I was first submersed into the baptistry water, a minister officiated at my baptism, and ever since I have witnessed hundreds more be dunked as I. The intent being, that the outward demonstration of water baptism reflects the convert's spiritual transformation and a potential, future regeneration of his soul. But, the text verse says that the convert must *change his mind* for the eternal better, *heartily* amending his wicked ways, with an abhorrence and a hatred for past sins!* I would however, like to mention that it is not just for our [lifestyle of carnality] past sins only, but all future acts of carnality as well. This evinces that should a person continue to live a lifestyle of carnality, after being once baptized in water, then it is also obvious that he has not been baptized in the water unto repentance! Consequently, he has not changed! This then, becomes the litmus test for a true conversion experience. **Truth #17: The fact that a person may be baptized with the water ceremonially, does nothing to regenerate the soul, for it must be accompanied with the revelation of the baptism in the water unto repentance. Otherwise, the new convert is left vulnerable to a relapse back into his carnality!** *(Heb. 10:26~29)*

Trees of Religion

Matthew 3:10
"And now the axe is laid unto the roots of the trees:...."

When you consider any fruit bearing tree, have you ever wondered to what purpose does the foliage serve? I certainly have. I was out walking along a tree line just recently and I asked the Lord to answer this very question. Immediately, my mind conceived this reply. *"The foliage of any tree protects and shields the fruit from the atmospheric elements, for without the leaves, the fruit would be damaged by them. Without the leaves, the ripening fruit could not grow into its full maturity."* So then, the foliage tents the growing fruit as though the fruit were in a green house, where humidity and temperature are properly regulated. When a fruited tree is in full bloom and its foliage is all dressed out for display, you could say that such a tree, is dressed out righteously. However, should a fruitless tree be in full foliage and have no fruit, then you could say that this fruitless tree, is not righteously dressed out. Apply this to a morally deprived churchgoer and the impenitent, and you could say that they possess a religious dress up only, but are thoroughly unrighteous in the eyes of God; because they lack fruit! *(cf. Psa. 1:4 – 6)* Once again, we see the combined application and effects of heat and water within the greenhouse. This again denotes that faith and repentance go hand in hand and that they are to be monogamous, just as a man's spirit and soul are to be. *More precisely that the heat of faith and the water of repentance exist to bring a saint into a spiritual green house effect.* The result of which, is that his leaves shall not wither and the fruit he bears, shall be as a healing for all the saint comes in contact with! *(cf. Psa. 1:1 – 3; Rev. 22:1 – 2)*

Matthew 21:18 – 19 AMP
"In the early dawn the next morning, as he was coming back to the city, He was hungry. And He saw one single leafy fig tree above the roadside, He went to it but He found nothing but leaves on it [seeing that in the fig tree the fruit appears at the same time as the leaves]. And He said to it, Never again shall fruit grow on you! And the fig tree withered up at once."

This fruitless fig tree resembles the myriad of churches that are as fruitless orchards! Jesus Christ cursed this tree of religious tradition [carnality] which must be recognized for what it is, carnal fruitlessness! **Truth #18: The fruitless branch and tree are cast into the hell fire of eternal judgment. Conversely, the fruitful branch and tree are pruned and baptized with the Holy Ghost and with the fire of righteousness!** Hallelujah! Again, *the reason why there are so many churches that are dead or dying is because their hands have become withered and the multipurpose tool of repentance [axe and shovel] as well as the knowledge of carnality [agriculture and horticulture], and the water unto repentance have all been ignored!* Since this is so, then it seems that they are not yet born of the water of repentance, which should be drawn from the well of salvation! *(cf. Isa. 12:3; Jn. 3:5)*

Whereas, the sap of any tree is the blood to that tree, similarly the life of any man is found in his blood. Jesus told Nicodemus that no man can enter the Kingdom of God unless that man is born of water and of the Holy Spirit. *(cf. Jn. 3:5)* **Truth #19: The water unto repentance, which speaks of the workings of righteousness within the soul, must be the means by which man's carnality is exfoliated, diminished and suppressed. Otherwise, there will be no dissolving of the layers of carnality within that soul, but only a further entrenchment of selfishness!** In other words, the water which Jesus referred to in *John 3:5*, is the same living water unto repentance which John the Baptist stated, and both speak of the workings of righteousness through repentance! Therefore, unless a man is born of the Spirit and the water unto repentance, he cannot enter the Kingdom of God! The Spirit of God is Son Light that warms the heart in faith believing, and the water unto repentance is the moisture the saint applies to his soul, for he has come to repentance! Together, the saint dwells in the tent of God in His divine green house!

Trees of Righteousness

Psalm 1:3 AMP
"And he shall be like a tree firmly planted [and tended] by the streams of water, ready to bring forth its fruit in its season; its leaf also shall not fade or wither; and everything he does shall prosper [and come to maturity]."

Isaiah 61:3b AMP
"...that they may be called oaks of righteousness [lofty, strong, and magnificent, distinguished for uprightness, justice and right standing with God], the planting of the Lord, that He may be glorified."

Those who have come to repentence are trees of righteousness, for they have been planted by the Lord! Like the tree of life and the tree of the knowledge of good and evil, which were planted by Almighty God in the garden of Eden, the righteous saint is rooted, grounded, pruned and firmly planted by God! Trees of righteousness are not planted in piles of refuse. Nor are they rooted in carnality! These trees are planted in holy ground, upon the mountain of God's righteousness. Their roots are imbedded in the soil of righteous judgment against the carnality within the soul of the penitent man. Consequently, trees of righteousness produce fruits of righteousness. **Truth #20: Through a lifestyle of repentance, the saint of God grows into a strong, magnificent tree of righteousness whose fruit is also righteous!** Since the tree is known by its fruit, likewise the fruit does not fall far from this tree! (For more insights with the mountain of God and of carnality refer to Freedom 3, chapter 32.)

A Condition of Stasis

John the Baptist, told the people to come to repentance, because their deeds were evil. He encouraged them to be enlightened with the revelation of repentance. In *Matthew 4:14 – 17*, we read that the societal conditions of darkness then were such as they are today. Whereas Isaiah the Prophet had previously stated to the people of his day, that they too sat in darkness, denotes that this darkness also covered an entire geographical region, yet they all saw a great light! Such territorial influence is known as *demographics* and *psycho graphics*, which are the studies of the migration and relocation of people as well as their collective psyche. *(cf. Dan. 10:13; Isa. 9:1 – 2; Mic. 3:1; Mt. 6:33)*

To sit in darkness and then to respond to the light requires a revelation of repentance! Darkness represents a blinded, obscured carnal mind with an impenitent conscience. The word *dull* comes to mind here. It means, "listless, muffled, stupid, apathy, weak." The thought that comes to mind now, is the person in a vegetated state. I'm not talking about an unconscious person or one who might be afflicted, such as in a coma, although these would be good associations. What I am addressing is the individual or society, who are in a condition of *stasis,* that is to say, where passivity resides. Medically and biologically, this condition pertains to a balanced equilibrium, but pertaining to the carnality of men, there is no activity of progression or a purposeful life! This condition goes beyond the passivity of routine, unassertive living. It pertains more to a mental condition of carnal mindedness, which bleeds into moral depravities and seeps into our conduct and behavior that is not God honoring!

The Four Faculties of the Mind
2 Corinthians 3:14 – 16 AMP
"In fact, their minds were grown hard and calloused [they had become dull and had lost the power of understanding]: for until this present day, when the Old Testament (the old covenant) is being read, that same veil stills lies [on their hearts], not being lifted [to reveal] that in Christ it is made void and done away. Yes, down to this [very] day whenever Moses is read, a veil lies upon their minds and hearts, But whenever a person turns [in repentance] to the Lord, the veil is stripped off and taken away." (cf. Eph. 4:23)

Whenever we allow ourselves to sit in darkness, which is influenced by either our surroundings, an authority figure or our own iniquity, a sort of hypnotic effect hovers, effectively dulling or numbing the spirit of the mind. It's much like the person who sits in front of a television for hours; the lights are on, but there's nobody home! Carnality does the same, for it has the same effect upon a soul. Such activity then inoculates the component elements of our mind, effectively desensitizing them to the spiritual things of God as well as dimming our susceptibility to God's Word; which is Light. There are many, many ministers who have caused and made to occur their respective congregations to become ineffective and non-working due to their ineffective, non-working, innocuous preaching! The result has become: that the anointing of God has waned, because of their preexisting and contagious condition of spiritual stasis!

Our iniquitous thoughts (Lie Based Thinking) preceed a carnal mind in all four of the cognitive compartments of the spirit of the mind. This is so because each of its four faculties have also become carnal. Specifically, *a mind is not carnal singularly; it is carnal collectively!* Scripture teaches that the carnal mind cannot receive the things of God, for they are spiritually discerned. This means that the *will* of impenitent men has not yet been submitted to the will of God. It means that the *conscience* of impenitent men has not acknowledged God nor have they identified Him as God. To these, a higher power is sufficient or that any mention of God is denied or eliminated, such as what is occurring presently within American society, and that of the world's. It means also that the faculty of *reason* has also been impaired, so much so that impenitent men are not capable of receiving sound instructions in righteousness. Finally, it means that impenitent men are void of the *intelligence [specific knowledge]* and therefore possess no understanding of spiritual things! Truly, their day in court shall come and they will not be acquitted for their ignorance, but shall be condemned for their stupidity! (See Freedom 1, chapter 4, The Head of the Bull is Cattle-Mindedness.)

Psalm 1:6 AMP
"For the Lord knows and is fully acquainted with the way of the righteous, but the way of the ungodly [those living outside God's will] shall perish (end in ruin and come to naught)."

Matthew 12:36 – 37 AMP
"But I tell you, on the day of judgment men will have to give ac-

count for every idle (inoperative, non working) word they speak. For by your words you will be justified and acquitted, and by your words you will be condemned and sentenced." (cf. Isa. 5:20, 51:1, 58:8)

The saints of God must do their part now, as they live, for a lifestyle of repentance demands personal involvement, *because the saint's involvement, is his personal atonement of his soul! (cf. Lev. 23:27 – 32; Phil 2:12; 1 Tim. 4:8)* Jesus has already accomplished His part then, as He lived. It is now up to us, the people of God, to seek and follow after His example (in His righteousness) throughout the days of our living. People who choose to be self-righteous are willingly ignorant of spiritual matters. Education or the lack of it, is not the issue. It's the lack of spiritual insight that Jesus Christ and all the writers of the epistles addressed. Jesus instructed the Pharisees to go and learn [spiritual things]. *(Mt. 9:10 – 13; Jn. 3:10)* We must do the same! *(cf. 2 Pet. 3:18)*

Colossians 2:23 AMP
"Such [practices] have indeed that outward appearance [that popularly passes] for wisdom, in promoting self-imposed rigor of devotion and delight in self-humiliation and severity of discipline of the body, but **they are no value in checking the indulgence of the flesh** *(the lower nature). [Instead, they do not honor God, but serve only to indulge the flesh]." (emphasis mine)*

Religious zealots are impenitent in their practice of will-worship. Their actions of ceremonial pomp and pageantry are only outward demonstrations of that which commonly passes as worldly wisdom, for that is exactly what it is! Where repentance is internal, that which is liturgical is external. The saint may discern between those who are of his spiritual caliber and above and those whose motives are contrarily carnal. God gives more grace [the power of the Holy Spirit to meet any tendency] to the humble. He sets Himself against the prideful. Likewise, the saint is to set himself against the carnal propensities of his own life. **Truth #21: Through a lifestyle of repentance, the saint learns to suppress his carnal, self-indulgent tendencies because a lifestyle of repentance is not an audacious public display of any religion!** *(cf. Jam. 4:6 – 7)*

Impenitence as Evidence Used Against Us
Matthew 11:20 – 22

"Then began He to upbraid the cities wherein most of his mighty works were done, because they repented not: Woe unto thee Cho-ra-zin! Woe unto thee, Bethsaida! For if the mighty works which were done in you, had been done in Tyre and Sidon, they would have repented long ago in **sackcloth and ashes***. But I say unto you, It shall be more tolerable for Tyre and Sidon in the day of Judgment, than for you."* (emphasis mine) *(cf. Heb. 12:17)*

Carnal men have a choice to come to repentance or to remain impenitent. They must never reject God's call to repent! If they do, then their refusal evinces their condemnation because they have not been born of the water (unto repentance) and the Spirit! *(cf. Jn. 3:18 – 19, 5:24)* **Truth #22: Moreover, should impenitent men reject repentance, then their decision to remain carnal, shall be the evidence of their iniquity which shall be used against them!** They fail to realize that a lifestyle of repentance will actually turn State's Evidence on their behalf and for their salvation. God's call to come to repentance is a call to a penitent lifestyle! **Truth #23: When Almighty God calls carnal men to repentance and that call is rejected or ignored, He shall hold the impenitent accountable for it! Failure to come to repentance is a criminal offense against Almighty God, for impenitence blasphemes the existence and the purpose of the Holy Ghost!** *(cf. Mk. 3:29; Jn. 16:7 – 11)* The decision to reject repentance, is as slapping God's gift of repentance back to Him or into His face! It's as though impenitent men are saying to Him that He has nothing important or necessary to say. In effect, carnal men tell Almighty God to mind His own business, while they tend to their own, because they won't take His Word seriously or to heart. Moreover, when a decision is made not to choose or to remain indifferent, as in a condition of stasis, then a choice has been made against repentance! *(cf. Rom. 11:29, 12:21)*

The Wisdom of Repentance

Matthew 12:41 – 42
"The men of Nineveh shall rise in judgment with this generation, and shall condemn it; because they repented at the preaching of Jonah; and, behold, a greater than Jonah is here. The queen of the south shall rise up in judgment with this generation and condemn it...she came from the uttermost parts of the earth to hear **the wisdom** *of Solomon; and behold, a greater than Solomon is here."* (emphasis mine)

The first thing that I notice in these two verses is that Jesus compares repentance with wisdom! **Truth #24: Therefore, a lifestyle of repentance is also the demonstration of the wisdom of God unto salvation. This means that the saints of God are to become sages of their carnality through their acquired wisdom of repentance!** In *Jonah 3:4*, eight words were spoken by the Prophet to the inhabitants of the great Babylonian city called, Nineveh. He said, *"Yet forty days and Nineveh shall be overthrown."* Immediately upon hearing this, the king and the entire populace came to repentance with sackcloth and ashes, whose repentance lasted nearly 150 years! (See Freedom 3, chapter 34)

Jesus said that the men of Nineveh shall rise in judgment against this generation, to whom Jesus was speaking. I've heard it said, that if God does not judge America for her sins in these latter times, then God owes Sodom and Gomorrah an apology. In light of the rampant outgrowth of corruption due to unsuppressed carnality, I have to agree with this statement. **Truth #25: A lifestyle of repentance affords the saint the wisdom of God so that, the saint may live uprightly before God, for repentance, as the doctrine of God, is to and for the saint, the hidden wisdom of God, which is for His glory and the saint's redemption!** In other words, except the glory of our righteousness exceeds that glory of the scribes and the Pharisee, in no case shall we enter the Kingdom of God! Only those glorified on Earth will qualify to reside in Heaven afterward. *(cf. Mt. 5:20; Jn. 3:5)*

1 Corinthians 2:7 – 8
"But we speak the wisdom of God in a mystery, even the hidden wisdom which God ordained before the world unto our glory: Which none of the princes of this world knew, for had they known it, they would not have crucified the Lord of Glory."

Why Sackcloth and Ashes?

Matthew 11:20 – 22
"…they would have repented long ago, in sackcloth and ashes…"

Why sackcloth and ashes? Sackcloth was worn as a symbol of mourning or penitence, often with ashes sprinkled on the head. Sackcloth was made of black goat's hair, which was a very course fiber and is very similar to the texture of burlap or wool. Natural resources such as jute, hemp, twine and the like were not readily available for the desert traveler. However, there were plenty of goats! The desert travelers entwined the goat's hair together on a warp (weaving machine) to make blankets of woolen sackcloth and other garments known as woof. *(cf. Lev. 13:48 – 49)* The ashes were obtained from the cooled residue of a fire known as a sin offering. Scripture teaches that the penitent either *sat, laid or wallowed* [flop about, squirm] in ashes. Ashes were also placed on the head, the face or beneath the one making penitence. This practice was a way of acknowledging to God, the carnality lodged within the soul of the penitent and the penitent's desire to suppress his carnality as indicated by those ashes beneath the penitent. *(cf. 2 Sam. 13:19; 1 Kg. 20:38; Est. 4:3: Job 2:8)* **Truth #26: Whereas, water submersion represents the death, burial and resurrection of Jesus Christ and the saint's identification to these, likewise, the wallowing in ashes represents the saint's recumbent position in the water unto repentance. Upon his surfacing, the saint becomes born of that meta-water!** This understanding gives the expression, "holy roller" a fresh new perspective, doesn't it? *(cf. Mt. 3:11; Jn. 3:5; Rom. 6:1 – 6)*

Just as water baptism is an outward display of the spiritual new birth from within, likewise, sackcloth was used as an outward display of penitence, which reflected the condition and the contrition of the heart, as that affliction of the soul. That condition being, iniquitous thoughts, evil imaginations and all ungodly fancies. **Truth #27: The blood of Jesus Christ identifies the love of God, who is first Love, for His love covers a multitude of sins. Similarly, the sackcloth portrayed that covering of God's expressed love towards the penitent. What's more, the sackcloth also represented the overlay of the sacrificial blood of the sin offering as well as the saint abiding in his first love!** *(cf. Rev. 2:4 – 5)* After all, God did not require that the animal's blood be smeared or applied to the person's own body, but the priest was required to throw the blood round about and against the altar. *(cf. Lev. 3:2, 8)* In like fashion, the sackcloth was a blanket that was thrown over and round about the penitent!

Sackcloth is a Symbol of the Blood

Truth #28: Like the pall that is used to cover a coffin, sackcloth was a covering, and symbolized the blood covering of

Christ. Since the penalty of sin is death and that a pall is used in death, it was very appropriate that the sackcloth, like the pall, be used in life! Sackcloth symbolized death to past sin and death in present and future carnality/sin. *(2 Tim. 2:11 – 12)* Through a lifestyle of repentance we save ourselves from the penalty of sin which is eternal death! Hallelujah! Therefore, a lifestyle of repentance must be consistent with a heart of faith. In Nineveh, from the king to the sack lady, all repented; that is, they all came to repentance having acquired the wisdom of repentance for the saving of themselves and their city! They even covered their animals with sackcloth representing for us, that they acknowledged their bullheadedness of a herd mentality! God desires all of us to become sack men and women! This presents a new twist on the old cliché, *"Hit the sack,"* doesn't it? Presently, the church has yet to *hit the sack*. Rather, she bellies up to the bar of denominationalism or whereever else the god of belly may lead.

As previously shown in Freedom 1, chapter 3, Almighty God incorporated repentance into the tabernacle, and that repentance was properly demonstrated by wearing sackcloth and ashes to declare one's penitence over carnality. However, due to the haughtiness of most, their sackcloth and ashes are spread beneath them as they bow like bulrushes over them. This mechanical routine makes the statement, *"My own self-righteousness is sufficient to atone for my sins!"* In my opinion, this is a direct blasphemy against the Holy Ghost, which shall not be forgiven of impenitent men in this world or the next! I personally drape a blanket or sheet over myself at times during prayer as I travail, which adds a whole other dimension to my prayer time. It shuts out all other distractions and it seems to help me focus on the task of suppressing my iniquitous thoughts, binding the spirit of my mind and all its component faculties (will, reasoning, intelligence, conscience) to the mind of Christ. (See Freedom 2, chapter 23, Ulterior Motives and Carnal Mind Sets)

Worthy and Unworthy
Hebrews 11:38 AMP
"[Men] of whom the world was not worthy -roaming over the desolate places and the mountains, and [living] in caves and caverns and holes in the earth."

Why did John the Baptist dwell in the wilderness? Because the world was not worthy of his presence, and so it is with every saint of this caliber! Yet, John the Baptist said that he was not worthy to bear the sandals of He who was to come after him. *(cf. Mt. 3:11)* I might add that even King Herod, who had John beheaded, considered John the Baptist unworthy of this world's pleasures and treasures as well. As I said in the Introduction of this book, Almighty God protects His wisdom from carnally corrupt men, who are not deserving of its benefits and treasures. In the wilderness, John was protected from the carnal influence of societal rule. On a personal note and based upon the ostracism directed towards me from the carnally influenced church, society and employment, I have come to accept the fact that the world is not worthy of me either! I say this not bombastically as though I am better than anyone else, but I do attest that the wisdom of repentance which Almighty God has shown me has protected me, thus far, from the ravages of carnal, impenitent men, but at the same time has pruned my soul for a specific purpose which God alone knows! Since John, whom Jesus applauded as being the greatest of all prophets, admitted of his own unworthiness, it's reasonable to say that neither are we, in and of ourselves, worthy! *(cf. Lk. 7:28)* (See also Chapter 19, "Men of Whom the World was not Worthy".)

The Customary Practice of Servant Hood
Matthew 3:11
"...whose shoes I am not worthy to bear;..." (cf. Lk. 10:4)

John referred to the customary practice of servant hood when he spoke of the sandals of Christ which he, John, was not worthy to bear or take off. According to the custom, the servant always walked behind, carrying the sandals of his master! The servant had the responsibility to maintain the appearance of his master's shoes. He would clean them so that no dirt would be seen on the shoe or under the soles of his master's feet. At times, the servant would even carry his master over and through the dirt or mud, just so his master's clothing would not get soiled. This gives fresh insight with what Jesus said to his disciples about shaking the dust of their feet as a testimony against those who would not receive them. *(cf. Deut. 23:12-14; Mt. 10:14; Rom. 6:9 – 23)* Conversely, in *Luke 10:4* Jesus instructs the disciples not to carry anything! It is evident then that Jesus was teaching them that they were worthy to have their needs cared for by others. Literally, the sandal was now on the other's foot!

Just as a lifestyle of repentance shall effect the multitudes, likewise, the wisdom of repentance, as the knowledge of one's own carnality, will also attract others to the water of repentance from the four corners of the earth. Sadly though, carnality has dulled their spiritual perspicuity. It's not that people are necessarily sold out to their denominational doctrines and dogmas, but it's the leadership who have inoculated them! *(cf. Mt. 23:15)* I remember while attending Bible School in Fort Worth, Texas that the school administrator said to me, *"Brother Ed, although God has called you to be a preacher of righteousness, know this, that there won't be many doors open to you or this word, because people don't want to be told what to do!"* Since then, I have personally learned this to be correct, however in time I know that doors shall open, because I'm working in concert with Almighty God!

In the midst of corruption and abomination, Almighty God still proves His love for impenitent man through the preachers of righteousness whom He sends to an unrighteous world. Spiritual leadership oppose themselves when they resist or contest those whom Almighty God has sent to them. Just as Jesus was sent to the spiritual leaders of His day and just as the prophets of old were sent to those leaders of their day and were killed by them, all because people rejected the preaching of righteousness (repentance), these men such as myself, have also been rejected. These men are in truth of a greater caliber than the existing leadership! **Truth #29: Therefore, the unrighteousness found in this world is not worthy nor is it to be compared to the righteousness of those saints of God whom God has destined to be righteous in this world!**

Consciousness of Guilt/Carnality Denotes Culpability

Matthew 12:41 – 42

"The men of Nineveh shall rise in judgment with this generation, and shall condemn it; because they repented at the preaching of Jonah; and, behold, a greater than Jonah is here. The queen of the south shall rise up in judgment with this generation and condemn it...she came from the uttermost parts of the earth to hear **the wisdom** *of Solomon; and behold, a greater than Solomon is here."*

In the legal arena, the expression, *consciousness of guilt,* which must be proven or determined, pertains to the perpetrator's personal awareness of his crime before, during and after the offense committed. Morally and criminally, this *consciousness of guilt* establishes his culpability; but the denominational premise is or has been for centuries, the predominant mind set of Christianity. Rarely can I find any churchgoer who possesses a knowledge of spiritual truth, who has an understanding of their iniquity or carnality, pertaining to the wisdom of God to function under the anointing of the very presence of God.

Consequently, the power and the anointing of God is absent from the church today due to an academic, intellectual and institutionalized dogma! Here in *Matthew 12*, Jesus spoke an indictment against the people of His day. He addressed their culpability in their carnality which denoted their guilt, for they refused to come to repentance! This is evident because of their blasphemy against the Holy Ghost. **Truth #30: Impenitence establishes the consciousness of guilt of one's carnality, for it denotes culpability! Conversely, repentance establishes the saint's righteousness, because his conscience is first pure and is not defiled!** *(cf. 1 Tim. 1:5, 3:9)*

Blasphemy of the Holy Ghost

Matthew 12:31-33

"Wherefore I say unto you, All manner of sin and blasphemy shall be forgiven unto men: but **the blasphemy against the Holy Ghost** *shall not be forgiven unto men. And whosoever speaketh a word against the Son of man, it shall be forgiven him; but whosoever* **speaketh against the Holy Ghost**, *it shall not be forgiven him, neither in this world, neither in the world to come.* **Either make the tree good and his fruit good, or else make the tree corrupt**, *and his fruit corrupt; for the tree is known by his fruit."* (emphasis mine, *cf. Heb. 10:29*)

Scripture does not provide a clue as to how long John the Baptist had been preaching repentance at the Jordan River. But from the context of *Matthew 3*, it is apparent that he had been preaching it for an extended and unspecified period of time, because all the people of Jerusalem, Judea and the surrounding countryside came out to hear him. Since these people, to include the Pharisees, knew of John's message, Jesus also knew. In fact, Jesus stated to Nicodemus, (in *John 3:5*) that no man shall enter the Kingdom of God unless he is first born of the water (unto repentance) and of the Spirit. This then establishes that Jesus referred to the water which John spoke of! Contextually and thematically, this then identifies the birth water! The two are not separate! Both statements are intrinsically connected by divine import! When impenitent men refuse or reject the doctrine of repentance, they are blaspheming the Holy Ghost!

Jesus spoke of the Holy Ghost as Comforter in *John 16:7-11*. He said in essence, that when He departs that He would not leave the disciples (us) comfortless, but that He would send the Holy Ghost as Comforter in His place. And when the Spirit is sent, this unrighteous world would be convicted of righteousness, of sin and of judgment. My point is this. **Truth #31: As long as carnal men refuse to come to repentance and they choose to reject the water unto repentance, which is the birth water that Jesus referred to in *John 3:5*, they are blaspheming the work of the Holy Spirit! Their rejection denotes their defiance and resistance to God's righteousness and at the same time hold fast to their immorality and sin!** Hence, the only other option for them is the judgment unto their own damnation! *(cf. Jn. 5:24)* It is evident then, that according to *Matthew 12*, blasphemy is associated to or with our conversation which pertains to one's conduct and behavior *(cf. 1 Pet. 3:11)* which carnal men speak and display against the Holy Ghost! This then identifies, at least for me, blasphemy which has been an undefined expression for many years! *(cf. Acts 7:51)* After all, Jesus Christ became sin, whereas the Holy Ghost did not! *(cf. 2 Cor. 5:21)*

Furthermore, I find that the last verse which states, *"Either make the tree good and his fruit good, or make the tree corrupt and his fruit corrupt..."* very significant. Specifically, that all men, whether carnal or not, bring about for themselves the reality of their own character and whether that character be godly or carnal. As pertaining to a lifestyle of repentance, any saint is afforded the opportunity to come to repentance and with God's grace the ability to recreate himself in God.

Wells Without Water

Like the famine stricken orchard or landscape regions, there are many churches that are wells without water! Without the water unto repentance, their people have no concept of the work of righteousness which is the Holy Ghost! The result is that unsuppressed carnality runs rampant within the congregations, and Almighty God shall hold these Pastors accountable! **Truth #32: Through a lifestyle of repentance, the saint no longer shall blaspheme the Holy Ghost, whose task is to convict impenitent men of their unrighteousness, sin and judgment! Otherwise, impenitent men are doomed, for they have condemned themselves to it!** The question remains, Just how many within the denominational church structure are truly saved, since repentance is altogether rejected? Scripturally, they have not been born of the water nor of the Spirit! *(cf. Rom. 3:5-6; 2 Pet 2:17)*

Whether a person is formally educated or not is never the issue with God. Most people, even those behind the pulpits, evade issues [of the heart]. Through neglect or fear, a mole hill soon becomes a mountain! Evading issues only permits an infiltration of carnality to entrench itself into the deepest recesses of the collective mind, thereby impeding and altogether frustrating the move and the ministry that God would have for a particular church, or individual and all because the Pastor chooses to avoid issues! *Spiritual maturity is the posterity of the knowledge of God's character!* The anointing and power of God must greatly influence our lives! Since the world is strategically designed to cause a saint to backslide, then it is essential that the spoken Word from the pulpit be words that lead others to turn towards repentance, and not towards blasphemy in their defiant carnality! *(cf. 2 Cor. 7:10 AMP)*

Transfigure Means Repent and Repent Means to Renew

Matthew 17:1-2

"And after six days Jesus taketh Peter, James and John his brother, and bringeth them up into a mountain a part, and was transfigured before them..."

Have you ever seen the glow of God's anointing or presence upon an individual? I have twice. In fact, on separate occasions, I've been advised by others that they have observed this aura of God's glory upon me! We even read of this in Scripture when on a certain occasion, Moses was said to have had such a shine and glow from his face and shoulders, so much so, that he had to wear a veil over his head whenever he spoke to the people or when out in public. *(cf. Ex. 34:29-35)* **Truth #33: Through a lifestyle of repentance, the saint acquires a transfigured countenance of righteousness!** There is a radiance of the glory of God's righteousness that can be observed by others! The word, *transfigure* means, "to change, repent and to renew." The word, *apart* means, "to separate" and the saint does so through a lifestyle of repentance, for through a lifestyle of repentance, he sanctifies himself for God's service and is therefore consecrated to Him. As we learned previously, this is in keeping with the Greek word, *meta*, which also means, *"to repent, change, metamorphose, to amend your ways, renew."*

We are all given ample opportunities to come to repentance.

Matthew 21:28-32

"But what think ye? A certain man had two sons; and he came to the first and said, Son, go work today in my vineyard. He answered and said, I will not: but afterward, he repented and went. And he came twain to the second son and said likewise. And he

answered and said, I go sir, but went not. Whether of them twain did the will of the father? They said unto Him, The first. Jesus said unto them, Verily I say unto you, that the publicans and the harlots go into the kingdom of God before you. For John came unto you in the way of righteousness [preaching repentance], and ye believed him not: but the publicans and the harlots believed him: and ye, when ye had seen it, repented not afterward, that ye might believe him." (cf. Acts 17:30, brackets mine)

Here, Jesus informed and advised the Pharisees of their insubordination, because they chose to reject the teaching of repentance. Scripture emphasizes that as long as a person lives, he shall be given ample opportunities to come to repentance. The text passages above show that a charge was given to the two sons to work in their father's vineyard. The same charge has been given to carnal men, but because they choose to reject repentance or put it off, they shall not enter the Kingdom of God! It's no different in the military where an officer would command his enlisted men to attack that hill and they either refuse to do so or they say, *"Sure thing sir, but we'll do it later!"* Their refusal and actions establish their insubordination to that order or command! So the question is, I wonder just how many are insubordinate themselves and exist within the unruly church structure? **Truth #34: Just as the enlisted know full well of their disobedience to an order given, whether prompt or otherwise, in like manner, impenitent humanity also are consciously aware of their noncompliance to God's command to all men everywhere to come to repentance!** *(cf. Acts 17:30-31)*

That Word which John Preached
Acts 10:35-38

"But in every nation, he that feareth him, and worketh righteousness, is accepted with him. The word which God sent unto the children of Israel, preaching peace by Jesus Christ; (he is Lord

*of all:) **That word**, I say, ye know, which was published throughout all Judea, and began from Galilee, **after the baptism which John preached;** How God anointed Jesus of Nazereth with the Holy Ghost and with power: who went about doing good, and healing all that were oppressed of the devil; for God was with Him."* (emphasis mine) *(cf. Prov. 2:19-22; Isa. 35:8-9; Rom. 6:19-22)*

Truth #35: A lifestyle of repentance is the way of righteousness! John the Baptist preached repentance to the multitudes. Jesus demonstrated and taught faith and repentance to the masses. *Ergo, coming to repentance precedes the way of righteousness, just as faith precedes repentance and righteousness precedes holiness, for without faith, why should anyone come to repentance? You see my friend, repentance is the process of sanctification just as sanctification is the cultivation of holiness!* Not only did John preach repentance, but the Apostles did as well, as did the Prophets of old! Their discourses on and about repentance may be found throughout their epistles, and yet in spite of this, the worldly church remains ignorant of this doctrine of God! Jesus preached repentance and instructed His disciples to do the same. *(Lk. 24:47)* Paul especially preached repentance. *(Acts 17:30; Rom.2:4; 2 Cor. 7:8-10)* Peter preached repentance. *(2 Pet. 3:9)* Even the two witnesses and the angelic host shall preach repentance! *(Rev. 11-16)*

Our Enemy Cannot Betray Us

In *Matthew 27:1-5*, Scripture tells us that Judas Iscariot repented after he betrayed Christ; but did he make it to Heaven? Judas felt remorse throughout his entire being, for he had squandered the blessings of his association with Christ so much so that he killed himself! The very heart of who he was, attacked his entire being! No doubt he trembled greatly to the core, because of this self-infliction! Obviously, Judas had the wrong impression of his atonement and repentance. Esau too, squandered his birthright and found no place of repentance. Through the carnality of his self-indulgence, Judas did the same. God desires not that impenitent men should commit suicide or to mutilate their physical person just to demonstrate repentance. However, He does expect each saint to die to selfish propensities and all manner of carnal proclivities. *(cf. Rom. 8:13)* Such repentance will lead the saints of God towards "220 Gospel" to be crucified, just as Paul the Apostle said!

Galatians 2:20 AMP
"I have been crucified with Christ [in Him I have shared His crucifixion]; it is no longer I who live, but Christ (the Messiah) lives in me; and the life I now live in the body I live by faith in (by adherence to and reliance on and complete trust in) the Son of God, Who loved me and gave Himself up for me."

We must nurture and protect friendships also; otherwise, we will betray others whether they are our brothers or sisters in Christ or not. And unlike Judas, we must never, intentionally injure an innocent party. The question is, can an enemy ever betray you? The answer is: No! You expect your enemies to be hostile towards you, but never someone close.

Judas did not simply return the tainted, blood money to just anyone. Judas returned this money to its rightful owners! He returned the thirty pieces of silver to the chief priest in the temple. The point being, when we consciously realize that Jesus Christ is Who the Word of God says He is, then we will likewise return everything the devil has given us, and all that which he has left in our soul is called carnality! **Truth #36: Through a lifestyle of repentance, the saint returns to his rightful owner, because he was bought with a price! Through a lifestyle of repentance, the saint of God renounces the carnality within his soul, just as a consumer would return a defective product!** *(cf. Gen. 4:1-11; Mt. 16:26; 1 Cor. 6:20)*

Chapter 2
Repentance in the Book of Mark

The Prophet

Essentially, the message of the Old Testament Prophet consisted of four elements. In brief, these elements were 1) to expose iniquity/sin, 2) to bring the people back to the moral, civil and ceremonial Law of God, 3) to warn the people of coming judgments and 4) to anticipate the coming Messiah. These Prophets of old, peered into the past for lessons and exhortations concerning their present and the future. In other words, they took that which was commonly known by the masses culturally and historically, and preached the spiritual truth, introducing the people to that which they were unfamiliar with. Consequently, their prophetic messages were twofold: 1) condemnation because of carnality and 2) consolation, because of the grace of God.

However, there are those celebrities, (Shepherds) not all, who have been brought to the forefront of pulpit address in ministry, solely on the gimmick of their worldly endeavors! These people are novices, in that they lack seasoning or time in grade in God's service to His Word. Their gimmick has been their worldly acclaim and yet their spiritual integrity remains suspect, at least in my estimation. Again, there are those ministerial celebrities who are self-proclaimed prophets or who are called prophets by others who have misunderstood the office of a Prophet! As I have shown throughout the 3 Freedom books and again in this work, you will learn that a true Prophet of God is first a preacher of righteousness! He is not a herald of material prosperity! Come to think of it, I cannot think of anyone preaching righteousness in these last days: Can you? In the Book of 2 Peter, chapter 2 verse 1, the writer charges false prophets as well as indicts false teachers in *verses 12 – 22*. The remaining verses, remind us of how and why God dealt with these people of the past. An example of this is also found in the *Book of Ezekiel* chapter 13, in which this Prophet denounced and exposed the false prophets of his day in the Old Testament, and later in chapter 34, he also incriminated and exposed the prideful Pastors, as well.

The following description and depiction of what a Prophet did was researched from the Vine's Expository Dictionary, pages 221, 222. "The Old Testament Prophets foretold of *future events such as divine judgments, of Messianic utterances, of repentance, and a return to morality.*" In fact, all seventeen primary Prophets proclaimed each of these; however, John the Baptist, as the first New Testament Prophet, preached repentance only. Because, in accordance to the purposes of God, John was not required to foretell of future events; as did his predecessors. "*Generally, and in accordance to the Old Testament text, the Prophet was one upon whom the Spirit of God did rest and one to whom and through whom God spoke.*" (Num. 11:17 – 29, 12:2; Amos 3:7 – 8) Because the message of the Old Testament Prophet was largely the proclamation of the divine purposes of salvation and glory to be accomplished in the future: the New Testament Prophet, is to be a preacher of the divine counsels of God's grace already accomplished and the foretelling of the intents and purposes of God in the future. This is because the charge of the New Testament Prophet's ministry is to edify, comfort, to encourage the saints, as well as to perfect the saints for the work of the ministry; *(cf. Eph. 4:11 – 14; 1 Cor. 14:3)* while its effect upon non-believers and the impenitent would show that the secrets of their hearts are already known by God, to convict them of their sin, and to constrain them to true worship. *(1 Cor. 14:24 – 25)*

Continuing, "with the completion of the canon of Scriptures, Old Testament prophecy apparently passed away. *(cf. 1 Cor. 13:8 – 9) In his place and measure, the Teacher has taken the place of the Prophet. (cf. 2 Pet. 2:1)* The difference is that, whereas the Old Testament Prophet's message was a desert revelation of the mind of God for the occasion, the message of the New Testament Teacher, is to gather from the completed revelations already contained in Scriptures. Though much of Old Testament prophecy was purely predictive, whether with reference to the past, present or future judgments of God upon all wickedness, prophecy is not necessarily, nor even primarily foretelling. *It is more precisely the declaration of that which cannot be known by natural means, and is therefore the foretelling of the will of God,* and this is not to be confused with a word of knowledge; which tends to pertain more to an individual with regards to personal issues. *(cf. Gen. 20:7; Deut. 18:18; Rev. 10:11; 11:3)* Prophets are gifts of our ascended Lord to His Church. Consequently, the office of a New Testament Prophet is placed after the Apostles, since none of the Old Testament Prophets of Israel are implied. *(cf. 1 Cor. 12:28; Eph. 2:20, 4:8 – 11; Acts 13:1)*"

PROPHETES: one who speaks forth or openly. a) *a herald of a divine message,* denoted among the Greeks are interpreters of the oracle of the gods. Hebrew: Roeh (a seer) Nabhi: *either one in whom the message from God springs forth or one to whom anything is secretly communicated.* (Note, that the predicting of future events is not necessarily intended)

PROPHETEIA: Signifies the speaking forth of the mind and counsel of God. Pertaining to the New Testament, it is used: a) of the gift; b) either of the *exercise* of the gift or of that which is prophesied. *(cf. 1 Cor. 13:8, 14:6; 1 Thes. 5:20; Mt. 13:14, 26:68)*

The Last Old Testament Prophet

Hebrews 9:18 AMP
"So even the [old] first covenant (God's will) was not inaugurated and ratified and put in force without the shedding of blood."

It is evident that what the traditional church considers to be the commencement of the New Testament, is of a truth, actually the very closing Books of the Old Testament. I'm speaking of the Books of Matthew, Mark, Luke and John. According to the Scripture above, since Jesus Christ had not yet died, our church view of the four Gospels has in fact been stymied; and so this would make the Book of Acts as the very first book of the actual New Testament and not the Book of Matthew! It is for this reason, why I stipulate that John the Baptist, as the predecessor to Jesus Christ, was the very last Old Testament Prophet, and keeping in line with the duty of all his predecessors, John the Baptist preached repentance as the doctrine of God providing the knowledge of salvation for the remission of sins.

John's Duty

John's character and work confirmed his name, which means: *Horn of Salvation*. And as any horn needs to be blown, his message of salvation, through the preaching of repentance, was to be further heralded by He, Who is our redemption and blows the horn, namely Jesus Christ! *(cf. 1 Cor. 1:30)* John was called, *The Prophet of the Highest,* by his dad Zacharias. *(cf. Lk. 1:15 – 17, 69)* As a Prophet, John's mission was to preach repentance for the remission of sins, and being a preacher of righteousness, he was to provide the knowledge of salvation to the people of God. *(cf. Lk. 1:76 – 77)* He did so by preaching the baptism of repentance for the remission of sins. *(cf. Lk. 3:3 – 4)* What John the Baptist preached then, today's ministers are also to teach. Present day spiritual leadership remains ignorant of repentance as a doctrine, and a message of God. Consequently, self-righteousness, carnal penchants and religious dress up and traditions are retained! What is needed is a paradigm shift from behind the pulpit! Spiritual leadership must come to repentance themselves, for their ignorance of this doctrine and their weak preaching, if they are to reacquire the power and force of righteous words! *(cf. Job 6:25)*

The Horns of the Altar and the Horn of Salvation

The word *horn*, implies strength or authority. It is an Old Testament expression which speaks of that which was affixed to the brazen altar for the intent of priestly duty. Whereas, the horns of the altar were corner posts of sorts, by which the penitent priest would grapple and travail on behalf of others once a year; similarly, John the Baptist was also a horn, through whom people who heeded and responded to his message of repentance, could come to repentance themselves in preparation of the appearing of their *salvation*, Who is the Author and Finisher of their faith—Jesus Christ! *(cf. Ex. 30:10; Titus 2:11; Heb. 12:2)* This therefore denotes that when they heeded the messenger, they also complied to his message. As it was then, so it must be today, that all men everywhere, no matter whether they are sinner or saint, must also heed the messenger and comply to his message! *(cf. Acts 17:30)* Ergo, I stipulate that any saint who preaches and teaches repentance today, is greater than John the Baptist and that person is God's messenger to his generation, just as John was to his! **Truth #37: When a saint comes to repentance, he has arrived at the horn of the altar, whereby he makes atonement for his own carnality, as the rule of action of the sin element within his soul! Moreover, repentance strengthens the saint's resolve to live righteously before God, because a lifestyle of repentance, is that demonstrated authority (horn) against all carnal propensities!**

The Power of Repentance, R R R

Mark 6:12 – 14 AMP

*"So **they** went out and preached that men should [come to repentance, and that they should change their minds for the better and heartily amend their ways, with abhorrence for their past sins]. And **they** drove out many unclean spirits and anointed with oil many who were sick and cured them. King Herod heard of it, for [Jesus'] name had become well known. He and they [of his court] said, John the Baptist has been raised from the dead; that is why these mighty powers [of performing miracles] are at work in him."* (emphasis mine) *(cf. Mk. 6:15 – 27)*

In the decade of the nineties, a very popular sitcom known as *Home Improvement* aired on television. The main character, Tim Taylor aka: the *Tool Man*, loved his power tools and was downright addicted to *"MORE POWER, R R R!"* Whenever he roared *"More Power"* his simian grunt sounded like the letters R R R. For the Tool Man, the association he made with his power tools (the bigger the better), bolstered his own masculinity.

Although Scripture does not specifically state that John the Baptist performed miracles of healing or the raising of the dead, here in these passages, Scripture does seem to indicate that John probably did perform powerful miracles! Moreover, Scripture teaches that John the Baptist came in the spirit and power of the Prophet Elijah, through whom Almighty God performed many dramatic miracles. *(cf. 1 Kg. 17 – 18; 2 Kg. 1:10, 2:8; Isa. 40:3; Mal. 4:5 – 6)*

So, to fully grasp the association made between the spirit and the power of Elijah, and John the Baptist, it is necessary to know what occurred in Elijah's life. According to Scripture, the Prophet Elijah controlled the weather, in that: according to the word of Elijah, it didn't rain for three years—*now that's power!* According to the word of Elijah, rain fell again ending the 3 year drought. *That's more power!* Elijah, called down fire from Heaven. Once, to consume a sacrifice on Mount Carmel and twice more, when two of the king's captains and their small detachments of 50 soldiers each, were consumed by fire for showing disrespect to the Prophet of God! *Now that's power, R R R!* Elijah raised the dead, and according to the word of the Prophet, the widow had an endless supply of oil! *Now that's power!* And finally, the man Elijah could split the Jordan River whenever he had to get to the other side! *Now that's power, R R R!*

The above passage, speaks of the disciples of Christ to whom Jesus had spoken to in the previous verses. Now King Herod testified that he believed that John the Baptist had been raised from the dead (reincarnated), and that is why he thought that these miracles were occurring. What is of interest, is that before Herod could make such a claim, he first had to associate these present miracles with something of the past! In other words: Could it be that John the Baptist did in fact perform miracles? This postulation of mine, is founded upon the miracles of which a few Old Testament Prophets had performed. For instance, Moses performed miracles as did the Prophets Elijah and Elisha. King Herod's proclamation inferred that he thought that John, whom he beheaded earlier, had been raised from the dead and was the one person responsible for all these healing miracles! So, here we have a devout enemy of God testifying on behalf of God and of John, and more specifically, of the *power of repentance, R R R!* **Truth #38: The ensuing power of a lifestyle of repentance, substantiates obedient faith, because repentance, is that which establishes saving faith in the life of a believer!** *(cf. Mk. 5:34; Lk. 7:50, 9:7 – 9)* **Although Jesus stated that faith can make a believer whole or that faith may save, a lifestyle of repentance qualifies that faith, for obedient faith is an essential condition of repentance!** Moreover, Scripture does teach that coming to repentance is a condition of health! *(cf. Isa. 6:10, 53:5; Acts 28:27)*

The Force of Righteous Words

Job 6:24 – 25 AMP
*"Teach me, and I will hold my peace; and **cause me to understand wherein I have erred.** How forcible are words of straightforward speech! But what does your arguing argue and prove or your reproof reprove?"* (emphasis mine)

The preaching of repentance, is first a righteous word, and as such—is forceful! No doubt that John the Baptist, as well as Jesus Christ infuriated many, and as it was then, so does it remain today. People don't want to be told what to do! *However, should one embrace the preaching and the teaching of the doctrine of repentance, that person will experience the force of this instruction in righteousness, because the force of this righteous word, targets the iniquity of the mind and the carnality within the soul.* The result of which transforms the saint, who has come to repentance to become a terror to his carnal self, as well as to others who remain carnally influenced! (See Freedom 2, chapter 24 for further insights pertaining to becoming a terror to thyself.)

You see, when a person finally comes to that point in life where he allows him/herself to learn the wisdom of repentance, and acquires the knowledge of carnality, as this investigation contains, he has become a student in the classroom of the Holy Ghost, for as the Scriptures above reads, *"...cause me to understand wherein I have erred."* **Truth #39: The preaching and the teaching of repentance, is intended to be forceful and must be presented as such. This however does not in any way imply or suggest that its presentation should be abused with railing intonations. The minister who hammers away at those who sit before him with a hostility towards sin, is mishandling this instruction in righteousness, and exploits the ignorance of others and demonstrates his own!** I liken this approach to a police officer who uses excessive force in enforcement contacts. By profession, the police officer is already in a position of subdued force. This force should only be activated or engaged, should a enforcement stop escalate in hostility.

Who Recognized John as a Prophet?

The Prophets of old prophesied in the desert. But for so many in the domesticated church, as well as in cultural Christianity, a Prophet is one who gives a specific, enticing word to an individual or a congregation. *It seems then that a misunderstanding of a Prophet's fidelity among the masses, promotes false prophets themselves!* And why not, since the false prophet would be a product of this same misconstrued demographic! To these, a Prophet is expected to tease itching ears and to speak of things people want to hear. However, a true Prophet will disappoint those who come to hear or see him. His words will be hard to receive and the spirit and power of delivery, shall convict their hearts of truth! His words will clash with the denominational doctrines, and the institutionalized dogmas of the worldly church! Many will be agitated and stirred to rage, because of his message of repentance!

In *Luke 7:24 – 28* Jesus, while applauding John the Baptist for his fidelity and service to the Kingdom of Heaven, asked the people one question three times. He asked, *"What did you expect to see?"* As an answer, Scripture states that John the Baptist was identified as a Prophet by several. He was recognized by the Prophet Malachi, by Zacharias, his paternal father, by his cousin Jesus Christ, as well as the local citizens, and King Herod and his court. *(cf. Mal. 4:6; Mt. 3:3; Lk. 1:65 – 66, 76, 7:28; Mk. 6:14 – 16)* In these passages, Jesus asked a very poignant question. He asked, *"But what did you come out to see?"* He asked this question, as He wanted the people to recognize that although the Old Testament Prophets, of which John was actually the very last, prophesied of the Messiah [then], John the Baptist prophesied of the evidence that pointed to Jesus Christ, [present]!

John was commissioned of God to prepare the hearts of the people to receive Jesus Christ as their Lord and Savior. Since Jesus Christ lived during the days of John's preaching, the Holy Ghost wants us to know that regardless of the corrupt world and all its sorrows, Jesus Christ is very much alive today, even during our life time. So, you could say with all things being equal, the sorrows of today, are no different than those of John's day! Just as Jesus appeared then, He lives today and He shall reappear again! *(cf. Isa. 57:15)* The New Testament Prophet's task is no different! Although John was a cousin to Jesus, the Christ, *(Lk. 1:36)* Almighty God wants His saints to become sons! *(cf. Rom. 8:14, 19)* This tells me the importance of relationships. The Prophet of God must possess a vibrant, lifelong relationship with Almighty God. As cousins, John the Baptist and Jesus Himself, both lived contemporaneously with each other. That is to say, they lived at the same time, and in the same locality. But get this; so do the saints of God today, for they serve a living God and a resurrected Savior! Hallelujah! So in this sense, there really is no difference: Is there?

A Prophet's Reward and a Righteous Man's Reward
Matthew 10:41

"He that receiveth a prophet in the name of a prophet shall receive a prophet's reward; and he that receiveth a righteous man in the name of a righteous man shall receive a righteous man's reward."

This verse begs the question: Just what is a Prophet's reward? In keeping with the theme of this investigation, *a Prophet's reward is the doctrine of repentance and the knowledge of salvation!* Worldly acclaim and wealth, shall never be the reward of a Prophet, as these things are temporal. However, as spiritual things of God, repentance and salvation, forever shall remain eternal! However, should a Prophet's message be rejected even in his own name, then the intended recipient shall receive the *reward of his iniquity*, which leads to eternal death! For the New Testament Church, a Prophet exists to bring the message of repentance as the knowledge of salvation! This remains his primary duty, as he has been charged of Almighty God to present repentance as God's instructions in righteousness. However, most people do not care to be told what to do, so their reward shall be their self-imposed condemnation and damnation. *(cf. Jn. 3:17 – 18, 5:24; Rom. 8:6)*

The other question is: What is a righteous man's reward? Obviously, his reward is eternal life, for he has been set free from the dictates of the law, since the law was never made for a righteous man; but it was made for the lawless and the disobedient, for the ungodly and the sinner. *(cf. 1 Tim. 1:9)* **Truth #40: Whereas, there is a duplicity of judgment, similarly, there is also a duplicity of righteousness. Where the former denotes the difference between righteous judgment which a saint applies to his carnality, the latter, denotes the indignation of Almighty God for man's impenitence. So then, when a saint comes to repentance, he levies righteous judgment against his own self-righteousness, thereby ensuring his salvation and conversion!**

John's Fidelity and Our Righteous Charge

John the Baptist did not foretell of future events in the fashion of his predecessors. Rather, he preached repentance for the remission of sins, exclusively. Why? Because Jesus Christ was alive and living among the people! So there was no need to prophecy of His coming, since He already existed. But John did testify of His appearing and existence, with the intent on fulfilling his divine charge to prepare the hearts of the people to accept Christ as the prophesied Messiah! Herein lies a truth of repentance, **Truth #41: The preaching and the teaching of repentance, is**

tantamount to the preparation of one's heart to acknowledge Jesus Christ as the prophesied Messiah and the Son of the living God, for without a lifestyle of repentance, impenitent men will never truly acknowledge Jesus as their Lord and Savior! This is why John preached repentance, as this was a divine mandate from Almighty God, given to all the Prophets, who were preachers of righteousness themselves! *(cf. Mal. 3:1 – 4; Lk. 1:15 – 17, 3:2 – 6; Mk. 6:16 – 28; Mt. 14:10)*

Today, all prophetic foretelling of judgments to come, are found in the Scriptures. However, true Prophets of God, in these last days, shall exist to preach repentance, not just because the coming of Christ is so very near; but also because, impenitent men live contemporaneously with a living God and a resurrected Savior now! Like John the Baptist, preachers of righteousness are to prepare the hearts of the people to receive Jesus as their Lord and Savior, before it is too late. *This diluted and convoluted pretense of a cornflake gospel which has been presented of late, undermines repentance, the doctrine of God, and preachers are going to be held accountable for this misuse of Scripture and for their abuse of the office in which they occupy! (cf. Jer. 10 :21, 23:1 – 2; Ezek. 34:1 – 10)*

Prophets were the greatest born of women! Mohammed Ali is not the greatest! He may claim to float like a butterfly and sting like a bee, but to Almighty God, he will be crushed like an annoying insect! Prophets are more honorable than kings and princes, and John the Baptist was the greatest of all Prophets before him. America and this corrupt world in which we all reside, do not realize the value and service, true Prophets present to the Church and nations! Yet, he that is least in the Kingdom of Heaven, is greater than John! *(cf. Mt. 11:11)* All ministers, who have obtained mercy of the Lord, are to be skillful and faithful in their calling! The hardest Apostle and the most righteous Prophet of old, have established for the New Testament Prophet, a standard to follow as preachers of righteousness who are employed under a more excellent covenant than they, and Scripture teaches that the New Testament Prophets occupy a more honorable office than even John the Baptist! These who follow *after* the Lamb (Calvary) far excel the greatest of those that went before them. Therefore, those of us who live after Calvary, under the Gospel of the New Covenant, have so much more to answer for! Whereas, Enoch was a preacher of righteousness, in that he foretold of divine judgments to come, John the Baptist preached repentance for the remission of sins. Therefore, judgment and repentance are clarion calls of the Prophet, especially in these last days! We are on borrowed time: Are you rapture ready? *(cf. Jude 14 – 15)*

Matthew 11:11
"Verily, I say unto you, Among them that are born of women there hath not risen a greater than John the Baptist: notwithstanding he that is least in the kingdom of heaven is greater than he."

Mark 1:4
"John did baptize in the wilderness, and preached the baptism of repentance for the remission of sins." (cf. Lk. 3:3, 24:47; Acts 13:25, 19:4; 2 Pet. 3:9)

Truth #42: Without repentance, there is no remission of sin; neither is there admission of carnality, for without repentance, man's carnality cannot be suppressed in his living. Whereas, the blood of Christ was shed for the remission of sin, in like manner, a lifestyle of repentance represents that covering, for they are parallel! *(cf. Lk. 3:3; Heb. 9:22, 10:18)* Now, the word, *remission* means, "acquittal, exoneration, pardon, discharge, forgiveness." This is more than an orchestrated church assembly and confessional, predicated by an evangelistic altar call! This is more than stating, *"I am a Christian,"* as so many impenitent men think themselves to actually be, based solely on their good person persona or a misunderstood theology. The word, *sins* in *Mark 1:4* means, *"to miss the mark and not to share in the prize [of that high calling]."* As you shall learn in chapter 6, *the greatest prize is eternal life, and the highest call is justification, and a lifestyle of repentance coupled with obedient faith, are the two means of acquisition.* Yes, God is merciful! Yes, God is loving! Yes, God is slow to anger! But in spite of His attributes for blessings, no sin or fashion of predominant carnality, shall enter into the Kingdom of Heaven, no matter what a particular denominational dogma may say to the contrary! *(cf. Rom. 1:18, 2:5 – 6, 8:5 – 6; 1 Cor. 2:14, 3:3; Gal. 5:1-5, 15 – 21)* Yes, I know that Jesus Christ shed His precious blood for the sins of the world, but unless impenitent men demonstrate faith in His blood, and take the appropriate corrective measures by coming to repentance, His blood shall not cover their sins of unsuppressed carnality! *(cf. Rom. 1:17, 3:25; Gal. 3:6 – 11)*

> *Hebrews 10:26 – 27 AMP*
> *"For if we go on deliberately and willingly sinning after once acquiring the knowledge of the Truth, there is no longer any sacrifice left to atone for [our] sins [no further offering to which to look forward to]. [There is nothing left for us then] but a kind of awful and fearful prospect and expectation of divine judgment and the fury of burning wrath and indignation which will consume those **who put themselves** in opposition [to God]."* (emphasis mine)

Repentance Heals the Withered Hand of Carnality
Mark 3:3 – 5
"And he said unto the man with the withered hand, Stand forth. And he said unto them, Is it lawful to do good on the Sabbath days, or to do evil? To save life or to kill? But they held their

*peace. And when he had looked round about on them **with anger** being grieved for the hardness of their hearts, he saith unto the man, Stretch forth thine hand. And he stretched it out: and his hand was restored whole as the other."* (emphasis mine)

Previously, I spoke of the shovel and the axe of repentance as tools. Well, if your hands were withered do you suppose you could handle these tools? I think not! Due to arthritic conditions, your hands would be gnarled and in much discomfort. I dare say, you would do good just to maintain minimal comfort, without taking on other strenuous activities which would inflame your malady. Well, this man had a withered hand and *in anger,* Jesus commanded him to stand forth! Almighty God is commanding all men to do the same. He is stating to us that we must stand up righteously before Him and be counted, for if we choose not to, then our unrighteousness shall become our demise. When a man stands uprightly before God, as an operation and work of righteousness, his withered hands are healed so that he may put the tools of repentance in hand and apply them to his heart and soul. Notice that the passage above states that Jesus was angry. This implies, that we too must acquire an *indignation* against our own carnality. **Truth #43: A lifestyle of repentance, heals the withered hand of carnality, so that the saint may stand uprightly before Almighty God, for he has cultivated his salvation and has pruned the righteous fruit of his character in God, through the use of these hand tools of repentance!**

The Timeline of Repentance
Zephaniah 2:1 – 3 AMP
*"Collect your thoughts, yes unbend yourselves [in submission and see if there is no sense of shame and no consciousness of sin left in you], O shameless nation [not desirous or desired]! [The **time for repentance** is speeding by like chaff whirled before the*

wind!] Therefore consider, before God's decree brings forth [the curse upon you], before the fierce anger of the Lord comes upon you–yes, before the day of the wrath of the Lord comes upon you! Seek the Lord [inquire for Him, inquire of Him, and require Him as the foremost necessity of your life], all you humble of the land who have acted in compliance with His revealed will and have kept His commandments: seek righteousness, seek humility [inquire for them, require them as vital]. It may be you will be hidden in the day of the Lord's anger." (emphasis mine)

As previously stated, each of the Old Testament Prophets were preachers of righteousness, in that they preached repentance to the rebellious people of their generations. Since the Old Testament's timeline extends for some 4000 years of antiquity, and since these Prophets lived during this era, it is reasonable to say that repentance also has a timeline of its own. Specifically, that its duration extends throughout the life of every single person in and throughout the days of their living! This is so, because iniquity, as the element of sin, exists throughout the lifetime of any person. So you can say that since all people have been conceived in sin, iniquity has its own time line as well! **Truth #44: Whereas, the timeline of repentance exists to avert the anger of God in the day of His wrath, the timeline of iniquity, exists to ensure that impenitent men will endure the indignation of Almighty God, as divine judgment against unremedied sin, caused by their unsuppressed carnality!**

– Timeline –

Old Testament Prophets	**New Testament Prophets**
Messianic Prophecies	Divine Judgments
Divine Judgments	Repentance
Repentance	Carnality
Carnality	

Your Spiritual Timeline

It is a spiritual truth, that every human being ever born, is first a spiritual being before he was ever a human being. This then signifies: that each one of us are eternal beings, whether inside or outside our physical body! For example, when I was an active law enforcement officer, as a routine, I had to attend a daily briefing prior to assuming my road patrol duties. Now these briefings, provided each officer the latest information pertaining to the road conditions and any pertinent facts which each officer had to know ahead of time. In like manner, Almighty God created all men as spirit beings first, prior to His dispatching us to patrol planet Earth during our respective shift (lifetime). So, as a briefing, Almighty God informed us of our responsibilities before we ever occupied our physical bodies! *(cf. Gen. 1:26 – 30; Psa. 8:6 – 8)* **Truth #45: A lifestyle of repentance, is the instruction previously given by and through which a saint is able to patrol the vast landscape of his carnality, as he patrols the many miles of unknown destinations within his soul, and as he does so, he effectively polices his beat during his shift. Thus enforcing righteous decrees against all crimes of his carnality!**

Now it seems, that every person whether living or dead, has within their own respective lives, two testaments of their own, and that Calvary's cross for each, is the defining moment within their respective lives. Let me explain: I was physically born on a certain month, at a specific day and time of a particular year and at a specific location, just as you were. This natural birth, represents all things physical. However, on Thursday morning, April 29, 1977, I was involved in a minor collision at a specific location at precisely 11:15, where I was born again, spiritually! Therefore, my spiritual rebirth, pertains to all things spiritual. So, it is evident that prior to my conversion, my life was Old Testament and since my conversion, my life that I now live, is for me a New Testament experience! Potentially then, everyone initially may live out their lives in their Old Testament living or be reborn into the one New Testament life. You see, a lifestyle of carnality, represents all things carnal, which includes, but is not limited to: self-centeredness, self-indulgences, all carnal propensities, moral depravities, all manner of immoralities, all manner of pride, lusts, fornications, etc. Anything that is of man's fleshly tendencies, would naturally fall in this category. However, all things that are spiritual, are not of the carnal nature, which the previous Old Testament timeline would naturally consider. **Truth #46: Just as the historical timeline of man's history involves the Old and the New Testament scripturally, so also does each and every man born again, live out his life individually, first in an Old Testament period in his carnality, and then upon his conversion and his adopted lifestyle of repentance, he lives out his new life in the New Testament of his living, spiritually!** *(cf. Rom. 6:1 – 23; Eph. 4:22; Col. 3:9 – 17)*

However, what is to be said of the majority of those who attest to their Christianity and yet they evince practically no evidence of true spiritual transformation? To wit, it is obvious then that these universal Christians, are perjuring themselves before God's court, in that their lives have all together misrepresented true godliness! Or it could be, that these carnally influenced people, were never in fact truly born again to begin with and are just fooling themselves with their religious hyperboles! Whatever the reason, iniquity has infiltrated the rank and file of the halls of Christendom and for the most part, has been accepted, even embraced by religious society! And the reason for this, is simply because all men everywhere are first in denial of their carnality. There was a time, when to be a true member of the Body of Christ—required discipleship. (Now a days, all that is required is a citizenship of a so-called Christian country!) They fail to see that what they call righteous is in fact self-righteous, self-serving and self-indulgent propensities of their own carnality! Truly then, a lifestyle of repentance is the only remedy to their carnal tragedy. **Truth #47: A lifestyle of repentance, evinces a man's New Testament life, where before his unrestrained carnality evinced his Old Testament living!**

The Decapitation of the Church

Mark 6:16
"But when Herod heard thereof, he said, It is John, whom I beheaded: he is risen from the dead." (cf. Col. 1:18)

Deuteronomy 32:1 – 2
"Give ear, O ye heavens, and I will speak: and hear O earth, the words of my mouth. ***My doctrine*** *shall drop as rain, my speech shall distill as the dew, as the small rain upon the tender herb, and as the showers upon the grass;"* (emphasis mine)

Repentance is a spiritual gift, and Almighty God saw to it, that His gift of repentance be given to all men of every generation. *(cf. Acts 11:18)* However, just as John the Baptist was beheaded, likewise have impenitent men decapitated this doctrinal gift of God! The beheading of any right reverend by the Church, is a premeditated decapitation. This *systematic* execution shall be used as evidence against a carnal church and its leaders! This repugnance, is the rejection of God's will and our obedience, and is perpetrated by self-serving, carnally minded church leaders! They have become the modern day Pharisee and guardian of dogmatic overtones! Whereas, capital punishment is determined based upon the heinousness of a particular crime of violence against another, the decapitation of the preaching of repentance, has become a capital offense within the existing mutinous church! **Truth #48: What capital punishment is to the judicial system of nations, the beheading of any preacher of repentance by the carnal church, shall be equated to a capital offense against Almighty God!**

Institutional preachers have become company executives, for their feet fill the shoes of pharisaic pomposity! I remember when an officer was promoted to the rank of sergeant, immediately he or she was absorbed into the higher echelons of the institution of the California Highway Patrol and such as it should be. But through this assimilation process, the new sergeant gradually became alienated from the troops from where he came. This managerial indoctrination, slowly caused the new sergeant to forget his roots, which caused all kinds of animosity. Scripturally, we must never forget our roots as the place from which we all came. If we do, then exclusivity, nepotism (favoritism shown to relatives) and special regard towards affluence shall exist, as it does now. *(Deut. 4:9, 6:10; Jn. 2:1-9)*

The New Testament Church, is built upon the foundation of the Apostles and the Prophets, but through default, the carnal church has evolved into the denominational church structure, so substantiated. *(cf. Eph. 2:20 – 22)* *Every wind of doctrine* that Scripture speaks of, denotes a myriad of dogmatic differences and denominational distinctions of religious sects and factions. *(cf. Eph. 3:21; 4:11 – 14)* We have forgotten that the Church is subject unto Christ, Who is the Head. Paul said this, when the infant Church was truly subject to Christ. This is the home plate of the Church in faith, and not in some hyphenated denomination! Hence, the carnal church has effectively lowered the bar, because denominational and institutionalized churches have allowed the New Testament Church to become substandard, so much so, that it has become subject only to the institutional indoctrination, and not unto Jesus Christ, Who is the Truth! Truly, we have a form of godliness, but deny His power, His grace, His glory, His anointing, and His presence; as these are attributes of Who God is. As the Head of the Church, Christ has been replaced with the traditional concepts of a western cultural perspicuity! *(cf. Eph. 1:22 – 23)* Literally, the dogma of carnal churches, has beheaded the true head of Christ, effectively decapitating the doctrine of repentance and the right reverend who presents it. For these, a capital offense has been committed, and I might add that capital punishment shall be executed, because Almighty God has held and will hold, every Gospel preacher in contempt of His High Court for this neglect!

Pulpit Puppeteers

I once heard a message entitled, *The Giant Ain't Dead till You Cut Off His Head!* By its title, you can see that this message referred to David and Goliath. This message basically asserted that knocking the giant down, was never sufficient towards overcoming adversity; but it was essential that we go one step further and lop off its head! This is precisely what King Herod did to John the Baptist! To King Herod, John was a giant, and this denotes that any right reverend, is also a giant in the service and commission of Almighty God!

So many times, we are our own worst enemy. Since any congregation is a cross section of any society, it stands to reason, that said congregations, consist of societal influences which are diametrically opposed to the overall intent of the local church. It used to be that the pulpit message was biting, even cutting to the bone. However, today most messages have lost their cutting edge, because the *pulpiteer* has lost his nerve to stand and address the giants of self-indulgence and carnality! **Truth #49: What the pulpiteer once was to the Gospel of the Word of His righteousness, has now become the puppeteer to the strings of his carnality and the selfish propensities of others; and what moral depravities and societal influences are or have become to our citizenry, denominational influence has conformed to the predominate mind set of unrighteous nations!** Hence, people are no longer subject to Christ, but to their respective institutions. *(cf. Eph. 5:24; Mk. 7:5 – 13)* The problem is that impenitent men love their denomination or institution and have despised the true New Testament Church which Jesus Christ died for! Nowadays, carnally minded men, would rather die for their *institution* than die for the *constitution* of the mystery of the Gospel! Perish the thought! Although, Jesus Christ did die for the sins of the world, He did not die for a carnal church! If that were the case, then He would have died for an adulterous church which occupies a red light district, and people who comprise this church, would all be a corporate cabal of effeminate men! But Scripture teaches He shall return to receive unto Himself, a glorious Church without spot or wrinkle; nor any such thing. Jesus Christ shall appear once again to receive those saints, who have heeded the call and have come to repentance, which is evident in the righteousness of their living. *(cf. Jn. 3:5; Eph. 5:27 – 32)*

Ephesians 4:14 – 15 AMP
"[That it might develop] until we all attain oneness in the faith and in the comprehension of the [full and accurate] **knowledge** *of the Son of God, that [we* **might** *arrive] at really mature manhood (the completeness of personality which is nothing less than the standard height of Christ's own perfection), the measure of the stature of the fullness of the Christ and the completeness found in Him. So then, we* **may** *no longer be children, tossed [like ships] to and fro between chance gusts of teaching and wavering with every changing wind of doctrine, [the prey of] the cunning and cleverness of unscrupulous men, [gamblers engaged] in every shifting form of trickery in inventing errors to mislead." (emphasis mine) (cf. Isa. 26:7 – 10; 1 Cor. 15:34)*

No longer does the preacher take his marching orders from God! His allegiance, is to the institutions of dead men, who have lost their minds to their carnality and tradition! They have eyes, but do not see, and ears, but they do not hear. Only a deaf and the dumb cadaver properly describes this condition of self-righteousness! Jesus Christ did not die for this, that His Church should remain carnal! He died for a glorious Church, without spot or wrinkle! His blood-work defined the New Testament Church in and through faith in that blood, responding to the call of repentance for the remission of sins, past, present and future! The free gift of the Word made flesh, Who gave His life in compliance to divine law, only substantiates a person's life through the gift of repentance, which validates the one, true faith and not a hyphenated psuedo faith or religion!

Grace is an Expression of God's Love

His free gift to us is called His grace. Denominational rights and rituals, are not attributes of grace as gifts, but are work ethics which negate the freedom and liberty we all should have in Christ! What the Word of His Gospel defines as grace, denominational dogma misconstrues as race! Like selfish, little children who fight and fuss over a toy, trifle or novelty. Similarly, it is for this reason there are at least 1500 denominations, and it is for this reason also, there are so many factions and church dissensions!

Paul, the Apostle, said he had run his race. So too, when we run or compete for the prize of the high calling of God, we enjoy God's grace. You see, GRACE is simply running our race God's way. As we do, we enjoy God's grace. And grace is never to be confused with a man's race, whether a competition or ethnicity, and just as any race is that which a man runs, it is also that which is beneath his feet. Likewise, when a saint runs his race God's way, then the saint comprehends all things are under his feet, just as they are under the feet of Almighty God! *(cf. Eph. 1:22 – 23, 5:24)*

Another point is this, since Scripture teaches that God is love, it is important that humanity realize and embrace the

Truth about Grace. [Let me explain: I had open heart surgery in 2011. I died after a 5 hour operation. I was brought back to life having been dead for 28 minutes. During my recovery, I asked Almighty God, Who is my Heavenly Father, to explain for me something about His grace. This is what He said: *"Son, I AM love and love must have an expression. My grace is the expression to all of humanity of my love to them and for them and whosoever understands this truth and embraces my love expressions, they will experience My loving kindness in their life."*]

James 2:17 AMP
"So also faith, if it does not have works (deeds and actions of obedience to back it up), by itself is destitute of power (inoperative, dead)."

Truth #50: It takes a physical act to release a spiritual force. The spiritual force of God's grace, must be released through a physical act, and that rule of action must be faith and repentance, as both are attributes of God's grace evinced in and through a godly character! When a saint's work is complete here and his race has been run during the course of his living, after he passes on, the gifts and callings of God, shall return to Him from whence they originated! Moreover, since Almighty God inhabits eternity, and knows the end from the beginning, He must wait for any penitent man to catch up with Him! This denotes God's grace keeps in step with man's pace. The gift of repentance therefore, is an attribute of the grace of God, for it is a spiritual thing of God which facilitates the salvation and the conversion of penitent men. When penitent men embrace the call of repentance, God's grace keeps pace in their race towards their final outcome of redemption!

The Remission of Carnality

What's more, repentance aids penitent men in the remission of their carnality! As previously stated, the word *remission* means, "to suspend, dormant, absolution, pardon, forgiveness." (Webster's) As an illustration, consider the remission of a cancer. By definition, although the cancer may be dormant or its growth may be suspended, the root microorganism, which caused it, still exists within the cancer stricken cell or organ. **Truth #51: Pertaining to carnality and a lifestyle of repentance, as long as a saint retains his acquired lifestyle of repentance, the iniquitous thoughts (Lie Based Thinking) as the microcosmic element of sin within his soul, shall also be in remission, for his carnality has been suppressed!** Moreover, a man's carnality shall remain within his soul; so long as he lives—it will not be eradicated *until* the day he dies! (cf. Isa. 22:14; Rom. 7:24)

The Copulative Characteristics of a Baptism

Mark 4:28
"For the earth bringeth forth fruit of **herself***; first the blade, then the ear, after that the full corn in the ear."* (emphasis mine)

Isaiah 5:14
"Therefore hell hath enlarged **herself***, and opened* **her** *mouth without measure: and their glory, and their multitude, and their pomp, and he that rejoiceth, shall descend into it."* (emphasis mine)

1 Peter 1:23 AMP
"You have been regenerated (born again, not from a mortal origin (seed, sperm), but one that is immortal by the ever living and lasting Word of God."

In order to present this concept, I must use the analogies of male and female genders in the manner of copulation. So I begin with a place known as Hell. I never knew that Hell had a gender, but as Isaiah indicates, Hell in fact does, and that gender has been determined by God to be *feminine*! In *Mark 4*, Jesus Christ implies that the planet Earth possesses a feminine gender, which also denotes that in order for fertility to take place, something else must be introduced to cause such fertilization to occur. That something else, is rain (humidity) and of course the warmth of natural sunlight (heat). In this sense, and as a physical ingredient of life, rain could be considered as Heaven's semen, for without life giving water, nothing could grow or continue to live.

> *Revelation 19:7*
> *"Let us be glad and rejoice, and give honor to him: for the marriage supper of the Lamb is come, and his **wife** has made **herself** ready."* (emphasis mine)

> *Ephesians 5:24 – 27*
> *"Therefore as the church is subject unto Christ, so let the wives also be subject to everything to their husbands. Husbands love your wives, as Christ loved the church and gave Himself up for **her**, so that He **might** sanctify **her**, having cleansed **her** by the washing of water of the Word..."* (emphasis mine)

Again, Scripture reveals the feminine gender of still another facet of humanity, specifically His Church! And please note that the word *might* is used, which implies a possibility, even a probability of doubt and uncertainty of man's compliance to divine law.

> *Jeremiah 3:14, 20*
> *"Turn O backsliding children, saith the Lord: for I am married to you...Surely as a wife treacherously departs from her husband, so have ye dealt treacherously unto me, O house of Israel, saith the Lord."* (cf. Jer. 3:1 – 3)

Hosea 10:12
"Sow yourselves in righteousness, reap in mercy, break up your fallow ground: for it is time to seek the Lord, till he come and rain righteousness upon you."

As His chosen people, backsliding Israel was also described as a wife and this is no civil marriage. So what's my point? My point is, that the rain from above, which comes in its due season, is symbolic of the consummating sperm of God, which fertilizes the seeds within the earth (egg). So in this sense, the rain baptizes the earth with its life giving flow. Moreover, just as a husband and wife come into union with each other, through their act of intimacy, the wife is baptized by the husband's semen, so that she may conceive. Once she does, and at the conclusion of her pregnancy, the child is birthed; but before the child's birth, the mother's water must break. In this, I find another illustration of a baptism into this natural life. In this sense, the wife is baptized twice! Once by her husband, and again during the birthing process. Finally, as pertaining to the new birth at conversion, when a sinner is converted, he is baptized into the family of God, just as two parents would have a new addition to their own family. Ideally, the new convert is soon baptized by a minister in water, which is symbolic of the birth of the new spirit man within. Still another baptism occurs, when the convert hopefully responds to the call of repentance and is baptized in water unto repentance, as Scripture indicates. Finally, the saint *might* be further baptized with the Holy Spirit, which Jesus Christ does officiate. All these are analogies of the copulative characteristics of a baptism. **Truth #52: The rain of righteousness upon a saint, exhibits the telltale signs of the consummating act of the baptism of repentance, which the saint is birthed into!** *(cf. Deut. 32:1 – 2; Titus 3:5)*

Salted Meat In God's House

Mark 9:49 – 50

*"For everyone shall be salted with fire, and every sacrifice shall be salted with salt. Salt is good: but if the salt has lost his saltiness, where with shall ye season it? Have salt within yourselves, and have **peace** one with another."* (emphasis mine)

Romans 3:17 AMP

"And they have no experience of the way of peace [they know nothing about peace, for a peaceful way they do not even recognize]."

Traditionally, churchgoers have heard *Malachi 3:10* quoted from pulpits, and specifically, as it pertains towards the tithes and offering; exclusively. Until the Spirit of God revealed something else, I too complied. However, upon investigation, I discovered a very significant truth about *Malachi 3:10*. Specifically, that the meat offerings of the Old Testament, were either cereal or grain offerings presented for sacrifice, and that a measure of salt was to be provided by the penitent, as a required ingredient before the cereal offering could be accepted for sacrifice. *(cf. Lev. 2:13 – 14)*

By application, the priest would then take this measure of *salt*, the oil, and the frankincense; and thoroughly mix them into the entire portion of the cereal or grain presented. In other words, this was not just a typical sprinkling, in the fashion of how salt is generally used with meals. But why was this done? As an answer, consider that the earth was cursed, due to the fall of man. *(cf. Gen. 3:14 – 17)* In Genesis, Almighty God informed Adam that the ground beneath his feet and everywhere that he would trod, would be cursed as a result of Satan's deception. This then intimates that all things that come from the ground then and now, is also cursed. So, this is the reason why the priest did intermingle the measure of salt with the cereal/grain offering.

Now the salt so mixed, had peculiar antiseptic qualities,

which suppressed the growth of microscopic pathogens within the grain/cereal offering. The salt did not remove these microorganisms, but it did impair their growth, thereby preventing this offering from being contaminated. **Truth #53: A lifestyle of repentance, is for the saint, who has given himself to repentance, the salt of God's righteousness, as this measure of salt suppresses the growth of his carnality, for he knows that it is the contaminant of the soul!**

Again, *Malachi 3:10* states in part, *"...that there would be meat in my house..."* Salt is a preservative, and in this sense is also an antiseptic. Salt, as a preservative, prevents deterioration. As an antiseptic, salt prevents infection, decay or rot caused by the growth of pathogenic microorganisms. (Webster's) This definition, then implies a condition of sterility which denotes a clean, uncontaminated state or condition. With regards to the meat in God's house, the New Testament Church, is that house and this house is made up of people who are the meat! Another way to look at meat, is the word *flesh*. Imagine walking through a slaughterhouse in which animal meat is processed. It's gruesome enough to see the animal enter the death house alive and to observe its body parts processed for market. *Similarly, it is tragic indeed to watch a convert enter into a denominational or traditional church organization alive with God, just to be cowed down, and then processed as another product of religious dogma!* The New Testament Church, is not a slaughterhouse! Yet, it remains a pack house where meat is permitted to putrefy, because of the lack of salt (repentance)! Jesus said, *"Have salt within yourselves..."* **Truth #54: Whereas, a donor may grant his body to science upon his death, similarly, carnal men dedicate their souls to religion, in their unsuppressed carnality!**

Romans 8:13
"For if ye live after the flesh, ye shall die: but if ye through the

Spirit do mortify the deeds of your body, ye shall live."

An Explanation of Frankincense
(as the Secret of Jeremiah, the Prophet)

Jeremiah 5:14
"Wherefore thus saith the Lord God of hosts, Because ye speak this word, behold, I will make my words in thy mouth **fire**, and this people wood, and it shall devour them." (emphasis mine)

Jeremiah 20:9
"Then I said, I will not make mention of him, nor speak any more in his name. But his word was in my mine heart as a **burning fire** shut up in my bones, and I was weary with forbearing, and I could not stay." (emphasis mine)

Ecclesiastes 3:10 – 11
"I have seen the travail, which God hath given to the sons of men to be exercised in it. He hath made every thing beautiful in his time: also he hath set the world in their heart, so that no man can find out the work that God maketh from the beginning to the end."

Levitcus 2:13 – 16
"And every oblation of thy **meat offering** [grain, cereal, wheat] shalt thou season with salt [of righteousness (Ma'lach); neither shalt thou suffer the covenant of thy God to be lacking from thy meat offering; **with all thine offerings thou shalt offer salt.** And if thou offer a meat offering of thy first fruits unto the Lord, thou shalt offer for the meat offering of thy first fruits green ears of corn dried by the fire, even corn beaten out of the full ears. And thou shalt **put oil [anointing]upon it**, and lay **frankincense** [gum or resin of tree] thereon; it is a meat offering. And the priest shall burn the memorial of it, part of the beaten corn thereof, and part

of the oil thereof, with all the frankincense thereof: it is an offering made by fire unto the Lord." (emphasis mine)

Matthew 23:27 – 28
"Woe, unto you, scribes and Pharisees, hypocrites! For ye are like unto white sepulchers, which indeed appear beautiful outward, but are within full of dead men's bones, and of all uncleanness. Even so ye also outwardly appear righteous unto men, but within ye are full of hypocrisy and iniquity."

Frankincense is not a spice in the typical sense. Rather, it is a combination of two ingredients! First, *Frank*: as used here is not a man's name. It applies to "a person, remark, etc. that is free or blunt in expressing truth or an opinion; unhampered by conventional reticence [control, restraint], or *candid*: implies a basic honesty that makes DECEIT or EVASION impossible to evade or avoid..." *Incense*: means to "kindle, inflame, to burn, shine. Any of the various substances as gums or resins producing a pleasant odor when burned." (Webster's)

Just as salt, oil and frankincense were to be added to the meat offering, and just as the wise men did present gifts of gold, frankincense and myrrh to the toddler, Jesus Christ *(See: Mt. 2:1 – 11);* so likewise, shall any man be seasoned with these same elements pertaining to himself as that living sacrifice, which is his reasonable service! *(See: Rom. 12:1 – 2)* So long as he pursues righteousness, having the oil of gladness (anointing), as well as the fire of God's *pathos* within his bones, he has made himself that living sacrifice, for he is a lively stone; even a hot rock! *(1 Pet. 2:5)*

He himself, as well as his words of straightforward speech *(Job 6:25)* would be first pure, truthful and honestly blunt, because the fire of God burns hot and bright within his heart and soul! Consequently, his words will incense a rage and fire in the hearts of all religious and carnal men. And this must be so, if the indignation of tradition is ever to be overcome! In other words, any preacher of righteousness (Prophet), will project these qualities of the Spirit, in and throughout his living! In effect, he will fight the fire of tradition with the fire of God. In this, he becomes a sweet and pleasant fragrance to Almighty God! This then is the secret to the fire which Jeremiah, the Prophet did speak of!

Amputations and Bodily Disfigurements
Isaiah 66:24
"And they shall go forth, and look upon the carcasses of the men that have transgressed against me: for their worm shall not die, neither shall their fire be quenched; and they shall be an abhorring unto all flesh."

In *Mark 9:43 – 50*, Jesus spoke of worms that dieth not in relation to severe bodily injuries, specifically amputations of the hand, foot and the bodily disfigurement of losing an eye. Left untreated, maggots would soon appear within the exposed site of injury. Soon, the untreated wound would putrefy and eventually the stench of rotting flesh, would permeate the air. Because the advances of medical science did not exist back then, salt was used as an antiseptic in its place. **Truth #55: Jesus took a common physical malady to teach a spiritual truth of salt, which speaks of a lifestyle of repentance, for through repentance, a saint salts himself with God's judgment and righteousness; in accordance to God's spice rack (His Word)!** As he salts his soul with the judgment of God's righteousness, he simultaneously assaults his carnality! **Truth #56: Whereas, a cadaver farm is that place in which medical and forensic science measures the process of rot and decomposition of bodies by time, ambient conditions and the appearance of worms and maggots. Likewise, organized religion, like cadaver farms themselves, have become the breeding grounds for carnal decomposition, due** to the process of carnal infestation of the worms and maggots, caused by the ambient conditions of immorality, ignorance and unsuppressed carnality!

> Psalm 119:123
> "Mine eyes fail for thy salvation, and for the word of thy righteousness." (cf. Dan. 4:27)

Carnal Snails

I'm thinking now of snails. You know, those slimy little worm like insects that gorge themselves in flower and vegetable gardens. I remember when I was a kid, how I often poured salt onto these slugs just to watch them bubble, sizzle and melt away. I was fascinated to see how the salt could have such an effect upon them! **Truth #57: Man's iniquity is like the snail that when left alone, his carnality will encroach upon and within the garden, which is his soul, and eat the heart away of any/all vestiges of eternal life! Repentance therefore, is like the salt, for when a saint applies the salt of God's righteousness upon the carnal snails within his soul, then these slugs are consumed by the conflagration of that salt!**

Carnal Maggots

We all have seen the little white critters that inch their way in, on and about a trash can. They are hideous to look at, and yet they are a fact of life. As you exterminate these maggots, you instinctively know that they exist due to a piece of discarded meat within the trash can. **Truth #58: Well, as compared to iniquity, as long as a man fails to suppress his iniquity and carnality, like maggots that inch their way in, on and about his soul. He becomes like that trash can, whose filth of rotting flesh serves as the meat for maggot infestation!**

Salt, Colloquially Speaking

Have you ever thought of the many ways salt is used colloquially? Here are just a few examples.

1. *The salt of the earth:* This denotes a person whose character is excellent, noble and of integrity.

2. *Salting the mine:* This phrase originated in places where unscrupulous men would place certain worthless iron pyrites within shafts, so as to deceive others into the value of the mine so salted. It means to give *artificial* value to anything that is in fact—worthless. It has the same import, as cooking the books.

3. *Old Salt:* This is a mariner's expression and is often used to describe a military career man.

4. *Salt as a spice:* Salt is generally used with its counter part—pepper.

5. *Medicinal Salt:* Often used as a soaking such as in a bath product called Epsom's salt. Also used as an antiseptic.

6. *Salt as a cure:* Salt is often used to cure meat, tobacco or fish.

7. *Below the Salt:* This expression implies something that is substandard or below average or par.

8. *Salt used as a superstition:* Throwing a pinch of salt over one's shoulder as a gesture of good luck.

9. *Salt as currency:* In days of antiquity, salt was used as a means of exchange/barter.

10. *Worth one's salt:* This expression intimates a quality of one's character as seen in his conduct and behavior. It asserts the potential of lack thereof with personal ethics and morality.

11. *Pillar of salt:* Speaks of Lot's wife, who was turned into a pillar of salt.

The Dung Hill of Self-Righteousness

Just as the animal sacrifices were offered in atonement for man's sin, and just as Jesus Christ laid down His life for the sins of the world, so too then must the saints of God become living sacrifices, and as such, they must have salt within themselves! *(cf. Rom. 12:1 – 3, 8:13)* Now salt is an emblem of the covenant relationship between God and His people. *(cf. Num. 18:19; 2 Chron. 13:5)* Therefore, as living sacrifices, the saints of God are required to have the salt of God's righteousness within themselves. This is not a superstition, but is a scriptural mandate! In other words, if you don't have the salt (repentance), don't bring the offering, for you are not an acceptable living sacrifice!

The Apostle Paul stated in *Philippians 3:7 – 8* that he counted all things but loss, as dung [waste matter fit for the dung heap (toilet or septic tank)]. In effect, he spoke of his own self-righteousness. He meant that his own efforts, abilities and accomplishments were worthless, inclusively! Consequently, and as a result of this revelation of himself, he recognized his own iniquitous thoughts as a rule of action from which his carnal tendencies did emerge. **Truth #59: As long as a man remains self-righteous, he is worthless in the eyes of Almighty God, although he may be considered a man worth his salt in an unrighteous world. However, should this man salt his soul with the salt of God's righteousness, he would at the same time, assault the carnality within his soul. This then would make him valuable in the sight of God, for this man is now worth his salt in the service to God!**

Substitution Salt

There are those folks whose physical condition, prevent them from ingesting natural salt. So to remedy this, science has produced an *imitation salt* which apparently, has the same taste as the real thing. Hence, these folks may enjoy the savor of a salt derivative with their food, although that is all its good for. Now, this substituted salt, does not possess any of the other qualities of natural salt; neither is it antiseptic. **Truth #60: What substituted salt is to self-righteousness and religion, natural salt is to God's righteousness and pure, undefiled worship!** On the surface, man's self-righteousness, seemingly possesses the savor of good salt; however, it does not possess any of the qualities of the salt of God's righteousness. This is because the assault of self-righteousness, as an attribute of carnality upon a man's soul—is an accursed thing. What's more, the fact that the earth was cursed, anything that grows from the earth, is also cursed. This then intimates, that since humanity is of this earth, anything and everything he does or that exists within him, is also cursed. Therefore, man's self-righteousness is wood, hay and stubble, which are those things deserving to be consumed in the flame! Remember what happened to Sodom and Gomorrah! These twin cities were assaulted from above, because they failed to apply the salt of God's righteousness to their souls, while they lived here below. *(cf. Hos. 9:1 – 4; Jn. 6:63)*

Harvested Salt

Whereas, one may salt the mine as previously mentioned, there are those salt mines, where natural salt, is harvested from the earth, as well as salt that is gathered from sea. The Holy Ghost has shown me this truth, salt water is pure, while salted Earth is not! *Salt from water represents God's righteousness, and the salt from the earth represents man's carnality!* This is due to excessive salting, which sterilizes the ground rendering it unproductive. *(cf. Gen. 3:14; Deut. 29:23; Judg. 9:45; Jer. 17:6)* **Truth #61: Salt that is harvested from the earth, equates to the salt of man's self-righteousness, and the salt that is harvested from the oceans represents the salt of God's righteousness!** This is due to the fact, that Scripture implies that water is indicative of either the Holy Spirit or of God's Word. Where God's righteousness produces all things added, man's self-righteousness, spawns only wood, hay and stubble, as those things lost (cursed). **Truth #62: A lifestyle of repentance, is the antiseptic to carnal tendencies, for repentance is the cure between self-**

righteousness and God's righteousness. Through a lifestyle of repentance, the saint processes his fleshly traits with the salt of God's righteousness, preserving his soul and transforming his character and heart in God!

The Anointing and the Salt

As applied to the traditional use of the word *wash*, soap suds come to mind, in that the loosened residue on any washable surface, would be washed away. Allowed to remain however, this dirt would only reattach itself to the surface just washed. Along with the soap suds and the filth, the thing just washed is twice more dirty. However, when the surface just washed is rinsed, the loosened dirt along with the soap suds, would be rinsed away, leaving the surface clean once again. As applied to the Hebrew word, *Ma'shack,* (anointing) the word *wash* possesses another utility; it is to rub. For example, an item of jewelry would have a luster about it, which may became dull from time to time. To reacquire the former brilliance, the jewelry would have to be cleaned and then polished, once again. I stipulate to you that the sheen does not vanish, but that it is a constitutional design of the jewelry itself, in that the sheen reappears, once it is rubbed out! **Truth #63: This then intimates that a man's carnality, must be rubbed with the abrasive known as repentance, so that the sheen of God's righteousness, may once again shine through his character, because ever since the fall of man, carnality has become the inherent tarnish within the soul of every man!** Now, the abrasive of repentance, is the application of the salt of God's righteousness, and used in this capacity, the Hebrew word *Ma'lack* (salt) is most appropriate. Ma'lack is translated salt and it means, "to rub into with intensity." This is significant, because the *Ma'shack* (anointing) also means, "to rub with oil, unction, ointment to anoint, to consecrate, etc." (Strong's Exhaustive Concordance, Heb. ref.# 4886, 4888, page 73 and ref. #4414, 1117, page 67 respectively)

The Curing Process of Repentance

Salt is used to cure meat, fish and tobacco. To *cure* something, is a process involving time and salt (heat). This cure counteracts ailments, evil and bad habits. Aging or drying, are also means of curing, such as used with concrete. In this, curing involves regulating humidity and temperature. (Remember the green house effect and the copulative characteristics of baptism?) But Paul said, *"...all things but loss..."* However, Jesus Christ said, *"Seek ye first the Kingdom of God and His righteousness and all these things shall be added unto you." (cf. Mt. 6:33)* What Paul counted as loss in the unsavory salt of his carnality [self-righteousness], Jesus Christ counts all things added in the salt of God's righteousness! **Truth #64: Therefore, as a cure for the constant outgrowth of carnality, a lifestyle of repentance is the spiritual curing process which requires a lifetime to realize!**

Self-Righteousness as a Sacred Cow

Matthew 5:20

"Except your righteousness exceed that of the scribes and Pharisees, ye shall in no case enter the kingdom of heaven."

Self-righteousness, whether in the guise of personal goodness or of religious diatribes, is a sacred cow, and as such, must be slaughtered and salted! The self-righteousness of man, is symptomatic of his carnal tendencies, his selfish propensities and his fleshly indulgences. The salt of repentance seasons and cures the saint, for a lifetime of reasonable service. He becomes a veteran, even an *old salt* in the battle against his flesh. Historically, the eastern nations consider salt as an emblem of fidelity and friendship. To eat of a person's salt, and so to share his hospitality, are still regarded among Arab nations today. Scripturally, salt is also emblematic of the covenant relationship between God and His people. *(cf. Num. 18:19; 2 Chron. 13:5)* As to the teaching of Jesus Christ, salt is also symbolic of that spiritual health and vigor, essential to godliness as an antiseptic to worldly carnal corruption. Salt also represents the holiness of Christ and the provisions of God's grace pertaining to salvation. To reject the saltiness of Christ, is to become salted with hell-fire! *(cf. Mk. 9:49; Judg. 9:45 – 52)* **Truth #65: A lifestyle of repentance, is the counter active agent against carnal corruption and all that is worldly!** A thoroughly salted soul, preserves the purity of the covenant relationship between God and His saint. Repentance therefore, is that which the saint does as a demonstration of his participation in this covenant of salt. When Jesus said, *"... Have salt within yourselves and be at peace one with another."* I believe this was His meaning.

Salt as Repentance

Mark 9:49
"For everyone shall be salted with fire, and every sacrifice shall be salted with salt." (cf. Mt. 5:45; Acts 10:34)

Of interest, is the fact that everyone shall be salted with fire. This insinuates that the fiery trials and circumstances in life, are equally the same for one and all, and at different seasons within our lives. So then, since the sun shines and the rains fall upon the just and the unjust alike; so too then, shall troublesome times befall every man. Given that, what makes the distinction between the saint and the sinner? There must be a difference between the two, so that the godly saint may be distinguished from the ungodly and the sinner. I attest to you that repentance, is that difference and distinguishing factor! *Whereas, many say they have faith, [albeit misconstrued] not all can say that they have come to repentance!* What humanity fails to acknowledge, is we are all held accountable for our words, deeds and thoughts. However, through the gift of repentance, a saint may distinguish himself while going through these arduous times. **Truth #66: Man's ignorance of his self-righteousness, spawns the mystery of his iniquity, and since iniquity is part and parcel to carnality, man's carnality is the mystery of his iniquity!** However, through a lifestyle of repentance, any man may acquire the knowledge of his carnality, which is the knowledge of salvation that dissipates this mystery! It is for this reason, why I have said, that as long as carnal men deny their carnality, they shall never come to understand righteousness! *(cf. Rom. 3:17; 1 Cor. 15:34)* **Truth #67: Through a lifestyle of repentance, the circumstances in life, are surmounted by the saint who has come to repentance. This is because the saint has realized that the effects of the fiery circumstances within his life, may be suppressed with the salt of his godly integrity within these circumstances!** He no longer sports a victim's mentality, but he does exhibit an overcomer's understanding with the audacity of obedient faith!

Notes:

Chapter 3

Repentance in the Book of Luke

The Birth of a Prophet

Luke 1:13
"But the angel said unto him, Fear not, Zacharias: for thy wife Elizabeth shall bear thee a son, and thou shalt call his name John."

Luke 1:15 – 17, 69
*"For he shall be great in the sight of the Lord, and shall drink neither wine nor strong drink; and he **shall be filled with the Holy Ghost**, even from his mother's womb. And many of the children of Israel **shall he turn** to the Lord their God. And he shall go before him in the spirit and the power of E-li-as, **to turn the hearts** of the fathers to the children, and **the disobedient to the wisdom of the just; to make ready a people** prepared for the Lord....And he hath raised up **a horn of salvation** for us in the house of his servant, David;"* (emphasis mine)

Luke 1:76 – 77
(Zacharias prophesied over his son saying,) *"Thou child shalt be called the Prophet of the Highest, for thou shalt go before the face of the Lord **to prepare His ways; to give knowledge of salvation (repentance) unto His people** by the remission of their sins."* (emphasis and parenthesis mine)

The role call was given! John the Baptist, although an infant, was announced publicly by his dad, Zacharias. No doubt he was aware of the prophecies of Malachi, which spoke of one, who would come in the spirit and power of Elijah. *(cf. Mal. 3:1, 4:5 – 6; Mt. 17:12 – 13; Lk. 1:16 – 17)* How proper for a father to announce the birth of his son and show such devotion, love and pride! In *Luke 1:63*, Zacharias named his son John, in compliance to the angelic instruction. The question was asked by another in attendance of John's dedication, *"What manner of child is this? For the hand of the Lord was upon him."*

The Wisdom of the Just

In verse 17 above, we read of the *wisdom of the just*. Keeping in theme with this investigation, I attest that this wisdom pertains to repentance as the doctrine of God, for how else shall any man be made ready and prepared for the Lord at His appearing? This then supports what has previously been stated regarding the wisdom of repentance, which is the knowledge of salvation. Although John preached repentance then, the preaching of repentance today, would still provide the same results now! As John preached repentance, he made ready a people prepared for the Lord. This infers that the preaching and teaching of repentance today, will get the saints ready, ahead of time. **Truth #68: Just as a bride would prepare herself for her wedding, likewise, a lifestyle of repentance, makes the saint ready ahead of time, so that he is prepared for the Lord's return!** I say this because of the current condition of the church family, and the violence in this world today, in which repentance, like the word faith, has not been preached or taught beyond a simple recitation of the word. Or if it has, then it probably has been inaccurate, incomplete or abusive. Secondly, *and the disobedient to the wisdom of the just; to make ready a people prepared for the Lord…* Depending on the translation, reading this passage is very intriguing. Primarily that it speaks of a change or reconsideration of societal mind sets for Godliness! Presently, the wisdom of the just (repentance), is nothing more than a recitation within the minds of the vast majority of humanity. And I believe this is so, because of their ignorance or stupidity. *Repentance has nothing to do with the sin consciousness which people possess! But it does have everything to do with the proper identification of truth! Truth that speaks of the acknowledgement of the proper identification of who an individual truly is, and not about what he thinks he is!*

He Tutored Me in Rabbit Trails

I remember when in the 1980s, the Spirit of God inspired me to write my name in the margin of my Bible next to an account of John the Baptist's life. I never knew that years later I would be writing this investigation on and about repentance! In April 1984, I had lunch with my spiritual mentor, Dr. Phil Oslin, now deceased, and during our meal, Brother Phil said to me, *"I have just one word to say to you Ed; it's steering!"* I asked him to clarify stirring or steering and he said, *"Stop thinking of food, Ed! I said, **Steering**, as in driving your patrol car!"* Now you have to know Phil to appreciate his methods. He tutored me in rabbit trails! That is to say, he would expound upon Scriptures, taking me in so many different directions. Talk about frustrating! I often would become irritated and bellow out, *"Phil, will you just get to the point!"* Perhaps you know someone like this. Now years later, I can appreciate his methods, because it's practically impossible to provide a short answer or explanation pertaining to the things of God.

For the longest time, I often wondered about this prophetic word, *steering*. So, I looked up the account of Zerubbabel, who was the governor of Judah. *(cf. Ezra 3:8; Neh. 12:47; Hag. 2:2)* As a priest, this man was instrumental in the reinstatement and reconstruction of the temple, and God used him to *steer* or turn a nation back to God. I also read of Moses, whom God used to *steer* a captive nation from bondage and turn them to worship the Lord their God. There are many examples which show men of God, particularly Prophets, whom God used to steer a people back to the Lord their God. And of all Prophets, Jesus said of John the Baptist, *"For I say unto you, Among those born of women, there is not a greater prophet than John: but he that is least in the kingdom of God is greater than he."* (cf. Lk. 7:28) But why did Jesus say this of John?

Since John preached repentance only, it could be that Jesus Christ stressed to the people that the message of and about repentance, is greater than all the prophecies of and about Him and of divine judgments to come. Could it be that the people of John's day, valued the Old Testament Prophets, above John the Baptist? If this were the case, and based upon my own observations of people today, who consider a Prophet to primarily foretell of things future, the people of John's day, probably considered John a lessor Prophet than his predecessors, all because he never foretold of future judgments or of the Messiah. But Jesus did not stop there. He went on to say, *"... he that is least in the kingdom of God is greater than he [John]."* The spiritual importance here is, that any other minister who preaches repentance after John, is greater than John! The preachers of righteousness after John and after Jesus' ascension, are greater than he, because these future right-reverends would believe even though they have not yet seen! *(cf. Jn. 20:29)*

The Preaching of Repentance

John the Baptist, never foretold of Messianic Prophecies, and Scripture does not state that he ever worked miracles, although I suspect that he in fact, did. He never spoke of divine judgments to come either. *It seems that all John did was preach repentance, for the remission of sins!* His preaching, steered an entire nation back to God, through the preaching of repentance! His preaching pierced the hearts and minds of everyone who heard him! He brought the social conscience of his day to a final end or to an ultimate conclusion. He forced the issue of their accountability and did not give anyone a way out, other than to come to repentance and learn of the knowledge of salvation (carnality)! Holy Ghost conviction fell upon the entire Hebrew nation, because John preached repentance! The conviction and force of these right words, fell upon the entire nation, and such as it should, for the Holy Ghost was sent to convict an unrighteous world of God's righteousness, man's sin, and of judgment. *(cf. Jn. 16:7 – 11)* His preaching was of such impact that the Holy Ghost could work! He did not present a sloppy, diluted rendering of the intent of God. Rather, John preached the explicit will of God, unlike today where weak preachers present a watered down rendering of what they think Almighty God's intent is or would be. **Truth #69: Whereas, the drug lord would cut the purity of a narcotic so as to extend his profit base, the anemic preacher has also cut the purity of the Gospel message of repentance with his insipid connotations, so as to extend his livelihood!** No wonder, carnality has run amuck in and through the halls of Christendom. Through the audacious preaching of repentance, John turned an entire nation back to the Lord their God!

Since a nation was turned back to God during John's day, such *steering* shall occur once again, during our day. However, I want to stress the point that John did not beat the people up with condescending preaching, unlike ministers today, who through the recent past have done just that. Never have I found where Jesus, Paul or any of the other disciples resorted to such abusive tactics. It's just my opinion, but the preaching of repentance has been mishandled by well meaning ministers. Their heavy handed tactics, have served only to browbeat their listeners with that which the people already knew, thereby alienating many from the Gospel and the Lord. Almighty God wants his ministers to realize that they shall be held accountable for any misappropriation of His Gospel! Ministers are to preach and teach, not scold or abuse.

We are to leave the conviction to the Holy Ghost, for that is His purpose. Ministers must present the Gospel in such a manner that the Holy Ghost may work. Anything less is not acceptable!

Recently, I spoke with a retired Pentecostal-Holiness minister about repentance. He in essence said to me, that God had called him to preach at the age of 19, and that he has never once preached repentance! He went on to say, he attended a regional conference recently, where some seventy-seven P/H churches were represented, and where the regional director thoroughly thrashed all the ministers for allowing their people to remain in sin! The director went on to say, that the ministers of this denomination have failed to address sin, and therefore have lowered the standard of righteousness! I told this minister that I attended an Assembly of God regional convention in Irving, Texas in September of 1996, and the regional director basically said the same thing to all the ministers of that conference. So it seems, when you consider the hundreds or thousands of ministers present at these two denominational minister conventions, that corporately, they have been derelict in their duty across the board! This is totally unacceptable!

The Force of the Doctrine of Repentance
Job 6:24 – 25 AMP
"Teach me, and I will hold my peace; and cause me to understand wherein I have erred. How forcible are words of straightforward speech! But what does your arguing argue and prove or your reproof reprove?"

Although I have already addressed this, it bares repeating. The preaching of repentance, is first a righteous word, and as such, is innately forceful! No doubt that John the Baptist, as well as Jesus Christ infuriated many, and as it was then, so does it remain today—people don't want to be told what to do! **Truth #70: How-**

ever, should one embrace the preaching and the teaching of the doctrine of repentance, that person will experience the force of this instruction in righteousness, because the force of this righteous word targets the carnality within the soul. The result of which transforms the saint, who has come to repentance, to become **a terror to his carnal self, as well as to others who remain carnally influenced!** (See Freedom 2, chapter 24 for further insights pertaining to becoming a terror to thyself.) You see, when a person finally comes to the point in life where he allows himself to learn the wisdom of repentance. And acquires the knowledge of his carnality, as this investigation contains, he has become a student of his own carnality and of repentance, for as the Scriptures above read, *"...cause me to understand wherein I have erred."*

That Word Which John Preached

Luke 3:3 – 4

"And he came into all the country about Jordan, preaching the baptism of repentance for the remission of sins. As it is written in the book of E-sa-ias the prophet saying, The voice of one crying in the wilderness, Prepare ye the way of the Lord, make His paths straight."

Acts 10:34 – 37

*"Then Peter opened his mouth, and said, Of a truth I perceive that God is no respecter of persons: But in every nation he that feareth Him, and **worketh righteousness**, is accepted with Him. **The word which God sent** unto the children of Israel, preaching peace by Jesus Christ: (He is Lord of all:) **That word**, I say, ye know, which was published throughout all Judea, and began from Galilee, **after the baptism which John preached;**"* (emphasis mine) *(cf. Acts 13:24 – 26)*

That word which John preached was the doctrine of God as

expressed through the baptism of repentance for the remission of sins, and everyone knew of it! Ever since Calvary, all ministers who have obtained mercy of the Lord are to be masters in their calling, and diligent in their office. But as long as repentance is ignored, they shall remain derelict, for they have chosen to abandon this doctrine of God, giving place to their denominational dogmas or their own carnal insecurities! Consequently, the Church as well as an entire nation anguishes in their carnality. Again, since Calvary, we ministers are employed under a more excellent dispensation (provision and not time) and are in a more honorable office than John the Baptist! Therefore, we have so much more to answer for! That word is the baptism of repentance. **Truth #71: The workers of righteousness, are to embrace the baptism of repentance, otherwise they remain workers of their own carnality, and those who embrace repentance—shall be accepted with God!** Here in *Acts 10:34 – 37*, Peter stated a spiritual truth of repentance, which Almighty God had sent by His voice [John the Baptist] to Israel.

As stated, God is no respecter of persons, no matter what their ethnicity. Of a certainty, all things written in the Word of God are truly written or stated; but not all things written are statements of truth! Verse 35 confirms this in that only those who are workers of righteousness qualify, and only these are intended! Therefore, although it is written plainly, that God is no respecter of persons, as saints of God, we must know that He is a respecter of the gift; as well as the fruit! If people can only get beyond the *exclusivity* which they suppose Christianity has, and come to realize and acknowledge, that Almighty God calls them as well. Then once they accept His calling, they too would understand that everyone *inclusively*, may be saved! We must understand, that righteousness must be evident in our living, and a *work ethic in righteousness* is the manner of its evidence and existence in our lives. This work of righteousness, is the operation of God, through the agency of the Holy Ghost, and His anointing upon the saint who is given, devoted or whole heartedly dedicated to His gift, the baptism of repentance! **Truth #72: A lifestyle of repentance, appropriates the operation of God, through the agency of the Holy Ghost working His righteousness within the saints of God!**

The Error of Tradition

Luke 3:8
"Bring forth therefore, fruits worthy of repentance and begin not to say within yourselves, We have Abraham as our father..." (cf. Zech. 1:1 – 6)

People have a common tendency to justify their actions, even when in the error of their tradition. John the Baptist preached repentance and his preaching hit hard, just like the preaching of all the prophets before him! John said, *"...say not within yourselves, We have Abraham as our father..."* John the Baptist wanted to persuade the people of his day, that they had to depart from their carnal traditions, and arrive at new spiritual transitions! Although Abraham was the father of a great nation, the rulers in essence said that their lineage was sufficient, and that repentance was unnecessary, at least for them because of their tradition! Due to their predetermined carnality, they were not going to be told by John, anything to the contrary, and surmised that since the hierarchy of the governing Roman officials had their own line of descendants of the Caesars, then Abraham would be their forefather in a similar fashion! *(cf. 1 Sam. 8:19 – 22)* Whereas, Caesar was considered immortal, the Pharisees perhaps, considered themselves or the institution of which they were a part, to be unending. In the *Book of Zechariah 1:2*, we read, *"God was sore displeased with your fathers."* Verse 4 picks this point up again with this statement, *"Be not like your fathers..."* And verse 5 asks the question, *"Your fathers, where are they?"*

In each of our lives, there exists foundations or fashions of men upon which we have patterned our livelihood, which also includes our established mind-sets and societal influences. Our thinking, our perceptions, our concepts and ideologies, all are based upon the former days, and former relationships, thereby making our present ways as demonstrations of previous progenitive ways! These are the result of societal influences, and the example of our forefathers. Just because you might have done something the same way, in the same manner, in the same place, with the same people and at the same time, does not necessarily mean that it is of God or that it is the only method, manner, place, people or time! So many people live out their entire lives, like assembly line robots. Few people want to lead; most choose to follow. Therefore, they continue to live out their lives, following their tradition and their past imitations and motivations. This evokes a narrow or shallow mindedness, which is contrary to the Spirit of wisdom and revelation. *(cf. Eph. 1:17 – 18)*

We must break this yoke of a parroting mentality and shatter into crumbs, this cookie cutter manner of living! We must go from traditions to transitions! Transitions, will require us to renew our minds (in each of its four faculties), and adopt a new lifestyle. Transitions, will require us to change relationships, localities, thinking patterns, and manner of speech. Categorically, transitions will demand that we exchange our carnality for godliness, because any transition, is as a right of passage! (Refer to Freedom 3, chapter 38 Repentance in the *Book of Zechariah*)

Vomit is Spewed Pre-Chewed Food

Isaiah 28:8
"For all the tables are full of filthy vomit, so there is no place that is clean."

The Word of God talks about vomit-laden tables. This verse applied to the oppressive rulers of Jerusalem in Isaiah's day. Similarly, in *Luke 3*, John confronted the religious leaders within the multitudes, who were also the rulers of the Jews in Jerusalem. Nothing had changed! The Lord's table continued to be vomit-laden, due to the self-indulgence of the religious leaders and the enterprising merchants! This was evident since Jesus cleansed the temple of all the merchants of whom the spurious Pharisees and corrupt priests, had allegiance in their sham to fleece the people. *(cf. Mt. 21:13)*

I remember while attending a service in the mid 1980s, I was approached by a merchandising acquaintance. This man was selling water filtration systems and he attempted to pursue me as another customer while at church. Suddenly, I am on a first name basis with this man! Before he could steam roll me with his pitch, I bellowed out, *"My Father's house shall be a house of prayer, but you have made it a den of thieves!"* Immediately, conviction fell upon this man and he repented of his merchandising priorities. This was not the only incident either, as there were many within this large Assembly of God church, who were involved in independent sales. For these people, the congregation was just a flesh pot, for their own self interests!

Jesus said, it is that which comes out of a man's mouth [spiritual vomit] that defiles him. *(cf. Mt. 15:18)* John the Baptist knew this as well; therefore, he told the people, *"...say not within yourselves..."* I believe he meant that since the salt of righteousness was absent, all that was within the hearts of the people, was as a festering, putrid food source, and when given the chance to exit, did so—as vomit! Hence, as *Isaiah 28:8* continues to state, *"...filthy vomit, so that there is no place that is clean."* When we come to the table of God, vomit shall not be found, for the Lord's table is always clean. Whereas, Esau found no place of repentance, similarly, impenitent men shall not find a clean place to sit at the

Lord's table either! This is because repentance denotes a clean heart in which there is no guile. However, when self-indulgent people choose to eat at the table of devils, vomit is always present for it is the main entrée, on this menu from Hell! *(cf. 1 Cor. 10:14 – 21)* **Truth #73: Through a lifestyle of repentance, the saint ensures for himself that which is within his heart, is first clean and proper!**

Health is a Fruit of Righteousness

Luke 5:31 – 32

"And Jesus answering said unto them, They that are whole need not a physician; but they that are sick. I came not to call the righteous, but sinners to repentance."

Why did Jesus say this? Analyzing these two verses, we learn that Jesus said the righteous are whole and the unrighteous [impenitent] are sick. Their sickness does not necessarily refer to any physical ailment alone, but is intended to include psycho-somatic illnesses as well, even demonic influences. In short, Jesus implied that a converted sinner, is a healed saint! So by taking God at His Word, I must ask another question. Why are there so many within the traditional church sick and dying prematurely? Obviously, the answer is that they are ignorant of their carnality; as well as, the spiritual truths of righteousness! As the following verses attest, people become sick through their own ignorance and carnal obtuseness! So, the remedy to reverse this carnal tragedy (this trend of personal assault and condemnation), is to obtain a working knowledge of specific truths of carnality and righteousness, whose influence transcends physical afflictions, traditions and societal influences! **Truth #74: Based upon a covenant relationship and by a constitutional necessity, the saint of God may choose to live in divine health, because a lifestyle of repentance, reverses the devil's own condemnation back towards and upon him (devil)!**

Biologically, our physical bodies regenerate brand new cells at the molecular level every six months or so. This total and complete regeneration denotes that our bodies were initially designed of God to live forever! It can't help but do so! However, if something is not done to correct future afflictions, then these new cells become tainted, thereby perpetuating the affliction. Because God created man's physical body to heal itself, by constitutional design, any and all illnesses must be eliminated from the body by way of the body's own defense systems. So, when a person allows his body to defend itself, he will eventually feel better because the body has been allowed to function as it should. For instance, if I were to accidentally cut myself, by design, my body's defense systems would be activated to heal or regenerate the injured tissues, even from a molecular or cellular level. It will do this because it can't help itself, for that is what it was designed to do! However, if I were to interfere with this healing process by neglecting my health through improper hygiene, then I suppress or hinder my body's defense systems, and the cut could become infected, thereby complicating the healing process. In effect, I resist or frustrate this constitutional preexisting condition. **Truth #75: Since all truth is parallel, and since carnality is a preexisting affliction of the unregenerate soul, then repentance, as the spiritual defense system of the soul is also a preexisting, constitutional condition, based upon a covenant relationship. Whereas, a man's body possesses preexisting defense systems to regenerate its health, likewise Almighty God has designed within the soul of man a spiritual defense system to regenerate its salvation, and that defense system within the soul, is the conscience of the individual that alerts him of the need for it. So whenever, and as long as impenitent men reject repentance, they work against the constitutional design of their soul's basic need for regeneration and salvation, even his own conscience, which is constantly urging him to come to repentance, and be**

converted! *(cf. Rom. 8:1 – 2; Heb. 2:14; 1 Jn. 3:8)*

Since people are in denial of their own carnality, they have no understanding of God's righteousness. *(cf. Rom. 3:10)* Before anyone may understand righteousness, he first must acquire a working knowledge of his iniquity, for it is man's iniquity that cultivates a carnal mind. The Apostle Paul said, *"for this cause many are weak and sickly among you, and many sleep [are dead]." (cf. 1 Cor. 11:27 – 30)* So the key to maintaining divine health is righteousness. **Truth #76: A lifestyle of repentance promotes healing, health, restoration and complete wholeness, for these are also fruits of God's righteousness!** *(cf. 1 Cor. 15:34)* What's more, Scripture tells us that through personal initiative, the saints of God are made the righteousness of God in Him, Jesus Christ because they aspire and seek after it. *(cf. Zeph. 2:1 – 3 AMP; 2 Cor. 5:21; Mt. 6:33)*

We Must Acknowledge the Justice of God

Luke 7:28 – 30 AMP

*"I tell you, among those born of woman there is no one greater than John; but he that is inferior [to the other citizens] in the kingdom of God is greater [in incomparable privilege] than he. And all the people who heard Him, even the tax collectors, acknowledged the justice of God [**in calling them to repentance and in pronouncing future wrath on the impenitent**], being baptized with the baptism of John. But the Pharisees and the lawyers [of the Mosaic Law] annulled and rejected and brought to nothing **God's purpose concerning themselves**, by [refusing and] not being baptized with the baptism of John."* (emphasis mine) *(cf. Acts 13:42 – 46)*

When a person comes to repentance, his subsequent lifestyle of repentance, denotes his acknowledgment of God's justice upon all unrighteousness. Through repentance, the saint applies righteous judgment against his own carnality, and in doing so, he saves himself from the future wrath of God's justice. **Truth**

#77: Whereas, the tribulation period is the pinnacle of man's heightened carnality as expressed through his self-righteousness and wickedness, the future wrath of God, is the judgment rendered on impenitent men for their crimes against God's moral law! So it is reasonable to state that the tribulation period, is induced by impenitent men! But more of this later.

As the crème of the crop, the Pharisees and the lawyers, were the best of society. As spiritual leaders and experts of the law, their stature was well known among the civilized masses. But despite their prestige and positions, they nevertheless had a particular character flaw. It was their contempt against Jesus, and specifically against what He had said about repentance, and that Word which John preached. You see, the call of repentance, requires all men to step down from their self-decreed superiority pertaining to their positions, their possessions and their piety, as this arrogance automatically disqualifies them from the Kingdom of God. Consequently, they judge themselves unworthy of salvation, and are very deserving of God's future wrath! *(cf. Prov. 15:25)*

A Lifestyle of Repentance Caters to Jesus

Luke 7:36 – 50 speaks of the woman with the alabaster box. **Truth #78: A lifestyle of repentance, is as a welcome that embraces the truth of God's Word of righteousness, whereas, a mere invitation, is only a formality with ulterior motives!** Through repentance, the saint caters to Almighty God. Through obedient faith in His Son, the saint takes special pains [Godly sorrow, repentance] in seeking those things that gratify the needs or desires of Jesus! That's right! Jesus has needs and desires. His need is for our fellowship, and His desire, is that none should perish in their iniquities and transgressions, but that all should come to repentance. *(cf. 2 Pet. 3:9; 2 Cor. 7:8 – 10; Jn. 3:16 – 18; Mt. 10:38 – 42)*

From time to time I have accepted invitations to attend social functions. Upon arrival, and during the time spent at these socials, I have rarely felt welcomed. How about you? How many times have you attended a function and were given a cold shoulder? Perhaps you were left with the impression that you were just a warm body occupying space. Well, the invitation that people give to God, is an inducement which the Holy Ghost responds to, but upon His arrival, He is rarely made to feel welcome, nor is He celebrated! In reflection, how many churches do the very same thing? As a rule of thumb, and this applies especially towards ministers of the Gospel, *go where you are celebrated and not just where you are tolerated.* To put it another way, go where you are truly welcomed and not just merely invited.

But Wisdom is Justified of All Her Children
Luke 7:35 AMP
"Yet wisdom is vindicated (shown to be true and divine) by all her children [by their life, character and deeds]."

Jesus told Nicodemus, that unless a man is born of the water and of the Spirit, that man could never enter the Kingdom of God. *(cf. Jn. 3:5)* Now, I don't know about you, but I was born of a woman who happens to be my beloved mother. In fact, all my five other siblings were also born of this same woman. Since this is a biological fact, you could say that all of us in the immediate Marr family, are children to dear old mom, and I'm sure it is no different for you.

In the *Book of Proverbs* and elsewhere, wisdom is described as strong drink and as a woman. The sexual attraction a man has toward a woman, compels (attracts) the man to certain activities of which I will not address here, for these activities are commonly known. Similarly, just as a man is attracted or pants after a whore [adulteress] in the natural sense, Almighty God desires that all men pant as a deer after the grace, truth and wisdom of His Word! *(cf. Psa. 42:1 – 2)* Moreover, just as an alcoholic craves the bottle, so likewise does God desire that all men, everywhere pant after the wisdom found in His Word of His righteousness. *(cf. Prov. 1:20 – 21, 8:1 – 36, 9:5; Isa. 55:1; Jn. 6:27)* **Truth #79: Whereas, a hooker walks the streets that lead to death; wisdom works the paths of righteousness which leads unto life! Likewise, what strong drink may be to inebriation; the new wine, as that spiritual thing of God, is to newness of life. The wisdom of repentance, is demonstrated in and through the sons of God, and validates their sobriety!** *(cf. 1 Tim. 2:9, 15)*

Titus 2:11 – 15
"For the grace of God that bringeth salvation hath appeared to all men, Teaching us that, denying ungodliness and worldly lusts, we should live soberly, righteously, and godly, in this present world..."

Children should be the natural outcome of a physical union between a husband and a wife, as this was God's design. Likewise, according to God's design, His children must also be born of the spiritual union of the water unto repentance and of the Spirit! God's children have acquired the wisdom of repentance, whereby they may *work out their own* salvation, even with fear and trembling. *(cf. Phil. 2:12)* But unfortunately, there are many who are the descendants of church as usual! They are not the children of wisdom, for they have never been born of the water unto repentance! Rather, they have become latch key kids, whose parents are out doing the town! **Truth #80: It is only through those born of the water unto repentance, that wisdom is vindicated, because they have been justified as true children of God, for they have been adopted!** *(cf. Rom. 8:14 – 17)*

A Walking Gospel

Luke 7:46
"My head with oil thou didst not anoint; but this woman hath anointed my feet with ointment."

Truth #81: Impenitent men fail to perceive that what repentance is towards the forgiveness of their sins, obedient faith is towards the salvation of their soul! They fail to acknowledge that faith and repentance go hand in hand, like a covenant hand shake between they and God. They fail to realize that without obedient faith and repentance, they are not marching in step with Almighty God! The impenitent fail to realize that a lifestyle of repentance, caters to Jesus! For instance, a platoon of recruits learn through close order drill, how to march in concert with each other as a platoon. These recruits learn to instinctively keep in step with the cadence they hear. No matter how the drill instructor may sound while singing his cadence, the platoon recognizes their D.I.'s cadence. So it could be said that their instinctive march, is the acquired anointing to march as a platoon.

When this penitent woman anointed the feet of Christ, the acquired ointment was the means of the anointing, for without the oil, the woman would not have anointed His feet! Notice that faith and repentance, were the key ingredients in this woman's contrition. The fact that His feet were anointed, tells me that Jesus walked uprightly and in perfect harmony and balance, in accordance to the scriptural mandate of Almighty God. Jesus kept in step with the cadence he heard. That cadence was the rhythmic beat of *faith-repentance, faith-repentance, faith-repentance...* (See Freedom 2, chapter 21 pages 170, 188 – 190 for additional insight.)

Obvious Success is Never a Reason to Gloat
Luke 10:17 – 20
"And the seventy returned again with joy, saying Lord, even the devils are subject unto us through thy name. And he said unto them, I beheld Satan as lighting fall from heaven. Behold, I give unto you power to tread on serpents and scorpions, and over all **the power of the enemy***: and nothing shall by any means hurt you. Notwithstanding, in this rejoice not, that the spirits are sub-*

ject unto you; but rather, rejoice that your names are written in heaven." (emphasis mine)

Although, it is common knowledge among students of the Martial Arts that they possess the acquired skill to kill, injure or otherwise incapacitate their attacker(s). They have learned as a discipline of attitude and motive, that they're never to flaunt their ability outside of proper ceremony. Or like the recruit platoon, who marches to the cadence of their Drill Instructor, the disciples were also students of their teacher (Jesus); and as such, they learned the spiritual discipline of attitude and motives, as well as the spiritual cadence *[faith-repentance]* of keeping in step with Christ. In short, it is for this reason, the spirits were subject unto the disciples, and just as it was for them, so shall it be for those saints of God today, who acquire the wisdom of God through a rhythmic application of obedient faith and repentance! The text verses states, ...*all the power of the enemy;* I attest to you, that this power of the enemy, is the resident carnality within our soul, for it is the rule of action of sin!

Psalm 94:12 – 13
"Blessed is the man whom thou chastenest, O Lord, and teachest him out of thy law; that thou mayest give him rest from the days of adversity [adversary, carnality], until the pit be digged for the wicked." (brackets mine)

It is just my opinion, but the reason why the predominant carnal church does not experience God's power, is simply because they have never been taught the principles of God's spiritual cadence! Ergo, their ignorance precedes their rejection of *repentance as the doctrine of God and the knowledge of salvation,* just as the Pharisees and the lawyers! However, those who do acknowledge their carnality, and who do respond to the call of repentance, these shall possess the power to tread on serpents and scorpions, as well as the power of their carnality. Because through a lifestyle of repentance, they have learned to assault this sin element within their souls! It is cause and effect. What's more, it's a law of necessity, based upon a covenant relationship. In fact, it could be said, that the serpents and the scorpions are nothing but, the attributes of one's own carnality; as that which must remain beneath our feet.

There is a Generation That...
Luke 11:30 – 32
"For as Jonas was a sign unto the Nin'evites, so shall also the Son of man be to this generation. The queen of the south shall rise up in the judgment with the men of this generation, and condemn them: for she came from the utmost parts of the earth to hear the wisdom of Solomon; and, behold, a greater than Solomon is here. The men of Nin'eve shall rise up in the judgment with this generation, and shall condemn it; **for they repented** *at the preaching of Jonas; and behold, a greater than Jonas is here."* (emphasis mine) *(cf. Prov. 30:11 – 14)*

It seems that at the time of the Great White Throne Judgment, Jesus Christ will not be the only one officiating. According to Scripture, the ancients of old, shall also sit as witnesses testifying against the impenitence of men after them! On the surface, this passage seemingly pertains to the generation to which Jesus was addressing. However, with all things being equal, that generation is no different than all succeeding generations that followed! *(cf. Eccl. 1:4)* Elsewhere, Jesus begged the question, *How shall I compare this generation to others?* He even said that His particular generation was evil! Although times may change, people really don't. This is because impenitent men, prefer their carnality over righteousness, and since no one seeks after righteousness, men remain predominantly ignorant of this divine virtue, and consequently, they remain in denial of their own carnality! *(cf. Rom. 3:10 – 18)* **Truth #82: Whereas, people perish for lack of knowledge, similarly they perish for lack of vision! And I might add, that they also perish for lack of wisdom! You see, righteousness must become a pursuit of spiritual knowledge founded upon scriptural text. It must become a divine vision through which the saint of God aspires to. Finally, the saint of God must acquire the righteousness of God, through the wisdom of repentance, for repentance is the knowledge of salvation!** *(cf. Prov. 29:18, 30:11-14; Isa. 5:13; Hos. 4:6; Lk. 1:77, 3:2 – 3)*

That Which Belongs to and is Intended for the Devil Alone

Romans 8:1 – 2
"There is therefore now no condemnation to them which are in Christ Jesus, who walk not after the flesh, but after the Spirit. For the law of the Spirit of Life in Christ Jesus hath set me free from the law of sin and death." (cf. Jn. 3:16 – 18, 5:24)

Therefore, because the saints of God have acquired for themselves the knowledge of their carnality, divine health is the outcome! *(cf. Jer. 17:14, 51:8)* Sin, sickness and death, are the devil's condemnation! They do not belong to the saints of God! They are not the works of God, as some surmise, but they are in reality, the devil's attempt to evade God's condemnation intended just for him. **Truth #83: Through the deceit of carnality in all its attributes, the devil effectively diverts God's condemnation intended for him, and redirects it onto the masses of unsuspecting humanity!** He has been successful with this strategy throughout history! Sin, sickness and death—never glorifies God! Only when the saint is filled with the fruits of righteousness, is God glorified. Now, imagine that you are bouncing a basketball against the wall in front of you. The fact that the ball rebounds back to you is illustrative of what Satan has successfully been doing to humanity. In other words, the ball is the condemnation, the wall is Satan, and you are the recipient! Whereas, God's condemnation is intended strictly for the devil, Satan has deflected God's curse intended just for him upon humanity. As saints of God, we are to take up the shield of faith, and redirect the curse of sin, sickness and death; thus, deflecting the curse back to the devil, who is its rightful owner and intended recipient! *(cf. Eph. 6:16)*

Philippians 1:11
"Being filled with the fruits of righteousness, which are by Jesus Christ, unto the glory and praise of God." (cf. Rom. 8:1 – 2)

Isaiah 6:10
"Make the heart of this people fat [greasy, waxed] and make their ears heavy [dull, severe] and shut their eyes; **lest they** *see with their eyes and hear with their ears and understand with their heart and be* **converted and be healed**.*"* (emphasis mine)

Isaiah 59:1 – 4 AMP
"Behold, the Lord's hand is not shortened at all, that it cannot save, nor His ear dull with deafness, that it cannot hear. **But your iniquities have made a separation between you and your God,** *and your sins have hidden His face from you, so that He will not hear. For your hands are defiled with blood and your fingers with iniquity; your lips have spoken lies, your tongue mutters wickedness.* **None sues or calls in righteousness** *[but for the sake of doing injury to others—to take some undo advantage]; no one goes to law honestly and pleads [his case] in truth: they trust in emptiness, worthlessness, and futility, speaking lies! They conceive mischief and bring forth evil!"* (emphasis mine)

Acts 28:27 AMP
*"For the heart (the understanding, the soul) of this people has grown dull (stupid, hardened, and calloused), and their ears are heavy and hard of hearing and they have shut tight their eyes, so that **they may not** perceive and have knowledge and become acquainted with their eyes and hear with their ears, and understand with their souls and turn [to Me and **be converted**] that I may heal them."*

The Things that Make for Peace

Luke 19:41 – 46 AMP
*"And as He approached, He saw the city, and He wept [audibly] over it. Exclaiming, Would that you had known personally, even at least in this your day, **the things that make for peace** (for freedom from all the distresses that are experienced as the result of sin and upon which your peace–your security, safety, prosperity, and happiness–depends)! But now **they are hidden from your eyes.** For a time is coming upon you when your enemies will throw up a bank [**with pointed stakes**] about you and surround you and shut you in on every side. And they will dash you down to the ground, you [Jerusalem] and your children within you; and they will not leave in you one stone upon another, [all] **because you did not come progressively to recognize and know and understand** [from observation and experience] the time of your visitation [that is, when God was visiting you, the time in which God showed Himself gracious toward you and offered you salvation through Christ]. Then He went into the temple [enclosure] and began to drive out those who were selling, Telling them, It is written, My house shall be a house of prayer; but you have made it a cave of robbers."* (emphasis mine)

Isaiah 32:17 – 18
"And the work of righteousness shall be peace; and the effect of righteousness quietness and assurance forever. And my people

shall dwell in peaceable habitation, and in sure dwellings, and in quiet resting places."

Romans 3:17 AMP
"And they have no experience of the way of peace [they know nothing about peace, for a peaceful way they do not even recognize]."

It's one thing to *define peace*, but it is quite another thing to *know the things that make for peace.* The things that make for peace, elude so many of us! I believe that this is due to the fact that people are ignorant of righteousness! *(cf. Rom. 3:10 – 11)* As stated in Scripture, the work and the effect of righteousness are quietness, assurance and peace. As a litmus test, to ascertain whether or not righteousness is at work within your dwelling, and to gauge its effects upon those who reside therein, it is essential that you acknowledge the fact that if turmoil remains or exists, then the work of righteousness has been neglected, and the effects of righteousness are absent. **Truth #84: As long as carnality thrives, exhibiting the objective symptoms of dysfunctional conduct and behavior, the things that make for peace shall never be known. This is due to the fact that people, across the board, remain ignorant of the rule of action of their own carnality, and are in denial of it!**

Just as we consider the grace of God to have many applications to man's life; similarly, man's iniquity also has many attributes evinced through his carnal living! Before peace can exist, everyone under your roof, must come to repentance and confess Jesus Christ, for He is our peace that breaks down every wall that separates! *(cf. Eph. 2:14)* Not only is Jesus Christ our Peace, He is also the Way of peace, which denotes the work and the effects of righteousness. *(cf. Jn. 14:14 – 16)*

Obsessive Compulsive Disorder or is it Unsuppressed Carnal Desires

I've read that millions of people have acquired a psychological disorder commonly known in its abbreviated form as (OCD), and it is defined as an anxiety disorder. My research has taught me, that this obsession, pertains towards the abnormal, premeditated thought processes, while the compulsion is the activity of these anomalistic premeditations. Moreover, OCD, is an acquired disorder at some time in a person's life, and that this disorder, is caused by a lack of a chemical known as serotonin within the brain. The therapy for this disorder, is either medical or a change in a person's lifestyle. **Truth #85: Where the medical may provide a quick remedy, the change of a lifestyle would require an endured alteration of living. Ergo, what the psychological expression is to a disorder, the spiritual import is to the unsuppressed *carnal desire*!** *(cf. Mt. 24:12 – 13)* In this age of quick fixes, most would prefer to take the medical therapy, so as to avoid the discipline of a lifestyle change. Few there would be that would choose to allow themselves to develop the discipline to amend their ways, having considered their present mannerisms. *Interestingly, the Word of God also speaks of these, and identifies them as iniquity and transgression. Where the iniquity pertains to the premeditation, the transgression pertains to the compulsive activity.* So in this sense, so long as a person chooses to remain in his/her carnality, that person has afflicted himself with Unsuppressed Carnal Desires (UCD). **Truth #86: What OCD may be to a psychological disorder, UCD is to the spiritual condition identified and described in Scripture as degenerate conduct and behavior! Therefore, so long as any man chooses to entertain iniquitous thoughts, and commits himself to them, then that man remains impenitent and is tormented with UCD!** *(cf. Rom. 8:13; Phil. 4:8)*

A Kingdom of Priests and the Politics of Religion
Luke 7:30-35 AMP

"But the Pharisees and the lawyers [of the Mosaic Law] annulled and rejected and brought to nothing God's purpose concerning themselves, by [refusing and] not being baptized by John. **So to what shall I compare the men of this generation? And what are they like?** *They are like little children sitting in the marketplace, calling to one another and saying, We piped (flute) to you [playing wedding], and you did not dance; we sang dirges and wailed [playing funeral], and you did not weep. For John the Baptist has come neither eating bread or drinking wine, and you say, he has a demon. The Son of Man has come eating and drinking, and you say, Behold, a Man Who is a glutton and a wine drinker, a friend of tax collectors and notorious sinners. Yet wisdom is vindicated (shown to be true and divine) by all her children [by their life, character, and deeds]."* (emphasis mine) *(cf. Acts 13:44 – 46)*

As an explanation to these passages, something must be known about the divergent back ground and hostilities of the Pharisees and the Sadducees against the Levitical Priesthood. The nation of Israel, was primarily predestined to be a priestly nation and to be a kingdom of priests; offering service to God. *(cf. Ex. 19:6)* Through Moses' brother Aaron, the Levitical Priesthood was initially intended to establish a kingdom of priests to minister unto the Lord their God at the tabernacle, until the prophesied Messiah appeared. However, there appeared in the rank and file of this spiritual hierarchy, a subversive movement to undermine the purpose and intent of the original priesthood. Consequently, and eventually, the Levitical Priesthood had been *abrogated* [nullified, invalidated, abolished] and in their place, there arose two distinct parties known as the Pharisee and the Sadducees.

"Now, the Pharisees were those pious men who were zealous for religion. They acted under the guidance of the scribes, and in opposition to the godless Sadducees. As a pseudo-political party, the Pharisees conspired to oppose the rightful high priest, while the Sadducees were a party of men who separated themselves from all things non-Jewish. The Pharisees were strictly legal-minded, and were the more popular party among the Jewish society. They deified the Mosaic Law and their attitude was more towards the pomp and pageantry of ceremonial observances. They did not put stress upon the righteousness of their actions, but upon its formal correctness. Consequently, their opposition to Christ and to John the Baptist; was inevitable. The teachings of John the Baptist and Jesus Christ, were essentially a condemnation to the doctrines and dogmas of these two pseudo-political parties. *(cf. Mt. 23)* This is why both John the Baptist and Jesus Christ denounced the societal influence(s) which these two parties had upon the people, and why the Pharisees and the Sadducees subsequently invalidated them. (Vine's Expository Dictionary pages 181 and 210, 211)

The Filibuster of Carnality

By comparison, these two factions resemble the political bipartisanship, that presently exists between the Democratic and the Republican parties, and the attempts to undermine the President's wall efforts and leadership strategies. The filibuster tactics of the senate, to bring nonsensical issues to the floor regarding judicial appointments, only frustrates the Constitution usurping the leadership of the President. According to the historical record, a filibuster was used exclusively to oppose legislature, not judicial appointments, such as Brett Kavenaugh as is the case today. However, pertaining to the Pharisees and the Sadducees, they filibustered the legislative mandates of God's intent, and placed their own agenda, as opinionated 9th circuit judges, ahead of God, Christ and John the Baptist. What's more, they conspired to eliminate the priesthood altogether, and assume this position and office upon themselves.

Now, consider the plight of the church today. Has it not filibustered the Constitution of God's Word of truth and righteousness? Sure it has! The fact that carnality has free reign within the myriad of denominations and other religious institutions, only supports this truth. No wonder Jesus stated to the Scribes and Pharisees: *"Full well ye reject the commandment of God, that ye may keep your own traditions...Making the Word of God of none effect through your traditions, which ye have delivered: **and many such like things ye do.**"* (cf. Mk. 7:9 – 13) (emphasis mine) Not to be overlooked, is the very last phrase of this passage. I attest to you that *the many other such things that we do* is called *carnality*. Such carnality, is displayed clearly through the addiction of ignorance, active and passive manipulation, control tactics, insecurities and all other forms and fashions of physical and spiritual abuse!

John the Baptist was born a priest, in that his father Zacharius was a Levitical Priest himself. As a Levitical Priest, who attended daily at the temple, he was also a spiritual leader of the true intents of God, but the Pharisees and the Sadducees were not. Sure they were leaders, but they possessed ulterior motives that were contrary to the full counsel of Almighty God. These two parties existed, to weaken the foundational supports of Jewish culture, as they were self-appointed prophets of civil disorder and religious unrest. Of interest are the apparent attempts of denominational and institutional leadership today, who have assumed upon themselves similar proclivities of self-serving penchants. Moreover, given the current state of affairs within America, where a socialist agenda is preferred over a republic, it does not take a rocket scientist to discover this ulterior societal influence. Lord help us!

The Sign of Judgment

Luke 11:29-32
*"And when the people had gathered thick together, he began to say, **This is an evil generation:** they seek a **sign**; and there shall*

*be no **sign** given it but the **sign** of Jonas the prophet. For as Jonas was a **sign** unto the Ninevites, so shall also the Son of man be to this generation. The queen of the south shall rise up in the judgment with the men of this generation, and condemn them: for she came from the utmost parts of the earth to hear the **wisdom** of Solomon, and behold, a greater than Solomon is here. The men of Ninevah shall rise up in the **judgment** with this generation, and shall condemn it: **for they repented** at the preaching of Jonas; and, behold, a greater than Jonas is here."* (emphasis mine)

I've often heard preachers relate that this sign of Jonah, speaks of the sign which Jesus Christ declared of and about Himself; specifically, *just as Jonah was three days in the belly of the fish, likewise, the Son of man would be three days in the belly of the earth. (See: Mt. 12:40)* Any *sign,* would be an *indicator* of something else, and in this case, that something else would be judgment and wisdom. *Repentance,* is the wisdom of God, and Jonah preached repentance. I attest to you, that it was this message of repentance, and not the fish, that Jesus refers to as the sign. Although on the surface, it would appear otherwise. In fact, you could correlate repentance and the resurrection, as being synonymous, just as Jesus Christ delivered those captives through repentance, righteous judgment, also delivers from evil, and leads towards salvation. *(cf. 2 Cor. 7:8 – 10)*

Again, Jesus compares *the wisdom of Solomon* to righteous judgment, which is repentance. But what of the wisdom of Solomon? To understand this, you must realize that the three books: *Song of Solomon, Ecclesiastes* and *Proverbs,* which were written by Solomon, contain the knowledge of carnality! They provide this knowledge, so that the Church might grasp hold of righteousness! **Truth #87: When carnal knowledge is acquired, the saint possesses the wisdom of God pertaining to a lifestyle of repentance, for without this knowledge, righteousness is misinterpreted and salvation is averted!** *(cf. Rom. 3:10 – 11; 1 Cor. 15:34)*

Jesus Christ, as the suffering Lamb, was the sign of righteous judgment against prevailing carnality, through the preaching of repentance to an evil generation! His death on the cross, establishes this truth. Although He did not come the first time to judge or condemn the world, *(cf. Jn. 3:16 – 18)* He shall return again as a presiding Judge, at which time the impenitent shall be sentenced to eternal condemnation, for they have condemned themselves to it! *(cf. Jn. 5:24)* Just as Jonah preached repentance to the great city of Ninevah, Jesus also preached repentance to the generation of His day, and through the agency of the Holy Ghost and His right-reverends, He is still preaching repentance to ours as well! Moreover, Jesus implies that those who do acquire the wisdom of repentance, would be as Solomon who recognized their own vexations and who would also acknowledge their carnality as the source of it.

Two News Worthy Events

Luke 13:1 – 5

"There were present at that season some that told him of the Galileans, whose blood Pilate had mingled with their sacrifices. And Jesus answering said unto them, Suppose ye that these Galileans were sinners above all the Galileans, because they suffered such things? I tell you, Nay, but **except ye repent**, *ye shall all likewise perish. Or those eighteen, upon whom the tower in Si-lo-am fell, and slew them, think ye that they were sinners above all men that dwelt in Jerusalem? I tell you, Nay, but* **except ye repent,** *ye shall all likewise perish."* (emphasis mine)

These verses address the horrific, unexpected and sudden death of certain Galileans whose blood was mingled with the pagan sacrifices and of a tower in Jerusalem which collapsed upon eighteen unsuspecting people, killing them. Three things come to mind here regarding these Galileans. *First,* either these

Galileans were antagonists against the established Roman rule and therefore were subsequently hunted down and captured by a Roman detachment. *Second,* perhaps they were offering sacrifices at the temple altar, as a Roman detachment apprehended them there, as in an ambush. *Third,* perhaps these Galileans were innocent of all insurrection against the established Roman government, and Pilate captured them for sport. Either way, Scripture relates that *their* blood was mingled with *their* sacrifices. The questions I have are these, What does the word, *their* represent? Does it mean that the Roman soldiers murdered the Galileans, while these Galileans were offering *their* own sacrifice to God? Or, does it mean that Pilate mingled the captured Galilean's blood with his pagan sacrifices while in the marauding sporting events within the coliseum?

Cruelty, never substantiates justice! True justice takes into consideration all evidence on both sides, and based upon the evidence and arguments presented, a just decree would be so rendered. However, when depraved men occupy positions of authority, justice becomes perverted. In its place, unfairness and tyranny rule! In this passage, Pilate could be portrayed as Satan, and as such, he would be a wholesale murderer, just as his father is! *(cf. Jn. 8:44)*

The Tower of Repentance

Proverbs 18:10 AMP

"The name of the Lord is a strong tower; the [consistently] righteous man [upright and in right standing with God] runs into it and is safe, high [above evil] and strong." (cf. Psa. 18:2; 2 Sam. 22:3; Jer. 6:7)

The other news worthy account, involved a tower that collapsed upon eighteen people, killing them. Jesus said, *"...except ye repent, ye shall all likewise perish."* Since He said this twice, it would be prudent of us to consider what He actually meant.

Here again is another paradoxical statement. From the perspective of repentance, Jesus intimated that unless the impenitent come to repentance, and allow the Lord to be their strong tower, impenitent men shall perish, unsuspectingly! **Truth #88: So, by way of this news worthy event, Jesus intimated that there is a tower of repentance, for if unrighteous men fail or refuse to come to repentance during their living, then the weight of a righteous tower shall fall upon them, killing them unawares!** This substantiates Scriptures, which denote that impenitent men are ignorant of their future. *(cf. Deut. 32:28 – 29, 36)*

But why did the tower fall? Was it an act of sabotage or terrorism? Perhaps, due to faulty construction, it collapsed? If this were the case, then on a surface observation only, it was an accident; for it was an unintended event. Maybe this tower was constructed decades or centuries earlier, and due to the effects of time and deterioration, the structural integrity eroded and it fell accordingly. Perhaps, there was an earthquake that caused it to topple? Either way, the blood of the eighteen people was also mingled with unseen forces beyond their control. **Truth #89: A lifestyle of repentance presupposes a preexisting condition of carnality within a man's soul. This then makes man's carnality completely within his control. Therefore, through a lifestyle of repentance, whatever happens, the saint of God is assured of his salvation, for if there is anything that he can be sure of, it is this: Almighty God will never leave him nor forsake him, for the saint has consistently made Him to be his strong tower!**

As a further explanation of these text Scriptures, I am reminded of the first rule of language and interpretation. Specifically, that if two people are ever to communicate effectively, then both must know and understand what the other is saying! As pertaining to Scripture, this rule could be applied to repentance as a spiritual gift of God, and since it is spiritual, a frame of reference such as an illustration is required, so that its spiritual significance may be comprehended. In these passages, Jesus used these two commonly known events, which were an experience or expression of life, and He introduced these people to that which they did not know, by way of metaphors or analogies. In short, Jesus used these two newsworthy events, to teach lessons about repentance and godliness.

Truth #90: Carnality, as a preexisting condition, gradually erodes the structural strength and vertical integrity of a man's relationship with Almighty God! We go through life conditioned to believe, that nothing out of the ordinary will ever occur. We say, *"Well, if it does, it will always happen to the other guy, but not to me!"* We fail to realize, that most everyone else is saying the same thing, until "it" happens to them! Now, advance history to 9-11-01. Do you see the urgency? Life is short—so unpredictable. We never know when "it" will happen, or where "it" will take place, or in what manner "it" may occur.

People often remark that God works in mysterious ways. *They fail to realize that life without God is mysterious and often is unexplainable.* Whenever tragedies take place, people everywhere ask the same questions, *"But why did this happen?"* or *"How could someone do this?"* Even in the law enforcement community, certain events are categorized as acts of God! When these tragedies do take place, they seem to be beyond our control. Well, as the first rule of necessity denotes, before anything occurs, there first must be a causative agent or factor which precipitated the event. *As this rule pertains to humanity, I wish to state that most everything that occurs in our lives is caused by our ungodly living or by our unrighteousness!* Things just don't happen without a reason or a cause! Only to the ignoramus and naive, those who look at life through primrose glasses, is life a mystery. Eventually, at the final judgment of impenitent men, Almighty God shall cause these to understand, that due to their actions being impenitent, the condemnation of their souls shall be the cause of their own eternal demise, which they themselves have prompted!

Preexisting Symptomatic Conditions of Carnality

Charles Finney wrote a very scholarly book entitled, *Finney's Systematic Theology*, in which he spoke of many spiritual usages such as: certain truths, sanctification, reprobation, even repentance, which has so inspired me in this investigation. **Truth #91: Taking a concurrent course, I wish to state that there are preexisting symptomatic conditions of carnality whose effects are unequivocally evident in the life of any man, and that a lifestyle of repentance addresses these symptoms!** Consequently, whenever carnality is not suppressed, by its very nature, it shall grow out of control or beyond the control of carnal men, because it can't help but do so. To clarify, please know, that a preexisting condition, is an after effect and is not a constitutional element of design. **Truth #92: Whereas, the constitutional element is an intended feature of design, a preexisting condition, is a glitch in the works. In other words, carnality was never an intended feature or faculty of man's basic design!** But it is a monkey *(burden)*, even a gremlin *(hindrance)*, that was injected after the fact, (conceived in sin) and this infers, that carnality can be controlled! **Truth #93: Whereas, over a period of time the body will regenerate its cells at the molecular level, likewise unsuppressed carnality will regenerate itself, for the very same reason, it can't help but do so!**

We Have Lost Control!

On the surface, when weather patterns become catastrophic events against man's existence, all of us are reminded that *we really don't have all things in our control,* and that in reality, humanity stands vulnerable, and is exposed to the weather's fury. *(Job 37:7 AMP)* When immoral men are able to terrorize a nation or community, and where innocent people are slaughtered for a particular deviant cause, *we have lost control!* Surely, when deviates can fly commercial planes into the World Trade Center Towers, the Pentagon, and the downed aircraft in Pennsylvania—*we have relinquished control!* When Judea-Christian symbolisms are removed from our government institutions and in their place the Gates of Baal, paganism and socialism is given equal footing—*we have lost control!* When any alternative deviant lifestyle is promoted above the norm, society has lost control! When any mention of God is stricken from judicial process and men and women who stand in protest to this insurgence are removed from office, truly *we have lost control!* When impenitent men consider darkness for light, wrong for right, and unrighteousness, in place of righteousness, truth and justice—*we have lost control!* May God help us to regain control! *(cf. Isa. 59:2 – 15)*

Where Have All the Leaders Gone, Long Time Passing...

1 Corinthians 1:18 – 20

"For the preaching of the cross is to them that perish foolishness; but unto us which are saved, it is the power of God [unto salvation]. For it is written, I will destroy the wisdom of the wise, and bring to nothing the understanding of the prudent. Where is the wise? Where is the scribe? Where is the disputer of this world? Hath not God made foolish the wisdom of this world?" (brackets mine)

Isaiah 3:1– 4

"For behold, the Lord of hosts, doth take away from Jerusalem and from Judah the stay and the staff, the whole stay of bread and the whole stay of water, the mighty man and the men of war, the [righteous] judge and the [true] prophet, and the prudent and the ancient, the captain of fifty and the honorable man, the counselor and the cunning artificer, and eloquent orator. And I will give children to be their princes, and babes shall rule over them." (brackets mine)

During the decade of the sixties, folk music became very popular. One of the songs begged the question, *"Where have all the flowers gone, long time passing?"* Well, these two passages of Scripture support and interpret one another. Nothing has changed! Whatever has occurred in the past, shall reoccur once again! *(cf. Eccl. 1:9, 3:15)* So it seems, that the Apostle Paul reiterated the Prophet Isaiah's discourse to the people of his day. In 1 Corinthians above, Paul asked the questions, Where are they? Where have they gone? He spoke this concerning the statesmanship and the whereabouts of prominent individuals and godly leadership. I ask the very same questions of you! Where are they? Has God called you to be a godly leader? What has happened to you? Where Paul had asked the question, Isaiah provided the answer! **Truth #94: Whereas, the heavenly articles of the Urmin and Thummin where taken away from impenitent men, similarly, righteous leadership shall also be removed by God from any society or culture whose social conscience remains carnal and chooses to stay altogether self-indulgent and immoral!** *(cf. Ex. 28:30, Rev. 22:11)*

We must come to repentance ahead of time and live a lifestyle of repentance, so that our blood won't be mingled with those who have already perished in their carnality and sin! Once again, I find the spiritual application of accountability here. God wants humanity to know that the sin problem is separate from us, individually. That's why Jesus died on the cross. He became sin for you and me! *(cf. 2 Cor. 5:21)* In fact, the Bible, in one way or another, testifies of His atonement [propitiation]. *(cf. Rom. 3:25, 5:11)* However, as long as impenitent men refuse to take the corrective measures to suppress their carnality through repentance, then God will destroy those who remain impenitent along with he who first spawned sin [devil],for as far as God is concerned, and based upon the evidence that He shall use against them, these impenitent men have mingled their life's blood with Satan! In this, they condemn themselves, for they have become one bloody cocktail with him!

Contaminated Blood is Useless

Contaminated blood is useless for analysis. As a California Highway Patrol Officer, I would arrest the intoxicated motorist. Often the violator would select a blood test. The nurse would arrive and the blood would be extracted from the motorist and stored in a small glass vial. Within the vial, the blood would be preserved with a white, anticoagulant powder, for without this powder, the blood would coagulate in the vial and become useless for laboratory analysis. The same is true for a pregnant woman, who happens to give birth outside a hospital setting. Similarly, no sin shall ever enter the Kingdom of God, for without a saving faith in the atoning blood of Jesus Christ under girded with a lifestyle of repentance, as a corresponding action, we are and thereby remain contaminated! *(cf. Gal. 5:19 – 21)* **Truth #95: A lifestyle of repentance is the anticoagulant that preserves the saint's life of faith in the blood of Jesus Christ! For without this anticoagulant, his faith would be dead and useless!** *(cf. Jam. 2:17 – 18)*

Through these two calamities, Jesus taught that all those who lost their lives, were contaminated with sin! This does not mean that all or some were in fact sinners, but He used these tragedies as illustrations about spiritual truths of repentance. We are not laboratory rats, nor are we test tube experiments in God's laboratory! We are however, spirit beings who occupy a physical body of whom God the Father, wants to come home! He truly misses our company! **Truth #96: Through a lifestyle of repentance, we remain ready for the unexpected, and we are free from the contaminants of habitual transgressions caused by unsuppressed carnality!**

Mingled Blood

Luke 13:1
"There were present at that season some that told him of the Galileans, whose blood Pilate had mingled with their sacrifices."

The word *mingle* as used in verse 1 means, *"to mix, to rub shoulders with, to associate with, to blend or become as one."* It could be that those Galileans who lost their lives at the hand of Pilate, had been commingling with the Romans. In other words, these people could have been caught up in the revelry of paganism. They might have been guilty by association! It is said that there is no honor among thieves. Well, these Galileans must have known in their hearts that they could suffer at the hands of Pilate. Perhaps these Galileans were true believers, and this verse means that these dear saints of God, perished at the hands of Pilate in the arena! *I've heard it said that sin will take you where you don't want to go, cost you more than you want to pay and keep you longer than you want to stay.* In any event, it is evident that these Galileans definitely paid with their very life's blood and I'm sure it wasn't to their liking or of their choosing, no matter what their association might have been!

Furthermore, how can we as saints of God ever think we could straddle the fence, living our lives in both carnality and spirituality? In doing this, we in effect, are also mingling our life's blood with the cup of devils! Can you imagine a hospital patient who is about to receive a blood transfusion? Imagine if the undefiled plasma were to be mingled with contaminated blood of say an AIDS victim. Do you suppose that this patient would be cured of his initial blood disease? If anything, he will be worse off: Wouldn't he?

1 Corinthians 10:20 – 22
"But I say, that the things which the Gentiles sacrifice, they sacrifice unto devils, and not to God: and I would not that ye should have fellowship with devils. Ye cannot drink the cup of the Lord, and the cup of devils: ye cannot be partakers of the Lord's table and the table of devils. Do we provoke the Lord to jealousy? Are we stronger than he?"

The Call of Repentance, Refused

Luke 14:16 – 24

"A certain man made a supper and bade many...For I say unto you, That none of these men which were bidden shall taste of my supper."

It is commonly believed that a sinner may acquire salvation upon his death bed or at the time of his passing. These passages seemingly refute this view. Notice Jesus said in verse 24 that these men which were bidden shall not taste of His supper! What He said, was that throughout a man's life, Almighty God, through the agency of the Holy Spirit, speaks to men, charging them to come to repentance. Yet they refuse out rightly or they make excuses, postponing their compliance to God's command.

I remember, when I was a Marine Security Guard overseas, my detachment would occasionally receive invitations to attend formal dinners or other diplomatic engagements. However, my Marine superiors would command us to attend these fancy-dress events. Although the invitations were extended to the Marine Guard Detachment of which I was a part, the import of these invitations, became more of a summons to appear! If we refused to honor them, then the host would have been offended, and the Marine Corp's image and reputation would have been tarnished, not to mention, that we would have been definitely reprimanded. Some of these diplomatic functions, required at least a representation of the Marine detachment. In this case, only one or two of us Marines would attend the function, for it did not matter who attended, only that a warm body in Dress Blues was present.

Well, my point is this. So often when a salvation call is given, it is always presented from the stand point of a simple invitation. The preacher would say something like this, *"The Holy Spirit is a gentleman and He will not force His will or way upon you, only accept this invitation and be saved: Won't you?"* Rarely, have I ever heard the consequence of a person's refusal to be converted! **Truth #97: Just as my Marine superiors commanded us Marines to attend Diplomatic functions, likewise the Holy Ghost is commanding carnal men to come to repentance! Whereas, Almighty God may extend the invitation to attend a formal banquet, through the agency of the Holy Spirit, humanity is commanded to come to repentance, because a lifestyle of repentance, is the calling card which gives the saints of God access!** *(cf. Acts 17:30; Jn. 16:7 – 11)* Verse 24 states it pretty plainly. If you don't accept this invitation [charge, order, proposal, instruction] while you live, and you choose not to respond to the opportunities granted, then in no case shall any impenitent man ever enter into the Kingdom of God and sit at His table! This is one reprimand, that I choose not to receive! Won't you comply and obey God's command to come to repentance, and join me at the Lord's banquet table?

Cast Sheep

Luke 15:5 – 10, is the parable of the lost sheep. In essence, this parable speaks of one lost sheep that has strayed from the flock of ninety-nine, and when the shepherd found this sheep, how he rejoiced upon finding it. As was learned in *Psalm 51* of Freedom 2, the word *cast* has at least three applications. Here, *cast* applies to a fallen or lost sheep. The expression describes a sheep that has been upended or inverted. If a certain sheep should stumble into a rut or ditch, and ends hooves up, that sheep has no way to right itself or up end itself. Literally, this animal becomes an easy kill for any predator. Sheep have no physical defenses. It's very survival depends upon the shepherd. Scripture says that, *"all we like sheep have gone astray."* This implies, that humanity has become estranged from God, our Chief Shepherd, and Jesus Christ, our Good Shepherd, and like sheep—we have no defense. Moreover, Scripture reveals that impenitent men shall be ditched, because of missed or lost opportunities to come to repentance. Thank God, that Jesus came to seek and to save that which was lost! *(cf. Isa. 53:6; Lk. 19:10, 42-44; Jn. 10:11; 1 Pet. 5:4)* Won't you allow yourself to be saved?

> *Psalm 40:1 – 2*
> *"I waited patiently for the Lord; and He inclined unto my cry. He brought me up out of a horrible pit, out of the miry clay, and set my feet upon a rock and established my goings."*

> *Psalm 51:11*
> *"Cast me not away from thy presence; and take not thy holy spirit from me."*

A Fireman's Carry and His Footprints in the Sand

Truth #98: Repentance is a fireman's carry, because the saint is carried away to safety on the shoulders of Christ! A fireman's carry, is a rescue technique. An injured person, is carried across the span of the rescuer's shoulders with a leg and arm grasped in the front by the rescuer. Imminent peril can make one vulnerable. A provision of a lifestyle of repentance, is that Jesus Christ carries the saint to safety from the rut of his carnality. We are delivered and safely removed from harm's way! Where once we were lost in the unfamiliar territory of the wilderness of sin, we are now found of Him and He has brought us to safety, all because of the knowledge of our carnality! It is said of the (Exodus) Hebrews, that their heel marks can still be seen as ruts across the desert, the lone footprints of Christ are also observed in the life of one who has come to repentance!

The Ninety-Nine Sheep

> *Luke 15:7*
> *"I say unto you, that likewise joy shall be in heaven over one*

sinner that repenteth more than the ninety and nine sheep which need no repentance."

Where's the party? It's in Heaven! Jesus said, *"...which need no repentance."* He spoke this in reference to the ninety-nine sheep. I'm aware of the comparison of some which say that the flock of sheep are the angelic hosts, but the simple truth is, Jesus Christ did not die for the angels. He died for fallen man. Therefore, the significance of repentance, is that the flock of ninety-nine [saints of God] sheep are altogether safe beneath the watchfulness of their shepherd, for His sheep know His voice and follow after it. *(cf. Jn. 10:3 – 5)*

Since the sheep are under the charge of their shepherd, there is safety and protection, so long as they abide in the presence of their shepherd. But should any go astray as this one sheep did, then the animal leaves itself open to danger, for it has removed itself from the safe boundaries of the flock and the shepherd's eye. Moreover, as a lost sheep which must be sought after, the remaining flock is also left unprotected, due to the carelessness of the one! This one lost sheep might also have been a cast sheep, and if so, its very survival depended upon its immediate rescue. Either way, the fact that this one sheep was found alive, intimates that perhaps this sheep would never forget the day his shepherd came to its rescue. From that moment on, a special bond existed between the sheep and the shepherd. And so it is with humanity, who are as many sheep that have gone astray! *(cf. Isa. 53:6)* Moreover, Jesus also inferred that those who are safe within the flock need no repentance, because of their position in the flock. But whoever strays off, does so through the influence of their own carnality. These therefore, would need to repent and return to the flock, where the Good Shepherd may keep watch over them all. *(cf. 1 Jn. 2:16)* Furthermore, the only time that repentance would never be needed, is after a saint is called home. You see, repentance, like faith and all the other spiritual things of God, returns to Him, from whence it and they came, upon the passing of a sinner or a saint. In other words, repentance, and all other attributes of God's grace, are needed on Earth. They are not required in Heaven!

Isaiah 22:14
"And it was revealed in my ear by the Lord of hosts, surely this iniquity will not be purged from you til ye die, saith the Lord God of hosts."

A Boxer Named Sabu

In the hot month of July in 1991, I acquired a 90 pound, 2 year old Boxer from a man who could no longer keep it. I named the dog, *Sabu*. Recognizing that Sabu would require a period of adjustment in his new and different surroundings, I patiently and therapeutically, spent time with him, so as to make his time of transition as comfortable as possible. Well, all was going well, until! I say until, because at this time, I had previously scheduled some reconstruction on my home in San Diego. This compounded Sabu's readjustment, as you could imagine. As a previously scheduled event, the carpet layer walked into my home with a rolled carpet padding upon his shoulder. Upon seeing the carpet layer for the first time, Sabu growled. The carpet layer in turn stomped his boots on the floor and thoroughly scared the tar out of Sabu! Sabu made a hasty retreat and ran towards the double wide screen door facing the backyard. Sabu, literally flew towards the closed screen and impacted it with his head. This impact, forced the screen door off its track, sending it flying into the back yard! Sabu however, kept running and was successful in escaping from the fenced yard. He darted at full speed out into the neighborhood, which was all completely new and strange to him. I immediately took off after him, but could not keep up. Calling out to him was not successful. However, I did manage to catch up with him in traffic. Sabu was dodging oncoming traffic on Palm Avenue as I was waving my arms on the sidewalk at approaching traffic to slow down and avoid killing my dog! Sabu cleared the traffic and continued into a large field. He then continued into another neighborhood, where he eventually exhausted himself, and collapsed. I finally caught up with Sabu as he laid there overheated and possibly suffering from heat exhaustion. Nearby, there was a man watering his front yard. I told him the situation, and asked him if he could give me a large bucket of water to cool Sabu's body temperature. As I gently applied the water with my hands, it wasn't too long, before Sabu's temperature had dropped, at which time I gave him water to drink.

At ninety pounds, I could not carry Sabu in my arms and walk four miles back to my home. So I placed him across my shoulders grabbing his legs together at my chest (the fireman's carry). That experience with Sabu, forever bonded us like I've never been attached to any dog before! From that time on, Sabu never left my side. He listened to my voice and responded accordingly. I never had any further problem with Sabu and neither did he. Sabu died in August of 1999 due to health complications, but my memory of him, still lives on—what a dog!

Boundaries Are Essential

The halls of Christendom, are filled with lost sheep who have strayed from the flock of God, of which they were born into. They have left the boundaries which ensure their salvation and have gone astray! Through the effects of their own carnality and their own self-indulgences, these impenitent and morally deprived people, need to be rescued from themselves!

It's one thing to ask Almighty God to enlarge your territory for His glory, but it is quite another to presumptuously go up the hill and expand your own borders on your own! *(cf. 1 Chron. 4:10;*

Deut. 1:43) Their estrangement from the family of God, proves their vulnerability to the predator of their soul. These people have justified themselves through the vanities of their own self-delusions. Such people are lost and they know it; but they couldn't care less, for that's how they choose to live their lives! They are ignorant of their addiction to their own ignorance, because they are in denial of their own carnality! But the joy that shall be in Heaven, speaks of a festivity going on! **Truth #99: Through a lifestyle of repentance, the saints of God become the "life of the party" because they have lived out their lives circumspectly, in and through a lifestyle of repentance!** *(cf. Eph. 5:15)*

2 Peter 2:10 – 12 AMP
"And particularly those who walk after the flesh and indulge in the lust of polluting passion and scorn and despise authority. Presumptuous and daring [self-willed and self-loving creatures]! They scoff at and revile dignitaries (glorious ones) without trembling. Whereas, [even] angels, though superior in might and power, do not bring a defaming charge against them before the Lord. But these [people]! Like unreasoning beasts, mere creatures of instinct, born, [only] to be captured and destroyed, railing at things of which they are ignorant, they shall utterly perish in their [own] corruption [in their destroying they shall surely be destroyed]." (cf. Isa. 26:1)

Coming of Age or Coming to Your Senses

Luke 15:16 – 21
*"And he would fain have filled his belly with the husks that the swine did eat; and **no man gave unto him**. And when **he had came to himself**, he said, How many hired servants of my fathers have bread enough and to spare, and I perish with hunger! I will arise and go to my father, and say unto him, Father, **I have sinned** against heaven and before thee. And am no more worthy **to be called thy son**; make me as one of thy hired servants. And he arose, and came*

to his father. But yet when he was a great way off, his father saw him, and had compassion, and ran, and fell on his neck, and kissed him. And the son said unto him, Father, I have sinned against heaven and in thy sight, and am no more worthy **to be called thy son."**

These Scriptures are identified as the parable of the Prodigal Son. Jesus said, that the younger son demanded of his father the inheritance that was to be his lot. What catches my attention, is the fact the younger son said this. Presently, it is common knowledge that young adults beneath the age of twenty-five, are required to pay higher insurance premiums than older, more seasoned drivers. It is also known, that when the younger comes of age and feels his oats, he is prone to rebellion against his parents, against established societal order, whether it be a school figure, a law enforcement officer or any other adult, whom he might perceive as the *establishment*, and therefore an encroachment upon his selfish indulgences. Here, in this parable, Jesus spoke of the younger son, who seemingly [in the biological and hormonal sense] had come of age; being that, this son, felt the urge to leave the nest and spread his wings! Like the one sheep that went astray, this young man strayed from the established boundaries of which he was born into! Rather than ask his father to grant him enlarged territories just for himself, this presumptuous young man, embarked on a journey, which eventually led to his own vulnerability! **Truth #100: It's one thing, to come of age biologically, but it's another, to come to your senses, spiritually. A lifestyle of repentance, is the span of time in a saint's life in which he does just that!**

We Have Only Ourselves to Blame

In verse 16, we read, *"...and no man gave unto him."* By this statement, it is evident that this eaglet of a son, succeeded in his own deficiency. He didn't need anyone else to help him accomplish this. He did this all on his own and of his own initiative.

Through an awareness of his own consciousness of guilt, he finally came to himself. He said in essence: Enough is enough! I'm sick and tired of being sick and tired! He, in effect, came to the end of himself, and yet to his credit, he chose to return to his father's house; as this was his only option. He did not allow himself to entertain the thoughts of despair, despondency and dismay, which would only have led to further destruction, personal suicide or criminal activities, for he had only himself to blame.

On January 11th, 1999, the Holy Ghost asked me a very poignant question. He caused me to hear in my ear this question. He asked, *"Does merely admitting, I have sinned, constitute true godly repentance?"* Since God had asked me, I immediately surmised that there is more to repentance than just saying, *"I have sinned!"* As pertaining to this young son, he recognized that merely admitting he had sinned, would not remedy his predicament, alone. He knew that if his condition were ever to change for the better, he would have to do something positive and constructive about his self-imposed quagmire. So he returned home and once again, was reestablished to his rightful position as the son of his father; although he never really lost it. In short, he surrendered his life, and having done so, he revered his father, having honored him. In verse 20, Scripture says that the father fell upon his son's neck. **Truth #101: The import here is that the wisdom of repentance, which the son realized, shall be for the saint an ornament of grace unto his head and as chains about his neck!** *(cf. Prov. 1:9, 4:9)* Upon reading this, I am reminded of what Michael Reagan, the *adopted son* said of his dad, President Ronald Reagan on the occasion of the President's funeral in June, 2004. He said, *"The best way that I can honor my dad is to meet him in Heaven."* What a son! The best way that anyone can best honor Almighty God is to be with Him in Heaven also!

Among the articles of clothing which his son was adorned

with, was the best robe which his father commanded to be placed upon his once wayward son. Traditionally, it has been accepted that this robe bespeaks of the robe of righteousness, which every saint shall receive upon their entrance into Heaven, and to this I do concur; although, Heaven's robe is white. *(cf. Rev. 3:4 – 5)* But what I want to point out is, that this young man probably arrived home wearing rags, perhaps an old filthy and tattered cloak, which means, he most likely was in need of a washing himself! But his father, upon greeting his son, commanded that he was to be immediately clothed in the finest of apparel. The message here is, that all that is necessary for the impenitent to do is to come just as they are and God, through the agency of the Holy Ghost, will see to it; that he is cleaned and washed! *(cf. Psa. 94:12 – 13; Titus 3:5)* But as for the best robe, when a sinner finally comes to his spiritual senses and acquires the wisdom of repentance, he goes from carnal rags to spiritual riches, and as verses 22, 23 indicates, a celebration will take place in his honor. **Truth #102: Through a lifestyle of repentance, the saint exchanges his old tattered rags of carnality for a breastplate of righteousness while he lives. Then, after his passing from Earth via his transport to Heaven, he shall once again exchange this breastplate of righteousness, for a gleaming white (light) robe of righteousness, which his heavenly Father shall adorn him with!** *(cf. Isa. 22:21, 61:10; Rev. 6:11)*

In summary, both parables (the lost sheep and the Prodigal Son) relate the same message of repentance. Where the former denotes that those who need no repentance, are those who have stayed within the flock, the latter denotes that repentance is the readmittance for the impenitent who have strayed from home, which for them is their established spiritual boundary, which God has intended for each of his sons. *(cf. Rom. 8:13 – 17)*

A Lifestyle of Repentance as Portrayed by the Rich Man and a Beggar

Luke 16 verses 19 – 31 is the parable of a certain rich man and a poor beggar named Lazarus. I noticed that this parable consists of four points of interest. *First*, verses 19 – 21 identifies for the reader, the two main characters and their lots in life. *Second*, verses 22 – 25 speaks of the death of each with the emphasis upon their after life experiences and encounters. *Third,* verses 26 – 27 identifies a final separation. *Finally*, verses 28 – 31 teaches that God's Word is sufficient for salvation. So let's embark on an survey regarding each point of interest, so as to obtain further insights of the things to take place for each of us after death.

Point of Interest Number One: A Desire for Crumbs

Luke 16:19 – 21

"There was a certain rich man, which was clothed in purple and fine linen, and fared sumptuously every day: And there was a certain beggar named Lazarus, which was laid at his gate, full of sores, And desiring to be fed with **the crumbs which fell from the rich man's table:** *moreover the dogs came and licked his sores."* (emphasis mine)

On occasion, I have preferred the company of animals over the companionship with certain people! People, nowadays are seemingly becoming more immoral and as they become increasingly decrepit, the standards of social morality, as a whole, follows suit. It's as though the whole of humanity is going in the toilet! But this really doesn't surprise me, for such moral decay and depravity, confirms the scriptural warnings regarding the human condition in these latter days. Lazarus, was evidently content having dogs lick his sores. His desire was for food, even crumbs, and not necessarily to develop a friendship with the rich man.

In contrast to the indifference of this rich man, I'm thinking of the good Samaritan who came to the aid of he who fell victim to robbers. *(cf. Lk. 10:30 – 36)* Moreover, I am reminded of the Canaanite woman who implored Jesus to have mercy upon her. On this occasion, Jesus asked her if it was proper to take the children's bread and throw it to the dogs? She responded and said, Yes, Lord, yet even the little pups eat *the crumbs that fall from their master's table.* Amazed at this response, Jesus stated, *"Great is your faith! Be it done unto you as you wish." (cf. Mt. 15:22 – 28)*

In these two accounts, Jesus spoke of the prejudices which existed between the house of Israel and the Gentile nations. You see, the house of Israel are the children of God, and the specific miracles and grace of God were intended just for them, as was the children's bread; but due to the long standing disobedience of Israel's history and culture, this bread (Jesus Christ) was not appreciated for who He was, but for what He could do on grand scales. On the other hand, this Canaanite woman, through the sincerity of her heart, begged mercy of Jesus. Unlike Israel, who rejected Jesus Christ (the Bread) as their Messiah, the Gentile nations have embraced the teachings of Christ. To this, did Jesus refer in this parable. You see, *her need compelled her presence, and her sincerity of heart, demanded His attention!*

The slightest scrap or crumb that falls from the master's table, as a residue or left over of the (Israel) children's bread, would be better than nothing at all, for the woman was already in a state of need. As they say, *"Beggars can't be choosey."* Because she was pleased to settle for the crumb, Jesus was most impressed with her faith, for faith is a crumb, even a muster seed and this woman would be satisfied with the least. **Truth #103: So, it may be inferred that the Bread of Life Israel rejected, has become the table scraps consumed by the Gentiles! This then implies that the Scriptures themselves are for the Gentiles the morsel of that which has fallen from the Master's table!** *So in this scenario, what* *has become one man's leftovers, becomes another's man's banquet!*

So the similarity between the Canaanite woman and Lazarus are striking. Both were beggars. This does not imply that the woman was as Lazarus, but nonetheless, she did beg mercy of Jesus, just as Lazarus begged mercy of the rich man. However, unlike the rich man, Jesus did respond to her need, whereas this rich man would not respond to the needs of Lazarus.

Point Number Two: My Father, Abraham
Luke 16:22 – 25

"And it came to pass, that the beggar died, and was carried by the angels into Abraham's bosom; the rich man also died and was buried; And in hell he lift up his eyes, being in torments, and seeth Abraham afar off, and Lazarus in his bosom. And he cried and said, Father Abraham, have mercy on me, and send Lazarus, that he may dip the tip of his finger in water, and cool my tongue, for I am tormented in this flame. But Abraham said, Son, Remember that thou in thy life time receivedst thy good things, and likewise Lazarus evil things; but now he is comforted and thou art tormented."

The fact that this rich man identified Abraham as father, is intriguing. Earlier, we learned of the traditions established by our forefathers. Specifically in *Luke 3:8*, John the Baptist, warned the Pharisees not to say, *"...we have Abraham as our father."* Here in this parable, we find this rich man did just that! He said, *"Father Abraham!"* Furthermore, although there is no mention of a particular vocation which this rich man lived, I do find it a plausible possibility, that perhaps this man was a Pharisee, because Scripture does show that Jesus had been speaking to the Pharisees previously as indicated in verse 14. These Pharisees lorded over the people, and were high-minded in their legal prowess. By and large, they wouldn't dare abase themselves by lowering themselves to assist lowly peasants! Let the dogs tend to their wounds! Perhaps you know somebody like this.

Moreover, I sense that perhaps Lazarus if he could, would actually attempt to relieve this rich man of his torments, because if anyone knows what it was like to suffer, Lazarus would! But Abraham did the speaking and not Lazarus. You might think that Abraham would extend certain privileges, since this rich man called him *father* and in life subscribed to Abraham as his father. But Scripture teaches that those who are dead, have no memory or portion in the rewards of the living. So, although this is considered a parable, Abraham would not have been cognizant of the rich man's allegiance towards him in his living, but Almighty God would! *(cf. Eccl. 9:6)*

Point Number Three: Lay up Uncertain Riches
Luke 16:26 – 27

"And besides all this, between us and you there is a great gulf fixed: so that they which would pass from hence to you cannot; neither can they pass to us, that would come from thence. Then he said, I pray thee therefore, father, that thou wouldest send him to my father's house:"

Apparently, this rich man [Pharisee], believed in the occult practice of communicating with the dead. I say this because his request to Abraham was that dead Lazarus would be sent to his father's house. It is evident that there are those most affluent in this life, even denominationally and politically, who dabble with the occult, such as in "Spirit Cooking", Cannibalism, Pedophilia, Human Trafficking and Abortions. No wonder Scripture charges the rich in this world not to be proud, arrogant and contemptuous of others. These who set their hopes on uncertain riches, are instructed in Scripture to set their hopes on Almighty God, Who richly and ceaselessly, provides His saints with everything for their enjoyment. First, Timothy charges them *that are rich to do good, to be rich in good works, to be liberal and generous of heart and ready to share with others less fortunate.* Should they do so, then they would lay up for themselves riches in Heaven that would endure forever. *(cf. 1 Tim. 6:17 – 19)*

Point Number Four: Salvation Through the Living Word

Luke 16:28 – 31

*"For I have five brethren; that he may testify unto them, lest they also come into this place of torment. Abraham saith unto him, They have Moses and the prophets; let them hear them. And he said, Nay, father Abraham: but if one went unto them from the dead, **they will repent**. And he said unto him, If they hear not Moses and the prophets, neither will they be persuaded, though one rose from the dead."* (emphasis mine)

This rich Pharisee had five brothers who were possibly Pharisees as well, or who were very influential. Abraham said to the rich man, your brothers have Moses and the Prophets. The intent being: that Moses and all the Old Testament Prophets were long since dead, as he and perhaps his surviving brothers should believe their words of righteousness while they still lived. The message for us today is simply, that unless impenitent men heed the Words of His righteousness and wake up to the righteousness of God, then they too, shall likewise perish and spend all eternity in flames of torments. However, should they come to repentance as they live, then their repentance will be accepted of God, just as Lazarus, for he begged to eat of the crumbs (word of faith and righteousness) that fell from the rich man's table, which intimates that his faith for the least, would satisfy his need for the much. Conversely, the rich man's desire for the much (pseudo-faith and self-righteousness) would never be satisfied with the least! **Truth #104: The doctrine of** repentance, has been deemed by the wealthy, carnal church, as the very least crumb of scriptural import. However, for the penitent saint, what the church considers a mere dainty, he knows as the nutritious staple of God unto eternal life! *(cf. Psa. 30:5; Mt. 5:3 – 11)*

Repentance Restores Health

Luke 17:12

"And as He was going into one village, He was met by ten lepers, who stood at a distance."

Scripture is replete with expressions that specifically state that when a man comes to repentance, he would be healed. *(cf. Jn. 12:40; Isa. 6:10, 53:5; Lk. 5:31 – 32)* So in this sense, repentance is applied medicinally as a remedy for a carnal tragedy! Even the Apostle Paul implied that many are sick and have passed on prematurely, all because these did not or would not examine themselves in relation to the body and the blood of Christ. *(cf. 1 Cor. 11:26 – 32)* **Truth #105: Whereas, carnality is said to be in remission, a lifestyle of repentance is the means of that suppression!** Consider here there were ten lepers and just one returned to worship at the feet of Christ; thanking Him. The result of this act of contrition, resulted in a permanent cure! *Whereas, faith may get one healed, repentance along with faith will regenerate a cure.* To wit, the other nine lepers received their healing, but their healing did not restore lost limbs. However, with this one leper, his cure not only healed him of his affliction, but also procured the lost limbs which rotted off due to his disease. *Where the others spent the rest of their days disabled, this one leper did not for he was cured through and through!*

Repentance is Not an Audacious Public Display of Self-Righteousness

Luke 18: 9 – 14

*"And he spake this parable unto certain **which trusted in themselves** that they were righteous, and despised others: Two men went up into the temple to pray; the one a Pharisee and the other a publican ... I tell you, this man [publican] went down to his house justified rather than the other: for every one that exalteth himself shall be abased and he that humbleth himself shall be exalted."* (emphasis mine)

It is evident that self-righteous people are ignorant of their own carnality! This is apparent, when you consider the prevailing attitude of the self-righteous in verse 9. There are people like this all around, even those behind the pulpit or political podium! These are the resident experts and the self-proclaimed *know-it-alls*, whose mission in life is, to convince everyone else of their arrogance! In this particular parable, the Pharisee had thoroughly convinced himself that he was a real piece of work! A class act and a class all by himself and to himself. Of a truth, he was a legend in his own mind! His insolence was the hallmark of his haughtiness. His head was up in the clouds; yet he was of no earthly use or spiritual good. The high horse upon which this Pharisee rode was named *Hoity-Toity*. Although this horse is not mentioned, the implication by Jesus was that self-righteous men are impenitent and presumptuous in their self-indulgences and over all carnal propensities. **Truth #106: A lifestyle of repentance is not an audacious public display of ceremonial regard or religious observation. Neither is a lifestyle of repentance a monastic existence which requires one to become a recluse from society. A lifestyle of repentance is however an audacious exhibition against carnal tendencies and this requires the saint may have to separate himself from all things worldly!** Since a snob considers himself as being high and mighty, in that he holds his nose high in the air; similarly, the self-righteous are those who, from their self-imposed lofty perch, look down the length of their noses upon others whom they perceive to be of less significance or importance. If this isn't partiality, I don't know what is; and you know something? God hates it!

Proverbs 16:5 AMP
"Everyone proud and arrogant in heart is disgusting, hateful, and exceedingly offensive to the Lord; be assured [I pledge it] they will not go unpunished."

Proverbs 8:13 AMP
"The reverent fear and worshipful awe of the Lord [includes] the hatred of evil; pride, arrogance, the evil way, and perverted and twisted speech I hate." (cf. Jam. 2:1-9)

Lost Opportunities

Luke 19:42 – 44 AMP
*"Exclaiming, Would that you **had known personally**, even at least **in your day**, the things that make for peace (for freedom from all the distresses that are experienced as the result of sin and upon which your peace-your security, safety, prosperity and happiness-depends)! But now **they are hidden from your eyes.** For **a time is coming** upon you when your enemies will throw up a bank [with pointed stakes] about you and surround you and **shut you in** on every side. And they will dash you down to the ground, you [Jerusalem] and **your children** within you; and they will not leave in you one stone upon another, [all] **because you did not come progressively to recognize and know and understand [from observation and experience] the time of your visitation** [that is, when God was visiting you, the time in which God showed Himself gracious towards you, and offered you salvation through Christ]."* (emphasis mine)

Once again, Jesus is addressing a social conscience of impenitence towards God, and the overall lack of faith in Him for their salvation. Notice that salvation is, also described as *peace*. God's grace is multifaceted and His salvation is applicable to all areas of a person's life. Specifically, salvation is pertinent just as faith. To understand this, you should know that salvation is not just a conversion event or experience, It is a process, that unfolds in and throughout life. Salvation however, is considered a spiritual thing of God and therefore a Truth. Accordingly, the saints of God should know something about its nomenclature. *Salvation* means, *"prosperity, safety, deliverance, health, forgiveness, preservation."* (Strong's Exhaustive Concordance, page 70, Gk. ref. #4991) Salvation then pertains towards the physical as well as the spiritual aspects of life, for the here and hereafter. *(cf. 1 Tim. 4:8)*

The dilemma is: people are not personally aware of these opportunities! They know and are familiar with other things and opportunities pertaining to their material lives, but are lacking in personal knowledge regarding the vulnerability of their own spiritual existence. These passages state, *"...at least in your day."* Scriptures tells us, *"that now is the day of salvation and of God's gracious welcome."* *(cf. 2 Cor. 6:1 – 2)* And yet, people today seemingly go about their business as if all were assured and secure. They fail to seize the opportunities of spiritual import and subsequently miss the opportunities for salvation! These lost opportunities jeopardize their eternal state! But what is hidden from their eyes is that which they have removed from their sight. As if 9/11 and all the other recent terrorist attacks elsewhere in the earth were not enough! There is coming a time and in greater measure, when righteous judgment by way of criminal indictments, military tribunals and executions, shall once again be levied upon an impenitent and self-indulgent people! And with President Donald Trump as America's 45 President, this greater measure has arrived! (I refer you to Freedom 2, chapter

25 for more insights regarding the measuring line of judgment and the abuse of the measure of faith).

The Theory of Relativity

Einstein's theory deduced the relationship between matter, time and space. But speaking of time, let's consider for the time being, the time of repentance as an opportunity. Perchance that impenitent men would seize the opportunity to come to repentance, intimates that time is equivalent to this opportunity. The theory of relativity in this sense pertains to the relative time of a person [matter], his life [opportunity], and the time [space of] in which the opportunity presents itself. **Truth #107: Since people occupy space as matter, then the space of their time on Earth provides them the opportunity for repentance. Coalesced, the time for repentance as a day of salvation denotes the opportunity seized!** Therefore, repentance shall require the time during a person's living! Both are crucial times in one's life, for should a man pass his time away without giving himself the time of day in which he lives, he shall remain ignorant of his future time [his latter end] and shall consequently experience another time to burn in the lake of fire, for without repentance, this man shall literally kill time and himself along with it. *(cf. Zeph. 2:1-3)*

Ability, Opportunity, Jeopardy

As a retired California Highway Patrol Officer, I evaluated my response towards hostile encounters with this simple rule of engagement: *Ability, Opportunity and Jeopardy*. The application is this: Every person alive has the *ability* to inflict injury or an offense upon or against another. Every person alive also has the *opportunity* to inflict injury or to be an offense towards another. When you consider each of these separately, there is no need for alarm, because these two elements are constitutional within each person alive. *Jeopardy* however, is the result of the two (ability and opportunity) coming together and due to the carnal condition of the soul, *jeopardy* is, the potential result! Whenever a state of *jeopardy* presented itself, only then would I be alarmed for my safety and overall well-being. My level of response would be the amount or type of force used to overcome the jeopardy. For instance, an officer pulls a motorist over for an observed moving violation. He doesn't know this driver, but he does know the violation committed. Now, the officer makes his approach on the left side [driver side] with his back to oncoming traffic. (Not a good tactic.) Now, suppose that the violator had a pistol on his front seat or lap and as the officer approaches from the left, the violator reaches for the pistol with his right arm and aims it towards the left front window of his vehicle, holding it close to his chest. There are two points of jeopardy to consider: First, the oncoming traffic poses a very real threat of injury to the officer. Second, the violator poses a very imminent threat towards the officer's life. As the officer arrives at the left front window, the perpetrator pulls the trigger just as the officer steps in the line of fire! The officer is shot and he stumbles into the traffic lane where he is mauled by oncoming traffic. If the gunshot did not kill him, surely the traffic would! Now, let's examine these three elements, individually.

- ***Ability:*** The officer had the ability to approach the stopped vehicle from the right side. He knew better, for his training has taught him the consequences if he did not. But, out of habit and complacency, he opted, as a choice, to make his approach on the left side, where he potentially would jeopardize his own safety, if not by the violator, definitely by the traffic! The driver on the other hand, also had the ability to conceal the weapon or choose not possess it at all.

- ***Opportunity:*** When the officer approached from the left, he stepped into a time of certain harm to his person. First, by the approaching traffic and second by the driver pulling the trigger. Had the officer approached on the right side, then he would have seen the furtive movement of the driver extending his right arm, reaching in the direction of his approach with gun in hand. These few, precious seconds would have alerted the officer of a gun, but since he approached from the left, he failed to consider the ability and the potential opportunity he just provided the driver to inflict mortal harm against his person, thereby placing himself in jeopardy!

- *Jeopardy:* is the result of the combined elements of ability and opportunity, and it goes without saying that from the standpoint of any offense, whenever the first two are neglected, the third will usually present itself! In short, the officer permitted his own demise because he chose to be negligent, thereby causing his own destruction! **Truth #108: A lifestyle of repentance demands constant attention to correct procedure. Should the saint allow himself to become complacent to proper instruction and methods, then his proficiency has waned, because he has relinquished his ability to choose the right path and has failed to seize the opportunity to protect his heart from certain carnal jeopardy!**

Proverbs 18:9 AMP
"He who is loose and slack in his work is brother to him who is a destroyer and he who does not use his endeavors to heal himself is brother to him who commits suicide."

Now, apply this to what Jesus Christ stated in this passage regarding the destruction of Jerusalem. In essence, He implied that Jerusalem as a whole possessed the ability to come to repentance and to acknowledge faith in Christ for her salvation, both physical and spiritual. Secondly, He implied that she also had a choice regarding the opportunity to come to repentance and to adopt a lifestyle of repentance ahead of time, but she squandered those opportunities away, effectively missing them altogether. As a consequence, the jeopardy which Jerusalem would eventually encounter would be of her own making! And so it shall be for all of impenitent humanity!

The Pointed Stakes of Carnal Jeopardy

The pointed stakes represent the jeopardy which impenitent men have given themselves to or have fallen upon. Presently, the pointed stakes of immorality, terrorism, high level corruption and the stripping of Almighty God from the foundations of government, just to mention a few, are gradually hemming us in, and in some respects have already run us through! The perforation caused by man's carnality has punctured his heart! He no longer comprehends immorality, because he has given place to the stabbing tip of what he considers to be—human rights! *The oughtness of his uprightness has been substituted with self-centeredness!* In other words, he has neglected his obligation to live in righteousness!

We are shut-ins, because carnality is all around! There is no escaping it. No matter what direction we turn toward or look, impenitent men have encased themselves, and society as a whole, in a barricade of unrighteousness, because people possess no understanding of righteousness or of their carnality! The tips of these stakes are at our throats and some have already impaled our hearts! *Whatever preaching takes place is sown among the thorns of preexisting carnality!* The Word preached falls upon and within the thorns which are at our throats, for these thorns are the deceitfulness of riches and the cares of this world! *(cf. Mt. 13:22)* **Truth #109: Where Scripture declares that God's grace should be as ornaments unto our head and as chains about our necks, these piercing tips have become the ornaments of necromancy about the neck of a dead or dying society!** *(cf. Prov. 1:9, 4:9)* These stakes intimate that the very heart and soul of impenitent men have been impaled by their own carnality! Consequently, our public conscience reflects the immoral parade of societal indifference and unrighteous! If you have ever seen either an animal or a man who has been impaled, you would better comprehend my meaning. As long as men remain carnally enterprising in their selfishness, then the stakes of their carnal endeavors shall continue to impale their hearts with deadly and eternal consequences!

Another example is the widow woman of Zarephath and her son as found in *1 Kings 17*. Traditionally, this account has been presented from the stand point that perhaps this widow gathered two sticks to cook what little meal and oil she had left. Upon reading this account recently, I noticed that contextually, Scripture does not say that she gathered these two sticks as fire wood, although it may be inferred. Suppose this widow gathered these two sticks for another sinister use. Suppose she intended to bake them having soaked them in the oil and coating them with the meal. Perchance she intended to feed one stick to her son while she ate the other! I say this because the alternative would be a slow, languishing death by starvation for both. She said to Prophet Elijah, *"...See, I am gathering two sticks, that I may go in and bake it for me and my son, that we may eat it-and die."* Perhaps this widow/mother had already premeditated their death by choking on these marinated sticks/stakes. **Truth #110: The similarities between the thorns that choke, and these sticks which could choke and the pointed stakes of carnality are striking, for each reference takes aim at the choke point of a man and his society! That choke point is his unsuppressed carnality!**

Suicides are very commonplace and whatever drives people to it, only they themselves know, or suppose that they know. I'm sure, that if you or I were medical doctors, we would be amazed to learn that those who have attempted suicide and failed, were brought to the dispossession of their right mind all on their own, due to the pointed stakes of carnality within their lives. Literally, these stakes have choked the very life out of them! As a law enforcement officer, I've had my share of suicidal attempts, most of which where successful. But for those that failed or those others who just wanted to draw attention to themselves as a final, last ditch effort and call for help, these survivors have conveyed to me, as the primary officer, their long standing heartache which had brought them to the breaking point. So it would seem, that this widow and her son were in a similar strait; to the point of breaking! Thank God for His mercy and grace!

A Heart's Desire for Incarceration
Luke 22:33
"And he [Peter] said unto him Lord, I am ready to go with thee, both to prison, and to death."

Peter, (aka: Simon), is known as a rather impulsive man, who often blurted out utterances seemingly without realizing the consequence of what he had said. He apparently had a compulsive disposition, which complimented his precipitous demeanor. A case in point would be his statements made towards Jesus Christ here in chapter 22. Peter probably, had never been incarcerated as of this event, so it could be that he possessed no experience as a actual prisoner within the dungeons and jail cells of the Roman rule, although he was aware. Compare Peter's brash statement in verse 33 with the penitent thief in *Luke 23:39 – 43*. The penitent thief knew firsthand what it meant to be incarcerated for possibly an extended period of time, whereas Peter did not. I do applaud Peter's heart felt desire to become a prisoner of the Lord, although prematurely spoken. Peter would have to grow into this level of grace by which he could be a credible prisoner of Christ. He would eventually develop a lifestyle of repentance, which would enable him to fulfill his heart's desire! **Truth #111: A heart's desire for incarceration denotes that the saint chooses** to pursue a lifestyle of repentance, for he realizes that coming to repentance is not just a pat-down search, as it is traditionally known. Rather, coming to repentance is a more invasive procedure, because a lifestyle of repentance is that intrusive inspection of the deepest cavities of the soul. So then, for the prisoner of Jesus Christ, repentance as the doctrine of God, is his strip search of those deepest recesses of his soul just as a body cavity search is for any correctional facility!**

Consider a young man in his teens who embarks upon a criminal career. Although he may be inexperienced at the start, he soon becomes associated with others who have been there and done that. As time passes by, this young man slowly and progressively develops a reputation and a criminal record, which documents his criminal exploitations. Eventually, as a hardened criminal, he reaches the pinnacle of his life of crime and makes it to the "Big House" where he would acquaint himself with the house rules of conduct and behavior.

As a prisoner, a lifestyle of penitence would be adopted whether he realizes it or not. From the penitentiary environment to the jump suit, there is no mistaking this house of replies! Herein lies a contrasting truth. Either way, and through individual choices we all must make, we either yield ourselves as instruments of righteousness or as vessels of unrighteousness, for the choice is ours alone. (cf. Rom. 6:16) **Truth #112: To condemn oneself to the Big House, all one must do is violate the law to qualify, and just as visitation rights are very limited and restricted within this house; similarly, a lifestyle of repentance limits and severely restricts carnal tendencies, immoral propensities and self-indulgences of all prisoners in God's House!** You see, repentance, as the doctrine of God and the knowledge of salvation, is for the saint desiring imprisonment, his incarceration instructions! **Truth #113: For a saint to qualify as a prisoner of the Lord, Jesus Christ, he must violate**

his carnality. Otherwise, his desire for God's House remains, just an insincere aspiration!

For the prisoner, the correctional facility would provide him a copy of the house rules emphasizing the expected conduct and behavior, which the officers would insist or otherwise ensure. To this inmate, such written policies are incarceration instructions which he must abide by. Interestingly, Jesus said the same thing in *John 15:4 – 7 "Abide in Me, and I in you...If ye abide in Me and My words abide in you..."* So as a prisoner of Jesus Christ implies, the saint must also grow accustomed to a new set of House Rules, for as a saint, he is within the House of God! (See Freedom 1, chapter 1 and Freedom 2 chapter 14 for further insights.)

Romans 11:32 AMP
"For God has imprisoned all in (a cell of) disobedience so that He may show mercy to all [Jew and Gentile alike]." (parenthesis mine)

Hebrews 3:6 AMP
*"But Christ (the Messiah) was faithful over His [own Father's] house as a Son [and Master of it]. And it is we who are [now members] of this house, **if** we hold fast and firm to the end our joyful and exultant confidence and sense of triumph in our hope [in Christ]."* (emphasis mine)

The Penitent Thief

Luke 23:39 – 43
"And one of the malefactors which were hanged railed on him, saying, If thou be the Christ, save thyself and us. But the other answering, rebuked him, saying, Dost thou not fear God, seeing thou art in the same condemnation? And we indeed justly; for we receive the due reward of our deeds, but this man hath done nothing amiss. And he said unto Jesus, Lord, remember me when thou comest into thy kingdom. And Jesus said unto him, Verily, I say

unto thee, this day thou shalt be with me in paradise."

If there was ever a passage that would seem to present the fact that there is a deathbed conversion experience, then this could be it. But let's face it, we really know nothing about this thief's personhood. We don't know his name, who he was, what his occupation was prior to his criminality, nothing! We don't know whether this man was a Jew or Gentile. We don't know his age, neither do we know his character. So actually, we really don't know anything at all about this penitent thief, other than what little Scripture relates to us in these verses! But upon closer examination, I wish to make the following postulation based upon some observations, for without a close scrutiny, any surmising on our part would be an injustice to our own souls today! First, a malefactor is a criminal. Either he was a career criminal or he did something wrong, for there is a difference. There are those imprisoned today who have never lived a life of crime and yet, they are just the same incarcerated as if they had. Take the murderer Scott Petersen for example. The criminal investigation and psychological profile revealed that he has never had a police record, and yet this one act of a double murder of his wife, Laci and his unborn son, Conner, was sufficient enough to qualify himself as a resident in the Big House; even death row!

And then there are the career criminals, those who have served time commensurate with their criminal activities throughout their lives. Of course, there are those serving time who are completely innocent, do to a perpetrated falsity against them! *For these innocents, although they are behind bars, they are not being punished for an actual crime committed, but they are suffering a persecution for a perceived offense perpetrated.* Scripture says in essence, that it is far better to suffer for righteousness sake than to suffer as a thief or murderer. *(cf. 1 Pet. 3:14 – 17)* But in the eyes of God, all have sinned [are malefactors], there is none righteous, there are none that understand, because none seek after God and His righteousness! *(cf. Rom. 3:10 – 11, 3:24)* But this thief was accepted of God, which implies that he was and perhaps had been, a worker of righteousness for quite some time, even in his cell. *(cf. Acts 10:34 – 37)*

As I wrote in Freedom 2, chapter 14, the penitentiary, as a city of refuge, is a *house of reply* for those imprisoned. It appears that this penitent thief came to terms with his crime during the time of his incarceration. Assuming that the time served was of long duration, then this thief came to repentance, having possessed true contrition for his deed and being in faith, accepted his execution. There are many cases where those incarcerated have come to Christ, having come to repentance during the duration of their lockup. Many a saint who were once criminally minded have been executed with the peace of God within their hearts. Death Row Prisoner Karla Faye Tucker was such a person, who although sentenced for the brutal pick-ax murder of another, through her death row experience came to faith and repentance years before her execution. (I recommend the true to life movie of her life behind bars, *forevermore* to you).

The fact that Jesus Christ was suspended between both thieves, was in all probability an answer to prayer for this penitent thief, for God hears the prayers of the righteous. *(cf. Prov. 10:24, 14:32, 15:29)* His time served accomplished its intended purpose, and that was the reconciliation of his soul. Consequently, Jesus served as this man's personal escort into paradise! This saintly thief recognized the opportunity to reconcile his soul back to God through repentance, for he was given the ministry of that reconciliation while incarcerated! *(cf. 2 Cor. 5:18 – 19)* Therefore, based upon this simple scrutiny, it is apparent that this thief did not have a deathbed conversion experience as some believe, but he did have hope and confidence even in the face of death, all because he came to repentance beforehand! He in effect, knew that he had the _ability_ to seize the _opportunity_ to come to repentance, to avoid eternal _jeopardy_!

That Which Must Be Taught and That Which Should Be Preached

Luke 24:47
"And that repentance and remission of sins should be preached in his name among all nations, beginning at Jerusalem."

Luke 21:22
"For these be the days of vengeance, that all things which are written may be fulfilled."

Matthew 28:19 – 20
"Go ye therefore and teach all nations, baptizing them in the name of the Father, the Son and the Holy Ghost: Teaching them to observe all things [repentance included] whatsoever I have commanded you..." (brackets mine)

To edify is to provide knowledge by way of instruction, so that others may learn. This work for example, is an attempt on my part, to contribute towards the edification of the Body of Christ. But what exactly is to be taught and what exactly is to be preached during these days of vengeance? **Truth #114: Using Scripture to interpret itself, I find that repentance as the doctrine of God must be taught to the saint and that the baptism of repentance for the remission of sins is that which should be preached to the sinner!** Specifically, Jesus Christ tells us to go and preach the Kingdom of God. *(Lk. 9:60)* Again and again, Jesus Christ gave parables that taught repentance and which contained insight into spiritual things and of the Kingdom of Heaven. **Truth #115: A lifestyle of repentance must be taught to the saint and the baptism of repentance must be preached to the sinner.** Likewise,

the Kingdom of God must be preached to the sinner, and the Kingdom of Heaven must be taught to the saint!

The Kingdom of God is the antithesis [contrast, opposite, reverse] to man and the worldliness within him and about him. The Kingdom of Heaven, as a place of residence wherein dwells righteousness, is also the antithesis to an unrighteous Earth. The earth is temporal in its fallen state, just as man is physical and is therefore temporal! The Kingdom of Heaven (spiritual) shall become the eternal residence of the saints of God, who are also spirit. Jesus said, that the Kingdom of God is within the saint. Therefore, to gain entry into the Kingdom of Heaven, the saint must be Kingdom-minded and not carnally minded. This means that the saint, as a prisoner of Jesus Christ, must acquaint himself with divine law as opposed to religious legalities. **Truth #116: Therefore, the baptism of repentance for the remission of sins is the reversal of carnality and a lifestyle of repentance is the contrast to carnality, as a life in sin! Where the baptism of repentance is the initial command of obedient faith in Christ, the corresponding action to this faith, is a lifestyle of repentance towards Almighty God!** *(cf. Acts 20:21)*

Consider for a moment, the creation of Adam and Eve before their fall. They radiated the very glory of God! There physical bodies were shrouded within a divine brilliance. However, after they fell, a drastic event occurred. No longer were they translucent with the Shekinah glory of God, even though the Shekinah Glory took years to fade away! They were as you and I are. Jesus said that the Kingdom of Heaven is within each saint. This then denotes that the very glory of God resides within and that it wants to express itself through our living. So, in order to be outwardly expressed, the Spirit of God within must be permitted to do so. And a lifestyle of repentance, as that profession (vocation) of faith, is the outward expression of the Holy Ghost! *(cf. Phil. 2:13)* Therefore, just as a spiritual *degeneration* occurred with

Adam and Eve, through a lifestyle of repentance, the saints of God shall also experience a spiritual *regeneration*! Hallelujah!!!

*Four Kingdoms and Then Some

There is a difference between the spiritual Kingdom of God and the spiritual Kingdom of Heaven. There also exists the natural kingdom of man and of the earth, which are both physical. And within this earth, there exists the animal kingdom, insect kingdom, aquatic kingdom, aviary kingdom as well as a microscopic kingdom, with regards to pathogens. But I want to address another kingdom which has been overlooked. It's the kingdom of *self* (Self-dom). *Self-dom* means, "the domain of self." (Webster's) Simple right? It is through *self* that each person knows of their independence and existence. As we shall learn later in Romans, *self* pertains to our conscience, which is one of the 5 furnishings of a New Testament Temple. *(1 Cor. 3:16 – 17)* But for now, suffice it to say that through *self*, each person is aware of his/her own personhood. Don't fret about this, for I shall not address the *id, ego or super ego* as some in the psychological and psychiatric professions do.

Any kingdom consists of a ruling body, a judicial body, an enforcement body, a currency, and its own unique custom. The word *kingdom* denotes a people or territory over whom or which a king reigns. The Kingdom of Heaven is the antithesis to that of Earth. That is to say, Earth's existence mirrors the existence of Heaven's Kingdom, which is Christ's domain and is within the Kingdom of God. Keeping kingdom at its simplest level, as applied to the sovereignty of Almighty God, Jesus tells us to preach the existence of God, and this includes His character, as the essence of Who He is. God's character, is contained within the pages of Scripture. God's Word, is His communication to humanity, but specifically to His Church. In this communication, we find memos, letters, commandments, spiritual laws, spiritual currency, etc. All these tell us of the existence of God's Kingdom, which is the sphere of His sovereign rule. Therefore, Jesus Christ lived on Earth as God and man, and wherever He was, the Kingdom of God was. Since this Earth and the world systems are in a fallen condition, the Kingdom of God is above, because sin cannot enter into the Kingdom of God, although within each true saint of God, His Kingdom does reside within them. **Truth #117: Through the wisdom of repentance, the saint becomes fully aware of his carnality and his mortality in the eyes of God. Accordingly, he comes to repentance making repentance a lifestyle so as to address the carnal kingdom within himself!**

Immigration is Translation

Colossians 1:13
"...we are translated into the kingdom of His dear Son."

The Kingdom of God, is the antithesis to the kingdom or domain of fallen man. That is why Jesus stated, we must be born again. *(cf. Jn. 3:3, 5, 7)* The Kingdom of God and the Kingdom of Heaven are often used interchangeably. As citizens of this spiritual Kingdom, the saints of God must be knowledgeable with the spiritual laws of the Kingdom, just as they would be to the law of the land. The United States, for example, has Immigration and Naturalization laws. These laws exist to permit and control the immigration of foreign nationals, who desire to exchange their citizenship from their homeland to that of America. However, these soon to be naturalized people must first learn or at least become aware of the language, the history, the laws of the land, as any other American must. The process of immigration is the relocation, the transplanting of and the transfer from one kingdom/nation to another! Therefore, as believers, it is essential that we know the requirements of the Kingdom of Heaven, which is within the Kingdom of God. A final note, the Kingdom of Heaven is always the Kingdom of God, but the Kingdom of God is not bound by the Kingdom of Heaven. Both Kingdoms are as they are, endless, for they abide in each other eternally. *(cf. Jn. 17:21, 15:1 – 10; 1 Jn. 5:7)*

Repentance as a Command

It seems that the pulpit ministry only invites people to repent. Jesus says we must be born again! This is an imperative expression and is therefore a command or a mandate as a term and condition of salvation. It is not an invitation, nor is it a suggestion! *The preaching of repentance is a forceful directive!* As a former Marine Corps Drill Instructor, I have an understanding of the intent of this Scripture. I only wish that I could blast away to all the nations this spiritual truth! *(cf. Jn. 3:3, 7; Acts 17:30)*

Throughout the epistles, the Apostle Paul taught repentance for the remission of sins and he preached the Kingdom of God, as well as all things pertaining to Jesus Christ. *(Acts 19:8, 28:31)* The Holy Ghost has just shown me that a watchman as a crier sounds out the alarm or commands! In *John 1:23*, John the Baptist, cried out *"REPENT!"* He did so with strong exhortations, which moved the people. Preaching the spiritual law of repentance must be with forcefulness and instruction, for it is with this urging and edification that moves people to receive the baptism of repentance and the subsequent lifestyle of righteousness. **Truth #118: Preaching repentance is a sound of alarm, and the call to repentance is a preparatory command. This then makes the call of repentance a command of execution declaring one to change. Ergo, the call to repentance is a challenge to renew the mind and then to change, while the call of is the Command of Execution!** *(Acts 17:30; Heb. 10:26 – 29)* Like the prison guard who is armed to the teeth and stands watch from the watch tower over the prison population, ensuring that all do in fact, live a life of penitence in compliance to House Rules, we too, must stand guard from the perimeter walls of our heart, ensuring that our carnality is forcefully suppressed, subdued and that the spirit of our mind, through the executive faculty of the will/choice, remains in control!

To qualify for the benefits of repentance, we must first come to repentance. The benefits are all found in and throughout the Word of God as this investigation Freedom Books attests; but before any saint can receive them, he must first acquire the instruction of righteousness, for it is the knowledge of salvation. Repentance then, must be preached to both sinner and saint alike. But the saint must also be taught (edified) the principle applications of developing a lifestyle of repentance. Like the renewal process of the mind, repentance is a daily activity which the saint must employ, if he is to suppress his carnality and keep it in remission.

The Call of Repentance

Philippians 3:11 – 17 AMP

*"That if possible I may attain to the [spiritual and moral] resurrection [that lifts me] out from among the dead [even while in the body]. Not that I have now attained [this ideal], or have already been made perfect, but I press on to lay hold of (grasp) and make my own, that for which Christ Jesus (the Messiah) has laid hold of me and made me His own. I do not consider, brethren, that I have captured and made it my own [yet]; but one thing I do [it is my one aspiration]; forgetting what lies behind and straining forward to what lies ahead, I press on toward the goal to win the [supreme and heavenly] prize to which God in Christ Jesus is calling us upward. So let those [of us] who are **spiritually mature and full grown** have this mind and hold these convictions; and if in any respect you have a different attitude of mind, God will make that clear to you also. Only let us hold true to what we have already attained and walk and order our lives by that. Brethren,*

together follow my example and observe those who live after the pattern we have set before you." (emphasis mine)

Truth #119: The call of repentance is the way of righteousness. It is that lifestyle to live, which emanates from the call to come to repentance. The call of repentance is a product of salvation, because it is a lifestyle which leads towards holiness! The call of repentance is a relief from the pain of sin and death, because repentance is a gift of God. Therefore, it belongs to and should be possessed by the saint of God. *(cf. Isa. 6:9 – 10)* The call of repentance is a specific designation and a command of God to all carnal men, everywhere! This call also means that each saint must shoulder the mantle of repentance, which is God's instruction of righteousness. **Truth #120: The call of repentance distinguishes one from all others, because a lifestyle of repentance qualifies the saint as a true citizen of Heaven, while on Earth! Therefore, this makes the call of repentance that higher call unto holiness, for it is the activity of personal sanctification unto Almighty God!**

Profane Views Against Nature and Nature's God
Isaiah 3:4
"And I will give children to be their princes, and babes shall rule over them."

Scripture indicates that when impenitent men choose to live in their carnality, by default, they permit themselves to become adolescent, even effeminate, although they may be a physically mature adults. The passage above implies that childishness and boys shall rule over the nation with an outrage against justice! This is alarming since Almighty God knows the end from the beginning. He included this in Scripture, because He thought that the impenitent people of this nation and they of all the earth would like to know their final outcome! However, there are those spoiled brats and rebellious children who have become adolescent-minded adults who shall not receive correction or righteous instruction, as they are hell-bent to have their own way, just as any youthful child would, who throws a temper tantrum! The fact that there are members of the judiciary, and so many politicians who impose their own profane views against nature and nature's God, only validates what Scripture states. These judges are not interested in justice; rather, they are more concerned with sabotaging the rule of God's law and weakening the very fiber of American society and culture, upon which this nation was built, with their godless; be it devilry! Talk about being a control freak! These societal and governmental leaders have forgotten that control is just an illusion, for the true power and authority resides with God and is often demonstrated through the people.

The Elephant in the House

You don't have to go on an elephant hunt, since there is a large pachyderm in the house! As to the same sex marriages, I want to ask you, is there an elephant in your house? Consider that this nation of ours is a very large house and all its citizens are the occupants of it. Now, since we all reside under the roof of this house, it is essential that the head of the house maintain order and discipline for the greater good of all. If he becomes negligent with his leadership or parental duties, then he has opened the door for all manner of rebellion to enter in. If this is done, then the question must be asked, just what kind of a gateway has been established and what sort of gatekeeper is he? You see, the head of any household is the gatekeeper to that which he or she permits to enter into his or her home, and he or she will determine the type of domicile in which he or she lives. As Scripture states, *"they of your on household will become your greatest foe." (cf. Mt. 10:36)* But it also states...

Proverbs 24:3
"Through skillful and godly Wisdom is a house (a life, a home, a family, a nation) built and by understanding it is established [on a sound and good foundation], And by knowledge shall the chambers be filled with all precious and pleasant riches." (cf. Mic. 7:6; Mt. 10:34 – 36)

False Peace is not Genuine Peace

So many times people will avoid confrontation by turning their backs on the elephant of carnality that has entered their home; and they do so to maintain a false peace! False peace is not genuine peace! Genuine peace is obtained through the work of righteousness, even if it means that a leader must impose righteous judgment against any wrongful deed or evil speech. Moreover, real peace is first, godly and is a work of righteousness. What's more, the effect of righteousness shall be quiet resting places and peaceful habitations! *(cf. Isa. 32:17 – 18)* Again, Scripture asks, *"How can a man rule the house of God, if he is unable to rule his own house well?" (cf. 1 Tim. 3:1 – 7)*

Same Sex Marriage and Nepotism

When other persons are respected, the partiality shown towards them shall be a witness against them for their nepotism! By this I mean, that should same sex marriages be legalized, the desired relationships between two so authorized, shall become a condition of nepotism, which means, *"the favoritism shown or extended to those relatives for positions of notoriety."* (Webster's) Now with regards to the gay agenda, it seems to me that there are certain institutions which do in fact show a respect towards those of an alternative lifestyle and who possess an ulterior motive, and they hide it not! Such as with the passing of the Gay marriage on June 25th, 2015, when upon this occasion, President Obama illuminated the White House with the Gay Pride

Colors! These same sex marriages are public attestations of their abnormal and deviant behavior *(UCD)*, and like Sodom, unless the leadership of this nation takes certain and specific measures to correct and stop this nonsense, America will force the hand of Almighty God's indignation against this nation for it! Personally, I for one do not want to become a recipient of God's wrath! Whereas, the homosexual movement declares its pretended rights for cultural recognition, their determinations will rebound against them for what it is, as an evil which they shall bring upon themselves for the reward of their abhorrent behavior! *Let it be known, Almighty God will not hold the impenitent guiltless, who have forced the hand of His indignation! (cf. Isa. 66:14 – 18)*

We Have Ruined Our Country!

Again, the Scripture states that such heightened carnality shall ruin the country, because the people who should oppose this insult and offense do nothing to prevent its cascading effect upon society. *(cf. Isa. 3:12 – 26)* And this cascading effect is occurring now, from one city in one county, in one state to another city and county in other states! Mayors and judges are skipping and prancing about like effeminate pasties and adolescent children, who stand to defy established law! *(cf. Isa. 3:11 – 26)* Should their crimes be allowed to continue, then the impression higher government leaves to all Americans, and they of the world would be: there is no longer a higher standard of righteousness and justice which leaders are obliged to abide by and enforce! *(cf. Eccl. 8:11)* And as Scripture reveals, the land itself will be defiled by the wicked due to their abominations! What's more, Almighty God will see to it that those in leadership positions now, who have abrogated their public service duties shall be expelled from their lofty positions, for they are not worthy of such offices! And this even applies to those of spiritual leadership as well! *(cf. Isa. 5:13 – 14; Jer. 16:5 – 7, 9 – 13)* Whereas, it has been said, *that we Americans don't live this way, nor do we do these things,* (relating to the recent acts of immorality in the Abu Ghraib Prison in Iraq) it is evident that some Americans actually do live this way and they really do condone these things, even in this house we call America! **Truth #121: Morality is never determined by ethnicity or locality. It is only determined by righteousness, as that by which man's universal carnality is suppressed! This then identifies righteousness as a virtue and that of repentance!**

Repentance, as the Doctrine of God Should Be Preached to All Nations

Luke 24:25-47 AMP

"And [Jesus] said to them, O foolish ones [sluggish in mind, dull of perception] and slow of heart to believe (adhere to and trust and rely on) **everything that the prophets have spoken!**.. *And that* **repentance** *[with a view to and as the condition of] forgiveness of sins* **should be preached in His name to all nations,** *beginning from Jerusalem."* (emphasis mine)

Now, our resurrected Lord caught up with His disciples as they journeyed on the road to Emmaus, and asked them a question regarding the topic of their conversation. Initially, these men did not recognize Jesus, as their heads and eyes were bowed low. However, as Jesus continued to speak, they did lift their eyes and they did recognize Him in His resurrected state. Of interest is the comment Jesus made to them pertaining to all the things the prophets had said. As such, Jesus Christ was the living evidence of their prophecies and He further reiterated their message of repentance by stating, that repentance must be preached in His Name to all nations! What comes to mind here, is that repentance must be preached in His Name. Why is this? **Truth #122: It is evident to me that since Jesus Christ did shed His precious blood for the remission of sins, His death validates this mandate that repentance be preached for the remission of sins as well, since nobody else fits this statement!** Repentance, as the doctrine of God is an essential condition for the forgiveness of sins, for without it, the reconciliation and the salvation of a soul is none existent! Furthermore, without this essential condition, a man's faith remains a fancy invention of his own carnal mindedness, because impenitence negates faith!

Notes:

Notes:

Chapter 4
Repentance in the Book of John

John 3:5 AMP
"Jesus answered, I assure you, most solemnly I tell you, unless a man is born of water and the Spirit, he cannot [ever] enter the kingdom of God."

It's Just a Matter of Interpretation

Regarding the water, the common interpretation has long been that this water represents only childbirth, naturally. But upon my further reading of this passage, in verses 3, 4 and 7 where Nicodemus asks, *how can a man go back into his mother's womb and be born again?* I recognized a traditional religious misunderstanding! As I read this, the Holy Spirit brought to my attention that this very question negates the natural birthing process! In it's place He meant that Nicodemus must be born from above! My awareness of this metaphor prompted me to ask several ministers of their opinion of these cited verses, specifically verse 5. *My question simply was which water was Jesus speaking of to Nicodemus? Was it the natural birth water or was it the water unto repentance which John the Baptist preached in Matthew 3:11?* These minister's were Evangelist J.D., Doctor D.L., Prophets D.S. and R. T., and Missionary Evangelist A.J.

Matthew 3:11 AMP
"As for me, I baptize with water because of [your] repentance [that is, because you are willing to change your inner self—your old

way of thinking, regret your sin and live a changed life], but He (the Messiah) who is coming after me is mightier [more powerful, more noble] than I, whose sandals I am not worthy to remove [even as His slave]; He will baptize you [who truly repent] with the Holy Spirit and [you who remain unrepentance] with fire and (judgment)."

To the man, each minister deferred to me saying in essence, *Man, you have something here Brother Ed. I would be interested in knowing what the Spirit of God has taught you!* Another said, *Brother Ed, I am so proud of you! Look how far you have come! This is my first conversation with anyone today, and to have it with you this early in the morning and about such a topic as this, WOW! You really have something here, brother!* And another said, *I never gave this much thought, but it seems to make sense.* Finally, only one understood! *He agreed with me that the water of repentance was inferred by John the Baptist.*

My observation is this: Because the Church and her preachers have neglected to speak of repentance, they would never understand this water which John the Baptist did speak of, was validated by Jesus Christ as He spoke with Nicodemus. My only conclusion must be, that there are only 2 levels of interpretation available. These levels, in my mind, are as the depths of water any person may choose to enter. The ankle deep water represents the natural birth process only, and the deepest water represents that interpretation which is over the head where anyone may choose to swim and see the wonderful works of God! *(Psa. 104:24 – 26, 107:23 – 24)* Therefore, I do believe that Jesus Christ and John the Baptist spoke of this deeper interpretation.

The Spirit of the Law

Romans 7:6 AMP

"But now we are discharged from the Law and have terminated all intercourse with it, having died once restrained and held

us captive. So now we serve not under [obedience to] the old code of written regulations, but [under obedience to the promptings] of the Spirit in newness [of life]."

Now, the discourse between Jesus and Nicodemus, which chapter 3 records is most intriguing. Specifically, in verse 10, wherein Jesus seemingly reprimanded Nicodemus. He said, *"Are you not a master of Israel, and yet you know not these things?"* What Jesus meant was that since leadership remains ignorant of the deeper things of spiritual import, how then shall the masses learn them? It seems then, that Jesus also implied Nicodemus was no different than other spiritual leaders, who remain ignorant of the deeper wisdom and revelation pertaining to the spiritual things of God! In this sense, Jesus encouraged Nicodemus to become a *Statesman of Theology,* rather than settle on remaining just another *Politician of Religion.*

As previously addressed, the water which Jesus spoke of, was the water unto repentance which John the Baptist did preach. Moreover, the Holy Spirit is named here as well, and not as an afterthought either. So I would like to introduce the [Holy] Spirit with a perspective of the Spirit of the Law, for Jesus even stated that His Words are Spirit and they are Life. *(cf. Jn. 6:63)*

In a court of law, *the judgment rendered for, would also include the intent of the spirit of the law towards.* This *spirit of the law* implies the moral obligation of the one party to do the right thing on behalf of the other party so offended/violated. Although the spirit of the law would not be so stated in the judgment, it is however implied just as the judgment *against* is not stated and is also implied. Without the spirit of the law, the legality of such law would pertain to only the restitution at face value. In other words, the only way restitution could be executed would be through the forced accountability; as deemed by a court order. Otherwise, such restitution would probably never occur. Herein is the intent of Scripture, which states that any offense against another should be compensated by as many as four or seven times the initial cost or value of the thing lost or the person offended. *(cf. 2 Sam. 12:6; Prov. 6:31; Lk. 19:8)* This compensation is as interest paid for a crime committed. So as you can see, crime really does not pay.

The spirit of the law denotes the willingness to comply with the full intent of the law. It is the due consideration that the violator has for the other so offended or victimized. This is because the spirit of the law denotes a genuine contrition, for having committed an offense. For example, a motorist would not normally violate the rules of the road intentionally, for he knows that to do so, could possibly endanger himself and other motorists. So, he willingly complies to the vehicle code, as he knows his compliance is *his obligation as the thing he ought to do*, in the best interest of the public good. His willingness to comply with the law, would be his best efforts, and therefore his due diligence to observe the spirit of the law of the road. This spirit of conformity, proposes the morality that one person should have as his due regard for others and their property. Hence, this motorist should expect and anticipate the same regard from others. This then is the golden rule of the road, and is the fulfillment of the spirit of the law, as it pertains to safe driving. **Truth #123: So, what the spirit of the law is towards one's obligation and compliance, the application of the law so offended is towards the execution of the law so violated! As pertaining to repentance, the saint's obedience becomes his righteousness, because his compliance evinces the spirit of the law so obeyed; while the impenitent remain disobedient to God's law, and are deserving of its execution for their carnality!** *(cf. Mt. 22:35 – 40; Rom. 6:16)*

Concerning repentance, without the Holy Spirit's intervention and a person's choice to do so, a lifestyle of repentance would become a practice of religion, which is counter productive to the intents of Almighty God. The Holy Spirit's involvement ensures that when a saint comes to repentance, that saint would become a worker of righteousness, because his compliance to the spirit of the law, would be the means of his transformation unto holiness and his admittance into the Kingdom of God, for without the agency of the Holy Spirit, the saint could not become a righteous citizen of Heaven. Rather, he would become an associated renegade in the society of self-righteous men! **Truth #124: Coming to repentance, necessitates that the saint fulfill his spiritual obligation to willingly comply to the Word of God, and not just observe the moral oughtness towards Almighty God or his fellow man!** So when Jesus Christ said, *"...unless a man is born of water and of the Spirit he cannot enter the kingdom of God,"* I believe this was His meaning, explicitly that without the leading and the agency of the Holy Spirit, it would be impossible for anyone to come to repentance, for carnality is always man's determination, as a choice and function of his will, in the mishandling of this gift of God.

The Technique of a Thorough Witness
John 4:7-26 – 30
"There cometh a woman of Samaria to draw water: Jesus saith unto her, Give me to drink....Jesus saith unto her, I that speak unto thee is he." (cf. Isa. 12:1 – 3)

These verses, speak of an engaging conversation between Jesus Christ and the woman of Samaria. To be called a Samaritan, meant that this woman was considered a *dog* by the Hebrews. Historically, Samaritans were the result of two racial descents; one of Hebrew and the other of Gentile. This bloodline of descent, was a moral breakdown, even a downfall to the Jews, because of what occurred further back in the history of this region of which the Old Testament speaks. She was of commingled blood, and therefore of a mixed race, because a Hebrew man married a Gentile woman against the commands of God! *(cf. Gen. 16:1 – 16; Ezra 10:1 – 3)* The fact that an interracial child would have no say with his/her conception and birth, insinuates that all children who are born physically into this world, is for them a right of passage into this world, nonetheless

This Samaritan woman had asked Jesus three different questions pertaining to Himself, to herself, and to her religious manner of worship. I am reminded of the skill which a salesman must possess in overcoming customer obstacles before he can close the sale. These obstacles, are a right of passage from the first question to the final conclusion. Well, in these verses: Jesus, although He is not a salesman in the traditional sense, did present a provision of salvation, which He knew this woman had need of. So as a right of passage towards closing this engaging conversation with a favorable, final outcome, Jesus patiently answered each of her three piercing questions, and in doing so, assured Himself of the final outcome, namely the conversion of this woman's heart. The result of which, was that many who heard of her testimony within the entire city where she lived, were also evangelized through this one certain woman!

Upon careful scrutiny, we find that Jesus presented His case to her, utilizing the three basic realms of truth, which must be proven before hand. They are proofs that are *true to Scripture* in that He spoke of Himself, proofs *true to Life,* in that He was thirsty and she was tired of carrying water pots, and proofs that were *true to Reason,* in that all who drink of that water would thirst again. The final outcome, was the woman asked Jesus to give her this living water! He did and the final outcome was she did receive. Consequently, all the citizens of this woman's home town heard of her testimony of conversion! Here in this account, Jesus demonstrated *the technique of a thorough witness.* The lesson being that the saints of God should learn this same technique, *which provides proof of specific truths that are pertinent to Scripture, to life and to reason.* By employing this method, Jesus pressed the issue of her carnality and forced her to acknowledge her position of hopelessness. Otherwise, her mind would not have been satisfied, since Jesus would have failed to dispel her doubts and eliminate her suspicion which were, for her—iniquitous thoughts. **Truth #125: A thorough witness, must dispel doubt and eliminate suspicion, if repentance, as the final outcome, is to be consciously realized!**

Pacifying Responses

But what does this have to do with a lifestyle of repentance? As an answer, the saint should know that before a lifestyle of repentance may be embarked upon, certain eternal questions about Almighty God, religious tradition, the saint himself, and the prospective convert, must be answered first with contextual truth and not some glib remark, as a pacifying response. For instance, I mentioned earlier that as a response to the question pertaining to *John 3:5 "Unless a man is born of water and the Spirit..."* the pacifying answer I have received from the pulpit, as well as the Bible School I attended, was the association made with the birthing of a child. Although this answer did not satisfy my mind as to its accuracy, I accepted it for the time being or until the Holy Ghost revealed to my mind the true meaning of it. And of course, that revelation did come to me during the writing of this investigation. Had I not embarked on this assignment, then with all things being no different and the same, I would have never acquired the knowledge of this spiritual truth!

There is an explanation for this. Consider for yourself the questions which you currently have, that have never been answered to your satisfaction and the questions that you once had. What's the difference? The difference is, that your mind innately desires to know truth, and there are some truths that need to be proven or demonstrated, before your mind will find rest! As for myself, and this particular question pertaining to being born of water, my mind did not find rest until this question was satisfactorily answered! **Truth #126: When the mind is satisfied, it immediately responds accordingly, because certain truths have been presented in such a manner, so as to answer specific questions, thereby eliminating doubts and suspicions!**

Paradox versus Paradigm

Paradoxically, contained within Scripture, you will find statements that seem contradictory to you. Immediately, your mind is perplexed, because, your mind demands answers! So to assist yourself in your understanding, simply apply the same technique of demonstration or proof to *Scripture*, to *life* and to *reason*, so that you may acquire the spiritual meaning. But most people are unfamiliar with this technique, so they simply give up! It is for this reason, why so much of the Bible is taken out of context, and why so many simply don't understand Scripture. Now the word *context* means: "To weave together, to join together, 1) the parts of a sentence, paragraph or discourse immediately following or preceding of certain words or theme and determining its exact meaning 2) the *whole* situation, background, or environment relevant to a particular event, personality or creation, etc." (Webster's) As a case in point, previously, I did address the penitent thief employing the three truths (Scripture, Life, Reason), and the result of which exposed so much more about the man than was previously considered or known: Right?

Most people fail to contemplate the *overall* intent of Scripture or they fail to compare Scripture with Scripture. This denotes that their powers of thought and their study and research skills are deficient. They fail to realize the Word of God was written in such a style so condensed, as to require much intense study. Through the Scriptures, a man may develop his powers of thought and his ability of critical thinking.

Now, critical thinking, is nothing more than thinking about how you think. Since Almighty God created mankind to think, He communicates to us as one intelligent being to another. Just by stating this, challenges the notion that the Spirit of God speaks directly and only to the *spirit* of a man. But which spirit does Scripture mean? My answer to this notion, is in the form of a question. Why then does Scripture tell us to be renewed in the spirit of our *mind*, which is an ingredient of the soul? *(cf. Eph. 4:23)* Why then does Scripture tell us to acquire the knowledge of God and to increase in it? *(cf. Hos. 4:6; Phil. 2:5; Col. 3:16; 2 Pet. 1:8 – 9)* Upon conversion, the spirit of a man is born again. However, the Word of God was written to address the iniquity component (carnality) within the soul. Therefore, the spirit of a man's mind as well as his soul, must be the intended targets of Scripture and not the reborn spirit of a man.

James 1:21 AMP
"So get rid of all uncleanness and the rampant outgrowth of wickedness (carnality), and in a humble,(gentle, modest) spirit receive and welcome the Word which implanted and rooted [in your hearts] **contains the power to save your souls.***"* (emphasis mine)

But what is a paradox? By definition, a *paradox* is "1) a statement that is contrary to common belief or discipline. 2) a statement that seems contradictory, unbelievable, or absurd, but that may be true in fact. For example: *"Water, water everywhere, and yet not a single drop to drink."* (Webster's) There are numerous scriptural examples such as that which is found in *John 2:18 – 21* in which Jesus spoke of the destruction of the temple and in three days He would raise it back up. *(cf. Mt. 26:61; Mk. 14:58)* The paradox was that Jesus spoke of His own body, but the Jews predictably thought that Jesus spoke of Solomon's Temple, which took some forty years to construct. In effect, the Jews were still living in their past. They failed to realize that that time had already come and gone! But Jesus was a man of the past, present and future, for He inhabits eternity!

Another example of a paradoxical statement which Jesus spoke, is found in *John 6:48 – 60* wherein Jesus spoke of Himself as the Bread of Life and unless the Jews ate His flesh and drank His blood, they would have no life in them. (See Chapter 26 for further insights into this paradoxical truth.) So for the Jew, Jesus' statements were to the people paradoxical statements, which they refuted and yet to Jesus, the Jews were as a paradigm (predictable), in that as a community of people, they had an overall concept of the temple alone, which took forty years to build, as well as the bread, which was something baked in the oven as a diet staple. The idea of eating His flesh and drinking His blood meant cannibalism, and this view was commonly accepted by most people in an intellectual society. All the parables which Jesus did teach, were paradoxical metaphore statements which contained spiritual truths, and yet in truth, even the disciples had difficulty understanding them. *(cf. Mt. 13:10 – 13)*

The Capacity and Utility of the Mind

But for us today, who are so far removed from antiquity, the ancient writings of scriptural text, seemingly create a contradiction to our way of thinking and living. This is so, because the capacity of a person's mind to receive insight is determined by the degree of understanding and functioning ability of their mind. For example, the powerful Pentium computers of today, far surpass the antiquated computer chips of just a decade ago. A 133 mhz. computer, for example, is slower than a 286 mhz. computer. And a 500 mhz. computer, although faster and possessing greater utility than a 133 mhz. machine, is much slower than the 3000 ghz. wonders of today! Our minds are no different. **Truth**

#127: So, the greater the mental capacity, the greater the inspirational utility. And the more a mind is renewed in all four of its faculties (will, intelligence, reasoning, conscience), the greater the utility of scriptural insight and revelation knowledge. This is because "true Christianity is consistent with progressive knowledge and holiness, and such other changes in thinking and in living as are demanded by increasing enlightenment!" (Charles G. Finney) As the late writer and physician, Oliver Wendell Holmes once stated, *"The mind once extended by a new idea can never return to its original dimensions."*

As to this Samaritan woman at the well, Scripture does not say anything more about this woman. Consequently, we don't know anything about her personal qualities, outside of her several husbands, neither do we know anything about her constitutional abilities pertaining to her insightfulness, her mental acuity or her cognitive utility. So, giving her the benefit of the doubt, it could be that this woman had more going for her than we realize. I personally don't believe that she was unable to manage her affairs. Pardon the pun. Upon conversion, this woman became an evangelist to her entire city! She caught the revelation of who Jesus was, and of her manner of traditional worship, acquired freedom from the bondage within her soul, all because of the technique of a thorough witness. Hallelujah!

Truth #128: Through a lifestyle of repentance, the Holy Ghost demonstrates or otherwise proves to the saint, certain truths pertaining to Scripture, which challenge religious tradition, to his life (character) and to his reason (carnal mindedness), thereby dispelling all suspicion, so that the saint may obtain rest for his heart and peace to his mind!

Give Me This Water!

In verse 15, this woman said to Jesus, *"Sir, give me this water, that I thirst not, neither come thither to draw."* Unlike those who heard John the Baptist preach repentance, this woman heard about the knowledge of salvation from Jesus Christ, of whom John spoke! For this woman, Jesus was the man with the water, for He was then as He is today—the Living Water! He was as the Man with the pitcher of water. *(Luke 22:10 – 16)* **Truth #129: A lifestyle of repentance, represents for the saint the abundant supply of water, for the Holy Ghost *is*, the person who carries the pitcher, and since He dwells within the saint, this makes the saint, the man with the pitcher of water also!** This woman had to carry heavy earthen jars, to and from the well for her daily need. Similarly, the saint of God must also carry his daily portion of Living Water. **Truth #130: Through a lifestyle of repentance, the saint may draw freely from the well of salvation, for he too has found the Man with the pitcher!** Where religion is a carnal work ethic, a lifestyle of repentance, is a spiritual discipline towards godliness.

Is There a Doctrine in the House?

John 7:15 – 18

"And the Jews marveled, saying, How knoweth this man letters, having never learned? Jesus answered them and said, ***My doctrine is not mine, but his that sent me.*** *If any man* ***will do his will, he shall know of the doctrine****, whether it be of God or whether I speak of myself. He that speaketh of himself, seeketh his own glory, but he that seeketh his glory that sent him, the same is true, and no unrighteousness is in him."* (emphasis mine) *(cf. Acts 4:13)*

Whereas, *1 Corinthians 2:7* indicates that the wisdom of God is for our glory, Jesus implies here in *John 7*, that the doctrine of God, is for His Glory. Where the former pertains towards a lifestyle of repentance, the later pertains to obedience to God's Word, in and through this lifestyle, via the spiritual discipline of repentance so acquired! **Truth #131: In other words, just as**

Jesus was obedient to His Father in all things, His obedience was publicly observed and known. His submission to this doctrine, manifested the wisdom of God in and throughout His physical life, thereby justifying this wisdom of repentance, for as Scripture states: This wisdom is justified by all Her children! *(cf. Lk. 1:17, 7:35)*

In verse 15, we read that these snobbish Jews, marveled at the wisdom which Jesus both spoke and portrayed. They asked, *"How can this man know such letters having never learned them?"* Academically, these letters represented the acquired wisdom of man's education from formal schooling of academia. Perhaps these Jews were speaking of the schools of Philosophy, whose societal influence was prolific. Because the Spirit of God was given to Jesus Christ without measure, He had no need for their Doctorates, for He knew all things. *(cf. 1 Jn. 2:27; Jn. 6:30)* Whereas, finite men are limited in their knowledge; similarly, their religious aspirations are also restricted. This is due to their ignorance of righteousness and their denial of carnality. **Truth #132: A thorough witness must dispel doubt and eliminate suspicion, if repentance, as the final outcome, is to be consciously realized!** I ask the question: Is there a doctrine (of repentance) in the house? This infers that presently, there is not, and this is due to the very same reason just stated. So many churches within this New Testament Church Age, are destitute of Almighty God's doctrine of repentance, and the current state or condition of these churches, validates its deficiency! *We must learn that this doctrine of repentance, is not only for our glory, but we glorify Almighty God through our compliance to it!*

The Will of God and the Doctrine of God

What is the will of God? In short, it is obedience, and obedience has many facets, which range from love to death, and everything in between! And just what is this doctrine of God? As an answer, doing God's will with a desire to satisfy the spirit of the law, shall reveal the doctrine of God, as His determination for all men! **Truth #133: In these two questions, I find that the will of God pertains to the doctrine of God, and keeping in line with the theme of this investigation, repentance is that doctrine, and therefore it is also His will, and His expressed determination, that all men everywhere must come to repentance!** *(cf. Acts 17:30)*

Earlier, we learned that the wisdom of God is found in His doctrine of repentance, for this *wisdom is justified by all her children.* Moreover, we learned that repentance, is *the wisdom of the just* or those who have been justified. *(cf. Lk. 1:17, 7:35)* This denotes that to be a true saint of God, will require a contrite, penitent heart and not just a sorrowful sensitivity, which is emotionally based alone. **Truth #134: Therefore, what the will of God is to His doctrine of repentance, the wisdom of God is to a saint's compliance in fulfilling His will, for without the wisdom of God, carnality shall not be suppressed and righteousness shall be averted!** After all, the entire Old Testament stressed obedience to God's law; similiarly, His moral law is stressed equally in the New Testament. So nothing has changed scripturally, pertaining to God's design and intent. However, the determination of carnal men has, in that they willfully choose to disobey, and their insubordination, reflects their ignorance of righteousness, and their denial of their own carnality! *(cf. 1 Sam. 15:22; Rom. 6:16)*

Scriptural Truth is Absolute Truth

Whereas, Jesus Christ is the King of kings and Lord of lords, it must be agreed that God's Word, is the greatest of all the great words ever spoken by carnal men. Scripture teaches that Almighty God, magnifies His Word even above His Name. *(Psa. 138:2)* Therefore, a reasonable verification may be *made, that the existence of divine truth is absolute, and there is no other truth besides this absolute!* Can you imagine what condition your own personal life would be in, if you conspired a new truth? And for many people, their own opinions, narrow perspectives and ignorance are to them *truths*, although greatly flawed, and their very lives attest to this deceptive reality. This is so because it is not within the ability of man to direct his own path.

Jeremiah 10:23 AMP
"O Lord [pleads Jeremiah in the name of the people], I know that [the determination of] the way of man is not in himself: it is not in man [even in a strong man or in a man at his best] to direct [his] own steps." (cf. Psa. 37:23; Prov. 20:24)

Any deviation from divine truth, in favor of a stunted or insipid denominational dogma or a philosophical constitution or opinion, shall be a distortion of God's Word and a shortcoming of perfect obedience to God's will! This biased *new truth,* then becomes a pretext, for spiritual truths have been taken out of context! As to God's will, the sum total and spirit of the whole Law of God, is properly expressed in one word—LOVE! *Therefore, it may be said, that God's will is equated to His love and our devoted love to His Word is equivalent to God's will!* As to the aspects and objects of love, love in and of itself, and by itself is not love, but is an expression of man's selfishness and carnal indulgence. This is because we fail to make a distinction between genuine love and carnal lust. So often we are confused by these two desires, since they are used interchangeably. Whereas, the letter "L" is found in both LOVE and LUST, it is not difficult to confound their respective meanings to those who don't know any better. *(cf. 1 Jn. 2:15 – 16; Mt. 24:12)*

The Four Quadrants of Love

Mark 12:30 AMP

*"And you shall love the Lord your God out of and with your whole **heart** and out of and with all your **soul** (your life) and out of and with all your **mind** (with your faculty of thought and your moral understanding) out of and with all your **strength**. This is the first and principle commandment."* (emphasis mine)

In Freedom 2, I discussed the four quadrants of self. They are the *open* self, the *hidden* self, the *blind* self and the unknown self. In this investigation, I also discuss the four faculties of the spirit of the mind. They are the faculties of *intelligence, reasoning, conscience* and *volition*. Now Scripture, introduces us to another four quadrants in which our love for God must exist. They are our *heart*, our *soul*, our *mind* and our *strength*. Here is a question: When the Scripture speaks of the spirit of a man, does it refer to the spiritual man as a twin of the physical man or does it address the spirit of his mind? My answer to this is, that the spirit of a man seems to be different from the spirit of the mind, because Scripture clearly states that upon conversion, the spirit of a man is born again, however the spirit of his mind must still be renewed, and that daily. *(cf. 2 Cor. 5:17; Rom. 12:1; Eph. 4:23)*

Unless we love God in all these areas, our love for God, should be suspect! Our ability to love others and ourselves, hinges upon the revelation of just how much Almighty God loves each of us! This rule of law, extends charity to our enemies and to our neighbor. Known as *the Golden Rule*, this rule is the rule of the Gospel. Therefore, if you suspect that your love for God is deficient in any of these four quadrants, then you have yet to be made completely perfected in God's love, whose direction is towards God, and whose effect is to yourself and others! *(cf. 1 Jn. 4:17 – 18; Jam. 2:8)* This deficiency, is so substantiated, given the plethora of domestic violence, suicides, murders, etc in society today.

A lifestyle of repentance, as the doctrine of God, which this investigation has shown time and again, is that doctrine! Whereas, obedient faith works by love, *(Gal. 5:6)* repentance is that corresponding action to this faith; and just as God's will conforms to His doctrine of repentance, His will becomes the saint's obligation. **Truth #135: True repentance, therefore, is a thorough reformation of heart and life! This reformation of heart consists in turning from self-gratification and self-indulgence, to benevolence as a lifestyle of repentance, because repentance is not just what the saint does for himself, but is his obligation towards God and what he does for others!** *(cf. Ezek. 9:4-6; Acts 20:21; 2 Tim. 2:19)*

Revelation versus Philosophical Pursuits
John 7:15-18
"And the Jews marveled, saying, How knoweth this man letters, having never learned? Jesus answered them saying, My doctrine is not mine, but his who sent me. If any man will do his will, he shall know of the doctrine, whether it be of God, or whether I speak of myself. He that speaketh of himself seeketh his own glory, but he that seeketh his glory that sent him, the same is true and no unrighteousness is in him."

A friend of mine once said to me, *"Ed, I have many acquaintances, who possess doctorates in theology, and whenever I talk with these people, our conversation hinges on what other men have said and what they have learned academically. But you Ed, whenever I speak with you, you don't tell me what any man has taught you or what you have learned academically. You tell me what Almighty God has revealed to you specifically! I learn more from you in a short visit, then I ever do with these formally educated theologians!"*

Similarly, the Apostle Paul said that the Gospel message

which he preached, came not by the instruction of man, but by the revelation given him by Jesus Christ; *(Gal. 1:12)* and here in *John 7*, Jesus intimated that the doctrine of God, is known only by revelation and not through academic or philosophical pursuits. Furthermore, Jesus said that if any man would do His Father's will, that man shall know of God's doctrine. Therefore, doing the will of God, is the same as keeping the sayings of Christ, which is to mean, obeying the commandments of God! *(cf. 2 Jn. 6; Jn. 14:24, 15:7 – 12; 1 Cor. 13:13)* Jesus said, *"Sanctify them through thy word; thy word is truth." (John 17:17)* The truth of the Gospel is the doctrine of God, for it is His instructions in righteousness. *(cf. Psa. 119:123)* **Truth #136: Therefore, this doctrine called repentance, delivers the saint from evil, and leads him towards salvation, for it cultivates his soul's regeneration. Through this knowledge of salvation, the saint of God acquires the wisdom of God, which before hand remained a mystery to him!**

Penance, Penitence and Repentance

I mentioned earlier, we must do God's will from a penitent (contrite) heart, with an understanding that we are satisfying the spirit of the law. Here, I would like to clarify what penitence is in relation to repentance. Although they are synonymous expressions, I want to point out that the root of each, is the word *PENT*, which means, *"held, confined, pent up."* From the idea of being *"pent up,"* it implies being introverted or to be caged as some animal would be. It also suggests an imprisonment as any criminal would be, and thus we are. *(Rom. 11:31 – 32)* The application is the same, but with an entirely opposite end result, and with a completely different motivation. Where an animal may be caged for sport or show, to satisfy greedy men, the prisoner is pent up as a requirement of law, hence the word, penitentiary. However, where penitence might imply bondage, repentance denotes freedom! **Truth #137: Where "Pent Up" suggests immobility, a stoppage and a cessation of forward progression in life, repentance, is the emancipation of a new lease on life and in this sense, a lifestyle of repentance is possessed! To be penitent, is first the person and what he does for himself, in saving his soul, because he has been made consciously aware of his carnality. Whereas, a lifestyle of repentance, is the activity of obligation to comply with the God's moral laws, thereby satisfying the spirit of His law!**

Now, the words, *repent, repented, repentance* are specifically used in scriptural text; whereas, *penitent, penitence, impenitent, impenitence and penance* are not found in the authorized writ. But this should not be interpreted as a violation of Scripture or as a perversion of God's truth, although denominationally it has. Let me explain: As a young boy growing up under the influence of Roman Catholicism, what I learned as repentance, was in all reality, just a form of institutionalized penance. The instructions I learned, required me to adhere to what the denominational tenets said or defined penance to be, if I was to receive absolution. Never mind what the Scriptures said about repentance as God's instructions in righteousness. In this context, penance is a counterfeit to true Godly repentance. This is because penance, in the guise of external endeavors, never equates to true godly repentance! **Truth #138: Whereas, penance is a denominational requirement for absolution, a lifestyle of repentance is God's mandate for conversion! Through repentance, a penitent saint has been liberated from bondage to his carnality, because his lifestyle of repentance has become the incarceration instruction of righteousness, which the saint complies with as a prisoner of his Lord, Jesus Christ!** Although the saint may be barred from the things of this earth, he nonetheless enjoys a freedom and a peace that this unrighteous world cannot ever know! *(cf. Jn. 14:27)*

Repentance and Judas Iscariot

John 12:4 – 6

*"Then said one of his disciples, Judas Iscariot, Simon's son, which should betray him, Why was not this ointment sold for three hundred pence, and given to the poor? This he said, not that he cared for the poor, but because **he was a thief,** and had the bag, and bare what was put therein."* (emphasis mine)

The question is: Did Judas ever come to repentance, obtaining eternal life? There are some who believe that Judas could not come to repentance since he existed solely for the purpose to betray the Son of God. Assuming that this to be correct, then my dispute to this assumption is as follows. If in fact Judas Iscariot existed solely for the purpose to betray Jesus Christ on that fateful night, then as far as God the Father is concerned, Judas rendered perfect obedience to His divine will! And if this was so, then Judas would have had no need to commit suicide, because true repentance never brings regret, right? *(cf. 2 Cor. 7:10)* His obedience to God's will, would make Judas a man of integrity in that he complied to the essential terms and conditions of God's Word of His righteousness, even for this one horrific event.

However, I believe that Judas Iscariot did not come to repentance on the premise that his godless character was the basis for his betrayal in the first place. Let me explain: The above passages tell us that Judas was first a thief, who had no genuine care or concern for the poor or for the devotion shown towards Jesus Christ. This morsel of information, provides a glimpse into his unscrupulous character, which he previously possessed prior to his betrayal. Since Scripture does not reveal anything more about Judas's past, it would be safe to consider that Judas lived a life of disobedience in the first place; and the preponderance of Scripture supports this postulation. For example: Rameses, the Pharaoh of Egypt, hardened his heart against God, and would not let

God's people go. *(Ex. 7:3 – 4)* Due to his insolence, he endured ten plagues of judgment, all because he chose [an act of his will], and refused to let them go. Then there was King Saul, who chose to disobey the prophet of God, having lied to him. *(cf. 1 Sam. 3:18)* And finally, there was Esau, whose promiscuous lifestyle, disqualified him from his birthright. *(cf. Obed. 1:6 – 7)*

In *John 11:47 – 53*, we read that the chief priests and the Pharisees convened together, to see how they might kill Jesus Christ. They felt threatened by Him, due to the following which He was acquiring. Consequently, these corrupt religious leaders conspired against Christ, to safeguard their positions, their possessions and their piety. As far as they were concerned, this man Jesus Christ was expendable and a threat, and therefore, it would be expedient that one man should die to protect their status, rather than many die, in a supposed revolt. (*Enter Judas Iscariot.*) Although the chief priests and the Pharisees conspired, they were waiting for the opportune time, by which they could effect their murderous plot. In their estimation, they needed some one, a pawn, who would willingly betray Christ, so as to deflect their true ulterior motives, aka: M.O. upon this stooge. When you think about it, anyone would do. Come to think of it, even today, there are corrupt politicians, corporate elites and bankers, who make up the Shadow Government or Deep State here in America, to overthrow President Donald J. Trump because of the wonderful work he is doing by over turning and exposing the deeply embedded corruption of the Deep State! President Trump is being used of God to provide a reprieve.

Consider the following Spirit Word regarding President Trump. Here is a fresh prophetic Word which the Holy Spirit spoke to my heart, back on November 9th, 2016. It's still very valid for today! Good Morning Folks. While I was in prayer thanking God Almighty for the Trump election victory on the morning of November 9th, the Spirit Who is Holy, sort of downloaded the following: I have granted America a season of probation!! This grace period is extended to the citizens of America for my righteousness to prevail!!! For as the fig tree that failed to produce any figs, so likewise has America failed to produce a righteous relationship with ME!!! Therefore, I the Lord God, the Commander of the Heavenly Hosts, do stipulate this additional season, this short period of reprieve as My grace period for America to come to repentance! *(Rom. 2:4)*

This grace period exists for America as another opportunity to come to repentance! It is does not exist for your parties nor for life as usual. But for a change of heart for My righteousness to prevail!!! If America fails to recognize this season for repentance, then I cannot protect you from yourselves and the consequences of judgement which she has self-sentenced herself to! *(Zephaniah 2:1-3* THEREFORE, Give to God that which is due Him *(Acts 20:21)*

No doubt that Judas Iscariot most definitely experienced shame and guilt for his betrayal of Jesus Christ. In his attempt to escape the torment and the pursuit of the dogs of Hell, which hounded his twisted conscience, he was driven to suicide, just so he could obtain peace of mind. All this to say that it comes down to choice, as that act of a man's will. Although Judas experienced a condemning shame, his guilt was misappropriated in the sense that Judas found no place of repentance, because he did not adhere to the law of the house of God, which is shame for his sin. *(cf. Ezek. 43:1 – 12)* Had Judas adopted a lifestyle of repentance beforehand, he would not have betrayed the Son of God; but since he preferred to live a life as a thief, his unsuppressed carnality, prevented him from being righteous in the first place. (See Freedom 3, chapter 31, **Just Who was Esau, Anyway?**) For anyone to disagree is perfectly fine. However, should you do so, then I must ask you to qualify your assertions to the contrary. I mean: What is your argument? If all you do is state your disagreement, and then provide no rebuttal, then it is apparent to me, that you really don't know what you are talking about! I'm sure you would agree.

Blinded Eyes, Calloused, Degenerate Hearts and Dementia

John 12:40 AMP
*"He has blinded their eyes and hardened and benumbed their [callous, degenerated] hearts [He has made their minds dull], to keep them from seeing with their eyes and understanding with their **hearts** and **minds** and repenting and turning to Me to heal them."* (emphasis mine)

My research has shown there are twelve cranial nerves which arise from beneath the brain. Three of the nerves are sensory in that they transmit information from the organ, directly to the brain. The others pertain to the olfactory nerve (nose); the optic nerve (sight); and the auditory nerve (hearing and balance). Any severe wound to the head, could damage any of these nerves, causing blindness, a loss of hearing or equilibrium and even the loss of smell. In this text verse, I find three areas of spiritual affliction. They are: *vision,* a degenerated *heart,* and spiritual *dementia.* As a parallel to the physical, let's examine in brief, each of these physical afflictions.

Vision: Should the optic nerve be injured, eyesight could be impaired, or be eliminated either momentarily or permanently; and as any person who has suffered such an injury could tell, this disability effectively interferes with a normal standard of living. Where once a person could see, now there are only blurs, shadows or darkness. As with the other two, the mental and emotional readjustments that must be mastered after the fact, presents new challenges in an alternate lifestyle initiated by that disability.

Heart: The heart of the matter of life, is the person's own heart, for without this blood pump, blood flow would not exist. If blood were not circulated within and throughout the cardiovascular system, then it would coagulate, developing clots. Stagnation would set in due to inactivity and a condition of stasis would exist. Not to mention the other heart diseases, which attack this blood pump/organ. *Scripture states that in the latter days men's hearts will fail them for the dreadful things that shall arise and come upon us. (cf. Lk. 21:26)* Since humanity is the highest of all of God's creations, and since the devil attempted to attack Almighty God and failed, we should know that Satan's contingency plan, is to attack the heart of mankind in his second attempt to usurp Almighty God.

In the text verse above, we read of a calloused and degenerate heart. Congestive heart failures, degenerative valves, hardened, clogged arteries and blood diseases all within the cardiovascular system are evident. However, what is not commonly known, is that there are remedies and cures for these physical diseases through proper nutrition and abstinence, as any nutritionalist would tell. However, another inference is intended, and that being the heart as the conscience. Scripture states that men's hearts shall fail them. This implies the conscience of a man has been defiled or seared, rendering him unconscious towards the things of God. But more on this later.

Mind: The third physical condition I see in the text verse, relates to the spirit of the mind. First off, the mind is not the brain! Where the brain is a physical organ of the body, the mind consists of four intangible faculties. Consider a computer once again. The computer could be compared to the brain, in that it is a tangible thing which can be handled and seen. Its capacity to produce imagery, is called cyberspace, and in this sense, is a form of (two or three-dimensional) virtual reality. Similarly, the brain is a tangible organ, which may be handled and preserved. It's capacity to produce imagery [psyche]; is self-evident, because everyone thinks in pictures within the theater of their mind. Just as there are three basic regions of the brain,(the forebrain, the midbrain, the hindbrain) and each region is further anatomically divided and identified as the two cerebral hemispheres, the *thalami,* and the *hypothalamus* and l*imbic* systems, likewise there are faculties of the mind. (Time's Atlas of the Body, pages 70, 71)

As shown previously, there are four faculties of the mind. They are: volition, intelligence, reasoning and conscience. Together, they are the four quadrants of the spirit of the mind intended for renewal in which the love of God should abide. As to the myriad of psychosomatic disorders and dysfunctions of the mind, medical science has identified dementia and its various derivatives such as insanity, Alzheimer, and senility. Each condition, greatly diminishes the persons cognitive abilities so much, that often the afflicted person is committed to a facility, where they perchance could spend the rest of their lives in this indignant state. So, having briefly examined each of these three degenerative physical conditions, let's apply these insights towards John 12:40 and see if there is any relationship, spiritually.

Vision: Aside from the obvious, the word *blinded* means, "to inflate with self-conceit, high-minded, to be lifted up with pride." (Strong's Greek ref. #5187, page 73) The Jews possessed no perspective of righteousness! Their eyes were shrouded in the smoke of their own carnality and self-indulgences, and as a man would grope along the wall in the darkness, unsure of his footing and his whereabouts, likewise, this condition of carnality, will cause impenitent men to fumble and stumble as if they had no eyes. **Truth #139: Through impenitence, there are many who have there eyesight set on their self-indulgence, yet they have no vision of righteousness as they are in denial of their carnality; but through a lifestyle of repentance, the smoke dissipates and the saint no longer fumbles about in the**

stench of his own self-righteousness, because he has an eye for *justice, truth, salvation and peace!* (cf. Job 12:25; Isa. 59:8 – 10)

Heart: The heart refers to the soul of man. More specifically, the heart applies to a consciousness of awareness, whether of guilt or of innocence. It is through the heart of a man that he possesses self- awareness. Expressions like, *"I love you with all my heart."* pertains to all that is within you or I. This denotes a complete and undaunted resolution for another. Just as love cannot be seen, for it is intangible, likewise, a heart cannot be observed, for it too is invisible. However, its nomenclature may be learned by its many and diversified descriptions and applications. So, in light of the text verse, heart pertains to the faculty of conscience.

Now, everybody has within him or her a God-conscience. This is evident, in that all men believe in something beyond themselves. As we will learn in chapter 6 (Repentance in the Book of Romans) a man's conscience is the credential of God, which He has placed within the mind of men, and it is through His credential, that all men must acknowledge for themselves, the reality and existence of Almighty God! When impenitent men fail to do so, then they shall experience heart failure. It is no different than any physical ailment of one's blood pump. If the condition is not acknowledged before hand, then heart failure will occur suddenly and unawares. **Truth #140: A lifestyle of repentance, is the identification of a heart condition ahead of time, because the saint has acknowledged his own carnality, and has become consciously aware of its detrimental effects!**

Psalm 77:6 AMP
"I call to remembrance my song in the night; with my heart I meditate and my spirit searches diligently:" (cf. 1 Cor. 2:7 – 9)

Mind: A dull mind is an inactive mind, and an inactive mind is a lethargic mind. The mind was so designed by God that it should respond to enlightenment, but due to indifference towards the things of God, people remain unconcerned and listless. The madness of unrestrained carnal propensities, hovers above all impenitent men, because they sit in darkness! Did you know that darkness possesses its own radiance? This is because black and white commingled, results in all things gray. Gray pertains to obscurity, dullness, cloudiness, fog and lead. Consequently, Scripture urges men to get the lead (carnality) out!

The absolutes of right and wrong, have become personal rights of self-indulgence, and therefore all things gray! These oppose that which *ought* to be done or that which should never be condoned. Light has become darkness and darkness light! Social conscience has given place to sub-cultural promiscuities! The imaginations of men's hearts have become all the more perverted. All arguments, theories and reasoning(s) have been set up against scriptural truth, and are contrary to the true knowledge of God! **Truth #141: Since the carnal mind is hostile towards the things of God, then neither can it know them, it is reasonable to say, that a carnal, unrenewed mind, is already in a state of dementia, and as institutions exist to house and care for those demented, likewise, Almighty God has reserved a place for those impenitent. It's called Hell!**

Other Synonymous Expressions of Conscientious Repentance

1. *Contrition:* Implies a deep, crushing, sorrow for sin [carnality, moral depravity] with a true purpose of heart for conversion. *(cf. Psa. 34:18, 51:17; Isa. 57:15, 66:2)*

2. *Compunction:* A prickling of the conscience and therefore, suggests a sharp, but passing sense of guilt. *(cf. Jn. 8:9; 1 Cor. 8:7; 1 Tim. 4:2; Tit. 1:15; Heb. 10:22)*

3. *Remorse:* A deep and torturing sense of guilt. *(cf. Rom. 3:19; 1 Cor.11:27; Gen. 42:21)*

4. *Regret*: May refer to sorrow over any unfortunate occurrence as well as over a fault or act of one's own. *(cf. Psa.13:2; Deut. 28:65; Prov. 15:13; Eccl. 5:17; Rom. 9:2)*

5. *Abhorrence*: To shudder intensely, to hate hence, to abhor. To turn oneself away from (as if from a stench) hence to detest. *(cf. Job 42:6; Rom. 12:9; Prov. 22:14)*

Notes:

List of Axioms
Truths of Repentance
Freedom IV

▶ **Truth #1:** To wit, what residual income is to a product continually sold, resident iniquity (Lie Based Thinking) is to Satan's reproduced deception in the history of the soul of humanity!

▶ **Truth #2:** The New Testament Church does not know her heritage pertaining to either, neither does she genuinely recognize her own long standing disobedience in her own carnality against the Word of God!

▶ **Truth #3:** Repentance as the Wisdom of the Just is the doctrine of God, which the saints of God should comprehensively know if they are to overcome carnal tendencies within their lives, for without this knowledge, righteousness remains unknown and the resultant holiness shall not be obtained!

▶ **Truth #4:** Repentance pertains to man's soul wherein his carnality resides, and righteousness is the expression of his true penitence. Without a working knowledge of his iniquity and carnality, man's disobediencce will never be suppressed and neither shall a soul be reconciled back to God!

▶ **Truth #5:** What metaphysical is to the supernatural, repentance is to the meta, as that which facilitates metamorphous!

Truth #6: Renew then, is to restore as repent is to change or turn! When a saint acquires repentance as that Wisdom of God, his soul is regenerated, because he has purposed in his heart to renew his mind so as to save his soul by and through a lifestyle of repentance!

Truth #7: Through a lifestyle of repentance, the saints of God shall learn God's will for their lives, because repentance must be based on the specific knowledge of carnality and not upon some slick trick of merchandising or religiosity!

Truth #8: Although he might be made the righteousness of God in Christ, spiritually, the saint's righteousness is not a quick acquisition, because a man's soul character takes a lifetime to develop; neither does righteousness ever pertain to fiscal achievement!

Truth #9: Therefore, what the shovel of repentance is to the dirt of our carnality, the axe is to the pruning of the fruit of our character!

Truth #10: Whereas, a withered hand prevents spiritual quickening, the arthritic condition of carnality impedes righteousness. This is due to the fact that the cultivation of a soul unto repentance and its pruning of the growth and fruits of repentance have been long since neglected!

Truth #11: A lifestyle of repentance shall become, for the saint who truly seeks after God's righteousness, a shovel to expose the root of iniquity (Lie Based Thinking) and an axe that cuts the traditions of carnality from beneath the saint so that he may stand uprightly before a holy and just God as a pruned tree of righteousness!

Truth #12: The water unto repentance as agitated water, is living water, whereas stagnant water is polluted and dead. This is because the water unto repentance brings life to an otherwise carnally tainted, dead soul!

Truth #13: Therefore, to be deserving of the provisions of a lifestyle of repentance will require one to become knowledgeable with the agricultural excavation process of his soul and the horticultural growth process of the fruits of his salvation!

Truth #14: The water unto repentance insinuates the gradual, gentle moistening of the saint's soul, so as to irrigate the sludge of his carnality so that his carnality may be exposed, acknowledged and identified for what it truly is, SIN! Unlike the deluge of Noah's day, which covered the entire Earth for forty days and nights as divine judgment against man's wickedness, the water unto repentance is the lesser judgment which the saint must levy against the iniquity/carnality within his own soul!

Truth #15: Similarly, coming to the Son in faith, oxygenates the soul facilitating its salvation, while the water unto repentance accelerates the growth of the fruits of repentance unto Godliness. This water unto repentance works in harmony with the saint to lead him towards and into a lifestyle of repentance, because repentance expedites the soul's cultivation and nutrition in righteousness, for without the Spirit and the water, the soil (soul) would not be moistened or cultivated!

Truth #16: Just like you or I would drink a glass of water to conduct the nourishment of the foods to our physical bodies likewise, when the saint drinks/assimilates the water unto repentance, he quickens the washing and cleansing of his soul from the carnality entrenched within it!

Truth #17: The fact that a person may be baptized with the water ceremonially, does nothing to regenerate the soul, for it must be accompanied with the revelation of the baptism in the water unto repentance. Otherwise, the new convert is left vulnerable to a relapse back into his carnality!

Truth #18: The fruitless branch and tree are cast into the hell fire of eternal judgment. Conversely, the fruitful branch and tree are pruned and baptized with the Holy Ghost and with the fire of righteousness!

Truth #19: The water unto repentance, which speaks of the workings of righteousness within the soul, must be the means by which man's carnality is exfoliated, diminished and suppressed. Otherwise, there will be no dissolving of the layers of carnality within that soul, but only a further entrenchment of selfishness!

Truth #20: Through a lifestyle of repentance, the saint of God grows into a strong, magnificent tree of righteousness whose fruit is also righteous!

Truth #21: Through a lifestyle of repentance, the saint learns to suppress his carnal, self-indulgent tendencies because a lifestyle of repentance is not an audacious public display of any religion!

Truth #22: Moreover, should impenitent men reject repentance, then their decision to remain carnal, shall be the evidence of their iniquity which shall be used against them!

Truth #23: When Almighty God calls carnal men to repentance and that call is rejected or ignored, He shall hold the impenitent accountable for it! Failure to come to repentance is a criminal offense against Almighty God, for impenitence blasphemes the existence and the purpose of the Holy Ghost!

Truth #24: Therefore, a lifestyle of repentance is also the demonstration of the wisdom of God unto salvation. This means that the saints of God are to become sages of their carnality through their acquired wisdom of repentance!

Truth #25: A lifestyle of repentance affords the saint the wisdom of God so that the saint may live uprightly before God, for repentance, as the doctrine of God, is to and for the saint, the hidden wisdom of God, which is for His glory and the saint's redemption!

Truth #26: Whereas, water submersion represents the death, burial and resurrection of Jesus Christ and the saint's identification to these, likewise, the wallowing in ashes represents the saint's recumbent position in the water unto repentance. Upon his surfacing, the saint becomes born of that meta-water!

Truth #27: The blood of Jesus Christ identifies the love of God, who is first Love, for His love covers a multitude of sins. Similarly, the sackcloth portrayed that covering of God's expressed love towards the penitent. What's more, the sackcloth also represented the overlay of the sacrificial blood of the sin offering as well as the saint abiding in his first love!

Truth #28: Like the pall that is used to cover a coffin, sackcloth was a covering, and symbolized the blood covering of Christ. Since the penalty of sin is death and that a pall is used in death, it was very appropriate that the sackcloth, like the pall, be used in life!

Truth #29: Therefore, the unrighteousness found in this world is not worthy nor is it to be compared to the righteousness of those saints of God whom God has destined to be righteous in this world!

Truth #30: Impenitence establishes the consciousness of guilt of one's carnality, for it denotes culpability! Conversely, repentance establishes the saint's righteousness, because his conscience is first pure and is not defiled!

Truth #31: As long as carnal men refuse to come to repentance and they choose to reject the water unto repentance, which is the birth water that Jesus referred to in *John 3:5*, they are blaspheming the work of the Holy Spirit! Their rejection denotes their defiance and resistance to God's righteousness and at the same time hold fast to their immorality and sin!

Truth #32: Through a lifestyle of repentance, the saint no longer shall blaspheme the Holy Ghost, whose task is to convict impenitent men of their unrighteousness, sin and judgment! Otherwise, impenitent men are doomed, for they have condemned themselves to it!

Truth #33: Through a lifestyle of repentance, the saint acquires a transfigured countenance of righteousness!

Truth #34: Just as the enlisted know full well of their disobedience to an order given, whether prompt or otherwise, in like manner, impenitent humanity also are consciously aware of their noncompliance to God's command to all men everywhere to come to repentance!

Truth #35: A lifestyle of repentance is the way of righteousness!

Truth #36: Through a lifestyle of repentance, the saint returns to his rightful owner, because he was bought with a price! Through a lifestyle of repentance, the saint of God renounces the carnality within his soul, just as a consumer would return a defective product!

Truth #37: When a saint comes to repentance, he has arrived at the Horn of the altar whereby he makes atonement for his own carnality, as the rule of action of the sin element within his soul! Moreover, repentance strengthens the saint's resolve to live righteously before God, because a lifestyle of repentance is that demonstrated authority (horn) against all carnal propensities!

Truth #38: The ensuing power of a lifestyle of repentance substanitiates obedient faith, because repentance is that which establishes saving faith in the life of a believer! *(cf. Mk. 5:34; Lk. 7:50, 9:7-9)* Although Jesus stated that faith can make a believer whole or that faith may save, a lifestyle of repentance qualifies that faith, for obedient faith is an essential condition of repentance!

Truth #39: The preaching and the teaching of repentance is intended to be forceful and must be presented as such. This however does not in any way imply or suggest that its presentation should be abused with railing intonations.
The minister who hammers away at those who sit before him with a hostility towards sin is mishandling this instruction in righteousness and exploits the ignorance of others and demonstrates his own!

Truth #40: Whereas, there is a duplicity of judgment, similarly there is also a duplicity of righteousness. Where the former denotes the difference between righteous judgment which a saint applies to his carnality, the latter denotes the indignation of Almighty God for man's impenitence. So then, when a saint comes to repentance, he levies righteous judgment against his own self- righteousness thereby ensuring his salvation and his conversion!

Truth #41: The preaching and the teaching of repentance is tantamount to the preparation of one's heart to acknowledge Jesus Christ as the prophesied Messiah and the Son of the living God, for without a lifestyle of repentance, impenitent men will never truly acknowledge Jesus as their Lord and Savior!

Truth #42: Without repentance, there is no remission of sin; neither is there admission of carnality, for without repentance, man's carnality cannot be suppressed in his living. Whereas, the blood of Christ was shed for the remission of sin, in like manner, a lifestyle of repentance represents that covering, for they are parallel!

Truth #43: A lifestyle of repentance heals the withered hand of carnality so that the saint may stand uprightly before Almighty God, for he has cultivated his salvation and has pruned the righteous fruit of his character in God through the use of these hand tools of repentance!

Truth #44: Whereas, the time line of repentance exists to avert the anger of God in the day of His wrath, the time line of iniquity exists to ensure that impenitent men will endure the indignation of Almighty God as divine judgment against unremedied sin, caused by their unsuppressed carnality!

Truth #45: A lifestyle of repentance is the instruction previously given by and through which a saint is able to patrol the vast landscape of his carnality as he patrols the many miles of unknown destinations within his soul, and as he does so, he effectively polices his beat during his shift, enforcing righteous decrees against all crimes of his carnality!

Truth #46: Just as the historical time line of man's history involves the Old and the New Testament scripturally, so also does each and every man born again, live out his life individually first in an Old Testament period in his carnality and then upon his conversion and his adopted lifestyle of repentance, he lives out his new life in the New Testament of his living, spiritually!

Truth #47: A lifestyle of repentance evinces a man's New Testament life, where before his unrestrained carnality evinced his Old Testament living!

Truth #48: What capital punishment is to the judicial system of nations, the beheading of any preacher of repentance by the carnal church, shall be equated to a capital offense against Almighty God!

Truth #49: What the pulpiteer once was to the Gospel of the Word of His righteousness, he has now become the puppeteer to the strings of his carnality and the selfish propensities of others; and what moral depravities and societal influences are or have become to our citizenry, denominational influence has conformed to the predominate mind set of unrighteous nations!

Truth #50: It takes a physical act to release a spiritual force. The spiritual force of God's grace must be released through a physical act, and that rule of action must be faith and repentance, as both are attributes of God's grace evinced in and through a godly character!

Truth #51: Pertaining to carnality and a lifestyle of repentance, as long as a saint retains his acquired lifestyle of repentance, the iniquitous thoughts (Lie Based Thinking) as the microcosmic element of sin within his soul shall also be in remission, for his carnality has been suppressed!

Truth #52: The rain of righteousness upon a saint exhibits the telltale signs of the consummating act of the baptism of repentance, which the saint is birthed into!

Truth #53: A lifestyle of repentance is for the saint, who has given himself to repentance the salt of God's righteousness, as this measure of salt suppresses the growth of his carnality, for he knows that it is the contaminant of the soul!

Truth #54: Whereas, a donor may grant his body to science upon his death, similarly, carnal men dedicate their souls to religion, in their unsuppressed carnality!

Truth #55: Jesus took a common physical malady to teach a spiritual truth of salt, which speaks of a lifestyle of repentance, for through repentance, a saint salts himself with God's judgment and righteousness; in accordance to God's spice rack (His Word)!

Truth #56: Whereas, a cadaver farm is that place in which medical and forensic science measures the process of rot and decomposition of bodies by time, ambient conditions and the appearance of worms and maggots. Likewise, organized religion, like cadaver farms themselves, have become the breeding grounds for carnal decomposition, due to the process of carnal infestation of the worms and maggots, caused by the ambient conditions of immorality, ignorance and unsuppressed carnality!

Truth #57: Man's iniquity is like the snail that when left alone, his carnality will encroach upon and within the garden, which is his soul, and eat the heart away of any/all vestiges of eternal life! Repentance therefore, is like the salt, for when a saint applies the salt of God's righteousness upon the carnal snails within his soul, then these slugs are consumed by the conflagration of that salt!

Truth #58: Well, as compared to iniquity, as long as a man fails to suppress his iniquity and carnality, like maggots that inch their way in, on and about his soul. He becomes like that trash can, whose filth of rotting flesh serves as the meat for maggot infestation!

Truth #59: As long as a man remains self-righteous, he is worthless in the eyes of Almighty God, although he may be considered a man worth his salt in an unrighteous world. However, should this man salt his soul with the salt of God's righteousness, he would at the same time, assault the carnality within his soul. This then would make him valuable in the sight of God, for this man is now worth his salt in the service to God!

Truth #60: What substituted salt is to self-righteousness and religion, natural salt is to God's righteousness and pure, undefiled worship!

Truth #61: Salt that is harvested from the earth equates to the salt of man's self-righteousness, and the salt that is harvested from the oceans represents the salt of God's righteousness!

Truth #62: A lifestyle of repentance is the antiseptic to carnal tendencies, for repentance is the cure between self-righteousness and God's righteousness. Through a lifestyle of repentance, the saint processes his fleshly traits with the salt of God's righteousness, preserving his soul and transforming his character and heart in God!

Truth #63: This then intimates that a man's carnality must be rubbed with the abrasive known as repentance, so that the sheen of God's righteousness may once again shine through his character, because ever since the fall of man, carnality has become the inherent tarnish within the soul of every man!

Truth #64: Therefore, as a cure for the constant outgrowth of carnality, a lifestyle of repentance is the spiritual curing process which requires a lifetime to realize!

Truth #65: A lifestyle of repentance is the counter active agent against carnal corruption and all that is worldly!

Truth #66: Man's ignorance of his self-righteousness spawns the mystery of his iniquity, and since iniquity is part and parcel to carnality, man's carnality is the mystery of his iniquity! However, through a lifestyle of repentance, any man may acquire the knowledge of his carnality, which is the knowledge of salvation that dissipates this mystery!

Truth #67: Through a lifestyle of repentance, the circumstances in life are surmounted by the saint who has come to repentance. This is because the saint has realized that the effects of the fiery circumstances within his life may be suppressed with the salt of his godly integrity within these circumstances!

Truth #68: Just as a bride would prepare herself for her wedding, likewise, a lifestyle of repentance makes the saint ready ahead of time, so that he is prepared for the Lord's return!

Truth #69: Whereas, the drug lord would cut the purity of a narcotic so as to extend his profit base, the anemic preacher has also cut the purity of the Gospel message of repentance with his insipid connotations so as to extend his livelihood!

Truth #70: However, should one embrace the preaching and the teaching of the doctrine of repentance, that person will experience the force of this instruction in righteousness, because the force of this righteous word targets the carnality within the soul. The result of which transforms the saint, who has come to repentance, to become a terror to his carnal self as well as to others who remain carnally influenced!

Truth #71: The workers of righteousness are to embrace the baptism of repentance, otherwise they remain workers of their own carnality, and those who embrace repentance shall be accepted with God!

Truth #72: A lifestyle of repentance appropriates the operation of God, through the agency of the Holy Ghost working His righteousness within the saints of God!

Truth #73: Through a lifestyle of repentance, the saint ensures for himself that which is within his heart is first clean and proper!

Truth #74: Based upon a covenant relationship and by a constitutional necessity, the saint of God may choose to live in divine health, because a lifestyle of repentance reverses the devil's own condemnation back towards and upon him (devil)!

Truth #75: Since all truth is parallel, and since carnality is a preexisting affliction of the unregenerate soul, then repentance, as the spiritual defense system of the soul is also a preexisting, constitutional condition based upon a covenant relationship. Whereas, a man's body possesses preexisting defense systems to regenerate its health, likewise Almighty God has designed within the soul of man a spiritual defense system to regenerate its salvation, and that defense system within the soul is the conscience of the individual that alerts him of the need for it. So, whenever and as long as impenitent men reject repentance, they work against the constitutional design of their soul's basic need for regeneration and salvation, even his own conscience, which is constantly urging him to come to repentance and be converted!

Truth #76: A lifestyle of repentance promotes healing, health, restoration and complete wholeness, for these are also fruits of God's righteousness!

Truth #77: Whereas, the tribulation period is the pinnacle of man's heightened carnality as expressed through his self-righteousness and wickedness, the future wrath of God is the judgment rendered on impenitent men for their crimes against God's moral law!

Truth #78: A lifestyle of repentance is as a welcome that embraces the truth of God's Word of righteousness, whereas, a mere invitation is only a formality with ulterior motives!

Truth #79: Whereas, a hooker walks the streets that lead to death; wisdom works the paths of righteousness which lead unto life! Likewise, what strong drink may be to inebriation; the new wine, as that spiritual thing of God, is to newness of life. The wisdom of repentance is demonstrated in and through the sons of God, and validates their sobriety!

Truth #80: It is only through those born of the water unto repentance that wisdom is vindicated, because they have been justified as true children of God, for they have been adopted!

Truth #81: Impenitent men fail to perceive that what repentance is towards the forgiveness of their sins, obedient faith is towards the salvation of their soul! They fail to acknowledge that faith and repentance go hand in hand, like a covenant hand shake between they and God. They fail to realize that without obedient faith and repentance, they are not marching in step with Almighty God! The impenitent fail to realize that a lifestyle of repentance caters to Jesus!

Truth #82: Whereas, people perish for lack of knowledge, similarly they perish for lack of vision! And I might add that they also perish for lack of wisdom! You see, righteousness must become a pursuit of spiritual knowledge founded upon scriptural text. It must become a divine vision through which the saint of God aspires to. Finally, the saint of God must acquire the righteousness of God through the wisdom of repentance, for repentance is the knowledge of salvation!

Truth #83: Through the deceit of carnality in all its attributes, the devil effectively diverts God's condemnation intended for him and redirects it onto the masses of unsuspecting humanity!

Truth #84: As long as carnality thrives, exhibiting the objective symptoms of dysfunctional conduct and behavior, the things that make for peace shall never be known. This is due to the fact that people, across the board, remain ignorant of the rule of action of their own carnality and are in denial of it!

Truth #85: Where the medical may provide a quick remedy, the change of a lifestyle would require an endured alteration of living. Ergo, what the psychological expression is to a disorder, the spiritual import is to the Unsuppressed Carnal Desire!

Truth #86: What OCD may be to a psychological disorder, UCD is to the spiritual condition identified and described in Scripture as degenerate conduct and behavior! Therefore, so long as any man chooses to entertain iniquitous thoughts and commits himself to them, then that man remains impenitent and is tormented with UCD!

Truth #87: When carnal knowledge is acquired, the saint possesses the wisdom of God pertaining to a lifestyle of repentance, for without this knowledge, righteousness is misinterpreted and salvation is averted!

Truth #88: So, by way of this news worthy event, Jesus intimated that there is a tower of repentance, for if unrighteous men fail or refuse to come to repentance during their living, then the weight of a righteous tower shall fall upon them, killing them unawares!

Truth #89: A lifestyle of repentance presupposes a preexisting condition of carnality within a man's soul. This then makes man's carnality completely within his control. Therefore, through a lifestyle of repentance, whatever happens, the saint of God is assured of his salvation, for if there is anything that he can be sure of, it is this: Almighty God will never leave him nor forsake him, for the saint has consistently made Him to be his strong tower!

Truth #90: Carnality, as a preexisting condition, gradually erodes the structural strength and vertical integrity of a man's relationship with Almighty God!

Truth #91: Taking a concurrent course, I wish to state that there are preexisting symptomatic conditions of carnality whose effects are unequivocally evident in the life of any man and that a lifestyle of repentance addresses these symptoms!

Truth #92: Whereas, the constitutional element is an intended feature of design, a preexisting condition is a glitch in the works. In other words, carnality was never an intended feature or faculty of man's basic design!

Truth #93: Whereas, over a period of time the body will regenerate its cells at the molecular level, likewise unsuppressed carnality will regenerate itself, for the very same reason, it can't help but do so!

Truth #94: Whereas, the heavenly articles of the Urmin and Thummin where taken away from impenitent men, similarly, righteous leadership shall also be removed by God from any society or culture whose social conscience remains carnal and chooses to stay altogether self-indulgent and immoral!

Truth #95: A lifestyle of repentance is the anticoagulant that preserves the saint's life of faith in the blood of Jesus Christ! For without this anticoagulant, his faith would be dead and useless!

Truth #96: Through a lifestyle of repentance, we remain ready for the unexpected and we are free from the contaminants of habitual transgressions caused by unsuppressed carnality!

Truth #97: Just as my Marine superiors commanded us Marines to attend Diplomatic functions, likewise the Holy Ghost is commanding carnal men to come to repentance! Whereas, Almighty God may extend the invitation to attend a formal banquet, through the agency of the Holy Spirit, humanity is commanded to come to repentance, because a lifestyle of repentance is the calling card which gives the saints of God access!

Truth #98: Repentance is a fireman's carry, because the saint is carried away to safety on the shoulders of Christ!

Truth #99: Through a lifestyle of repentance, the saints of God become the "life of the party" because they have lived out their lives circumspectly, in and through a lifestyle of repentance!

Truth #100: It's one thing to come of age biologically, but it's another to come to your senses, spiritually. A lifestyle of repentance is the span of time in a saint's life in which he does just that!

Truth #101: The import here is that the wisdom of repentance, which the son realized, shall be for the saint an ornament of grace unto his head and as chains about his neck!

Truth #102: Through a lifestyle of repentance, the saint exchanges his old tattered rags of carnality for a breastplate of righteousness while he lives. Then, after his passing from Earth via his transport to Heaven, he shall once again exchange this breastplate of righteousness for a gleaming white (light) robe of righteousness, which his heavenly Father shall adorn him with!

Truth #103: So, it may be inferred that the Bread of Life Israel rejected, has become the table scraps consumed by the Gentiles! This then implies that the Scriptures themselves are for the Gentiles the morsel of that which has fallen from the Master's table!

Truth #104: The doctrine of repentance has been deemed by the wealthy, carnal church as the very least crumb of scriptural import. However, for the penitent saint, what the Church considers a mere dainty, he knows as the nutritious staple of God unto eternal life!

Truth #105: Whereas, carnality is said to be in remission, a lifestyle of repentance is the means of that suppression!

Truth #106: A lifestyle of repentance is not an audacious public display of ceremonial regard or religious observation. Neither is a lifestyle of repentance a monastic existence which requires one to become a recluse from society. A lifestyle of repentance is however an audacious exhibition against carnal tendencies and this requires the saint may have to separate himself from all things worldly!

Truth #107: Since people occupy space as matter, then the space of their time on Earth provides them the opportunity for repentance. Coalesced, the time for repentance as a day of salvation denotes the opportunity seized!

Truth #108: A lifestyle of repentance demands constant attention to correct procedure. Should the saint allow himself to become complacent to proper instruction and methods, then his proficiency has waned, because he has relinquished his ability to choose the right path and has failed to seize the opportunity to protect his heart from certain carnal jeopardy!

Truth #109: Where Scripture declares that God's grace should be as ornaments unto our head and as chains about our necks, these piercing tips have become the ornaments of necromancy about the neck of a dead or dying society!

Truth #110: The similarities between the thorns that choke, and these sticks which could choke and the pointed stakes of carnality are striking, for each reference takes aim at the choke point of a man and his society! That choke point is his unsuppressed carnality!

Truth #111: A heart's desire for incarceration denotes that the saint chooses to pursue a lifestyle of repentance, for he realizes that coming to repentance is not just a pat down search, as it is traditionally known. Rather, coming to repentance is a more invasive procedure because a lifestyle of repentance is that intrusive inspection of the deepest cavities of the soul. So then, for the prisoner of Jesus Christ, repentance as the doctrine of God, is his strip search of those deepest recesses of his soul just as a body cavity search is for any correctional facility!

Truth #112: To condemn oneself to the Big House, all one must do is violate the law to qualify, and just as visitation rights are very limited and restricted within this house similarly, a lifestyle of repentance limits and severely restricts carnal tendencies, immoral propensities and self-indulgences of all prisoners in God's House!

Truth #113: For a saint to qualify as a prisoner of the Lord, Jesus Christ, he must violate his carnality. Otherwise, his desire for God's House remains, just an insincere aspiration!

Truth #114: Using Scripture to interpret itself, I find that repentance as the doctrine of God must be taught to the saint and that the baptism of repentance for the remission of sins is that which should be preached to the sinner!

Truth #115: A lifestyle of repentance must be taught to the saint and the baptism of repentance must be preached to the sinner. Likewise, the Kingdom of God must be preached to the sinner, and the Kingdom of Heaven must be taught to the saint!

Truth #116: Therefore, the baptism of repentance for the remission of sins is the reversal of carnality and a lifestyle of repentance is the contrast to carnality, as a life in sin! Where the baptism of repentance is the initial command of obedient faith in Christ, the corresponding action to this faith, is a lifestyle of repentance towards Almighty God!

Truth #117: Through the wisdom of repentance, the saint becomes fully aware of his carnality and his mortality in the eyes of God. Accordingly, he comes to repentance making repentance a lifestyle so as to address the carnal kingdom within himself!

Truth #118: Preaching repentance is a sound of alarm, and the call to repentance is a preparatory command. This then makes the call of repentance a command of execution declaring one to change. Ergo, the call to repentance is a challenge to renew the mind and then to change, while the call of is the Command of Execution!

Truth #119: The call of repentance is the way of righteousness. It is that lifestyle to live, which emanates from the call to come to repentance. The call of repentance is a product of salvation, because it is a lifestyle which leads towards holiness!

Truth #120: The call of repentance distinguishes one from all others, because a lifestyle of repentance qualifies the saint as a true citizen of Heaven, while on Earth! Therefore, this makes the call of repentance that higher call unto holiness, for it is the activity of personal sanctification unto Almighty God!

Truth #121: Morality is never determined by ethnicity or locality. It is only determined by righteousness, as that by which man's universal carnality is suppressed! This then identifies righteousness as a virtue and that of repentance!

Truth #122: It is evident to me that since Jesus Christ did shed His precious blood for the remission of sins, His death validates this mandate that repentance be preached for the remission of sins as well, since nobody else fits this statement! Repentance, as the doctrine of God is an essential condition for the forgiveness of sins, for without it, the reconciliation and the salvation of a soul is none existent! Furthermore, without this essential condition, a man's faith remains a fancy invention of his own carnal mindedness, because impenitence negates faith!

Truth #123: So, what the spirit of the law is towards one's obligation and compliance, the application of the law so offended is towards the execution of the law so violated! As pertaining to repentance, the saint's obedience becomes his righteousness, because his compliance evinces the spirit of the law so obeyed; while the impenitent remain disobedient to God's law and are deserving of its execution for their carnality!

Truth #124: Coming to repentance necessitates that the saint fulfill his spiritual obligation to willingly comply to the Word of God and not just observe the moral ought ness towards Almighty God or his fellow man!

Truth #125: A thorough witness must dispel doubt and eliminate suspicion if repentance, as the final outcome, is to be consciously realized!

Truth #126: When the mind is satisfied, it immediately responds accordingly, because certain truths have been presented in such a manner so as to answer specific questions, thereby eliminating doubts and suspicions!

Truth #127: So, the greater the mental capacity, the greater the inspirational utility. And the more a mind is renewed in all four of its faculties (will, intelligence, reasoning, conscience) the greater the utility of scriptural insight and revelation knowledge. This is because "true Christianity is consistent with progressive knowledge and holiness, and such other changes in thinking and in living as are demanded by increasing enlightenment!

Truth #128: Through a lifestyle of repentance, the Holy Ghost demonstrates or otherwise proves to the saint, certain truths pertaining to Scripture which challenge religious tradition, to his life (character) and to his reason (carnal mindedness), thereby dispelling all suspicion, so that the saint may obtain rest for his heart and peace to his mind!

Truth #129: A lifestyle of repentance represents for the saint the abundant supply of water, for the Holy Ghost is the person who carries the pitcher, and since He dwells within the saint, this makes the saint, the man with the pitcher of water also!

Truth #130: Through a lifestyle of repentance, the saint may draw freely from the well of salvation, for he too has found the Man with the pitcher!

Truth #131: In other words, just as Jesus was obedient to His Father in all things, His obedience was publicly observed and known. His submission to this doctrine manifested the wisdom of God in and throughout His physical life, thereby justifying this wisdom of repentance, for as Scripture states that this wisdom is justified by all Her children!

Truth #132: A Thorough witness must dispel doubt and eliminate suspicion if repentance, as the final outcome, is to be consciously realized!

Truth #133: In these two questions I find that the will of God pertains to the doctrine of God, and keeping in line with the theme of this investigation, repentance is that doctrine and therefore it is also His will, and as His expressed determination that all men everywhere must come to repentance!

Truth #134: Therefore, what the will of God is to His doctrine of repentance, the wisdom of God is to a saint's compliance in fulfilling His will, for without the wisdom of God, carnality shall not be suppressed and righteousness shall be averted!

Truth #135: True repentance, therefore, is a thorough reformation of heart and life! This reformation of heart consist in turning from self-gratification and self-indulgence to benevolence as a lifestyle of repentance, because repentance is not just what the saint does for himself, but is his obligation towards God and what he does for others!

Truth #136: Therefore, this doctrine called repentance delivers the saint from evil and leads him towards salvation, for it cultivates his soul's regeneration. Through this knowledge of salvation, the saint of God acquires the wisdom of God, which before hand remained a mystery to him!

Truth #137: Where "Pent Up" suggests immobility, a stoppage and a cessation of forward progression in life, repentance is the emancipation of a new lease on life and in this sense, a lifestyle of repentance is possessed! To be penitent is first the person and what he does for himself, in saving his soul because he has been made consciously aware of his carnality. Whereas, lifestyle of repentance is the activity of obligation to comply with the God's moral laws, thereby satisfying the spirit of His law!

Truth #138: Whereas, penance is a denominational requirement for absolution, a lifestyle of repentance is God's mandate for conversion! Through repentance, a penitent saint has been liberated from bondage to his carnality because his lifestyle of repentance has become the incarceration instruction of righteousness, which the saint complies with as a prisoner of his Lord, Jesus Christ!

Truth #139: Through impenitence, there are many who have there eyesight set on their self- indulgence, yet they have no vision of righteousness as they are in denial of their carnality; but through a lifestyle of repentance, the smoke dissipates and the saint no longer fumbles about in the stench of his own self-righteousness, because he has an eye for justice, truth, salvation and peace!

Truth #140: A lifestyle of repentance is the identification of a heart condition, ahead of time, because the saint has acknowledged his own carnality and has become consciously aware of its detrimental effects!

Truth #141: Since the carnal mind is hostile towards the

things of God and neither can it know them, it is reasonable to say that a carnal, unrenewed mind is already in a state of dementia, and as institutions exist to house and care for those demented, likewise, Almighty God has reserved a place for those impenitent. It's called Hell!

Notes:

Notes:

"A large part of why men have trouble understanding God is: They don't understand themselves."

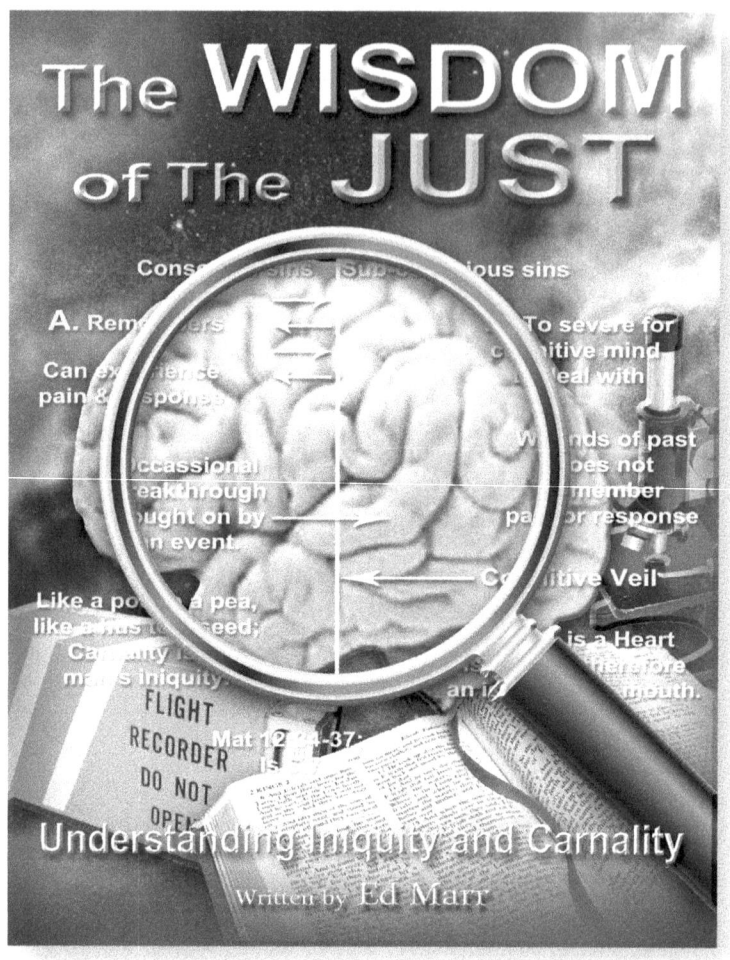

Wisdom is the principal thing; therefore get wisdom: and with all thy getting get understanding.
– Proverbs 4:7 KJV

A MUST READ! GET YOUR COPY TODAY!

Available through this ministry, Bold Truth Publishing, and Amazon.com

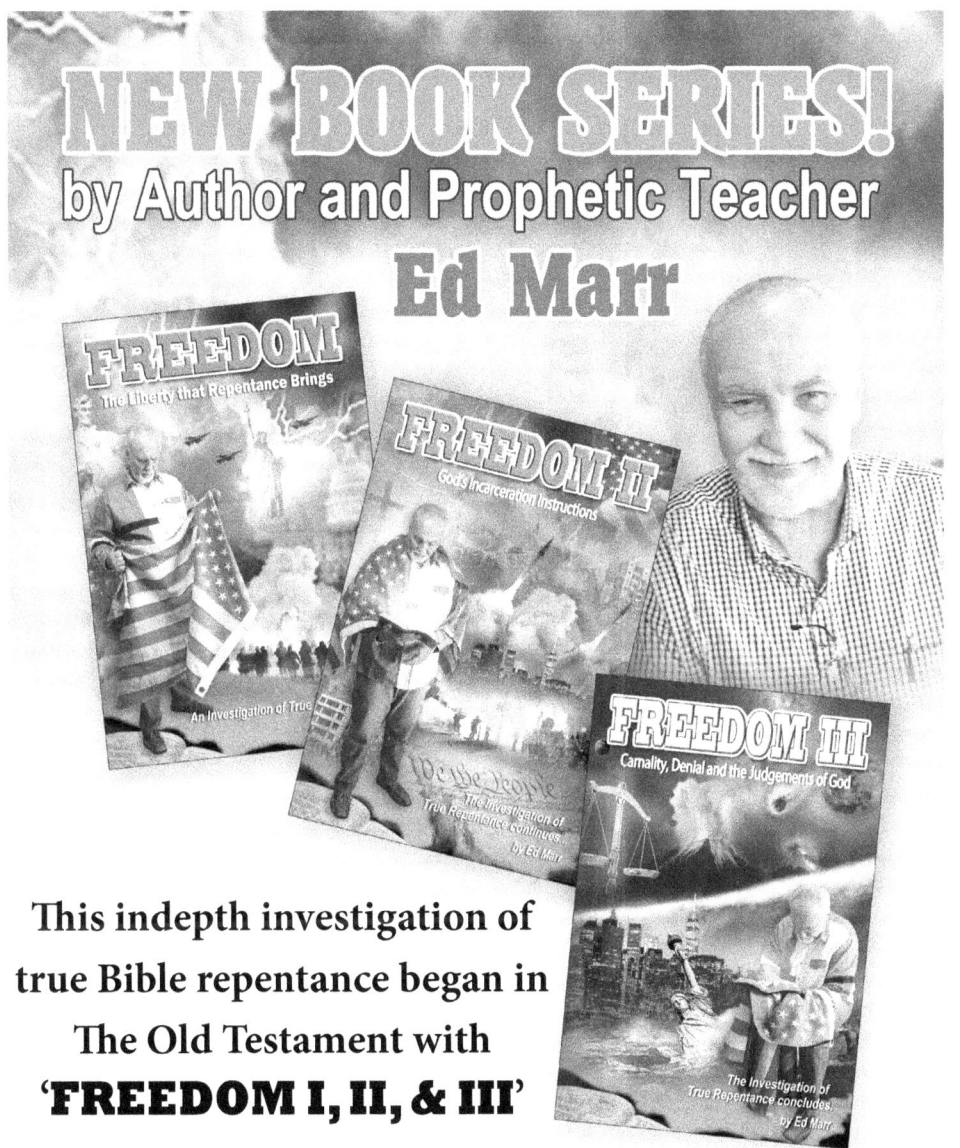

Check out these other Great Books from BOLD TRUTH PUBLISHING

by Adrienne Gottlieb
- **The Replacement Theology LIE**
The Book Jews wished every Christian would read

-----

by Daryl Holloman
- **Seemed Good to The Holy Ghost**
Inspired Teachings by Brother Daryl
PLUS - Prophecies spoken in Pardo, Cebu, Philippines

-----

by Steve Young
- **SIX FEET DEEP**
Burying Your Past with Forgiveness

-----

by Paul Howard
- **THE FAITH WALK**
Keys to walking in VICTORY!

------

by Deborah K. Reed
- **THE GIFT of KNOWING Our Heavenly Father**
Abiding in Intimacy

------

by Martha Johnson
- **Our Story for His Glory**
The Birth of a Church

------

by Dr. Marilyn Neubauer
- **PRAYING for the Sick**
— GUIDELINES —

-----

by Caleb Agadagba
- **STRATEGIC PRAYER**

by Jerry W. Hollenbeck
• The KINGDOM of GOD
An Agrarian Society
Featuring The Kingdom Realities, Bible Study Course,

---

by Mary Ann England
• Women in Ministry
*From her Teachings at the FCF Bible School - Tulsa, Oklahoma
(Foreword by Pat Harrison)*

---

by James Jonsten
• WHO is GOD to YOU?
The path to know the most misunderstood name in the universe.

---

by Judy Spencer
• TURN OFF THE STEW

---

by Wayne W. Sanders
• EFFECTIVE PRISON Ministries

---

by Michael R. Hicks
• KINGDOM of LIGHT I / kingdom of Darkness
Truth about Sprital Warfare

---

by Aaron Jones
• In the SECRET PLACE of THE MOST HIGH
God's Word for Supernatural Healing, Deliverance and Protection

---

by Marcella O'Banion Burnes
• MENE, MENE, TEKEL UPHARSIN
Prophetic Poetry for these Perilous End-Times

See more Books and all of our products at
www.BoldTruthPublishing.com

A MUST READ

Powerful testimony of what God did in, to, and through one State Traffic Officer.

"Action-packed, an intriguing mix of lawful AUTHORITY and Holy Ghost POWER. I thoroughly enjoyed it!"

- Pastor Kenn Watson
VICTORY Assembly of God

Available at select Bookstores and
www.boldtruthpublishing.com

www.ingramcontent.com/pod-product-compliance
Lightning Source LLC
Chambersburg PA
CBHW060114170426
43198CB00010B/893